A Field Guide to the
Grand Canyon

A Field Guide to the
Grand Canyon

STEPHEN WHITNEY

ILLUSTRATIONS BY THE AUTHOR

QUILL

New York 1982

To my parents

Copyright © 1982 by Stephen Whitney

Grateful acknowledgment is given to the following:
Northern Arizona University, Emery Kolb Collection; U.S. National Park Service; and Tom Bean

Library of Congress Cataloging in Publication Data

Whitney, Stephen, 1942-
  A field guide to the Grand Canyon.

  Includes bibliographies and index.
    1. Natural history—Arizona—Grand Canyon—Guide-books.
2. Grand Canyon (Ariz.)—Description and travel—
1960-   —Guide-books.   I. Title.
[QH105.A65W44   1982]   917.91'3204   82-3676
ISBN 0-688-01326-0   AACR2
ISBN 0-688-01328-7 (pbk)

Text design: LEVAVI & LEVAVI

Printed in the United States of America

FIRST QUILL EDITION

1 2 3 4 5 6 7 8 9 10

ACKNOWLEDGMENTS

The author is indebted to many individuals for their generous and skilled assistance in the preparation of this handbook. Special thanks are due to:

William Kemsley, Jr., founder of Foot Trails Publications, who dreamed up the project, invited me to do it and provided unfailing moral and financial support;

Stewart Aitchison, who not only read the entire manuscript, but assisted in the revision of the chapter on mammals, offered numerous suggestions and corrections, scouted for photographs, led me to still other reviewers and offered needed encouragement;

Grand Canyon National Park Superintendant Richard W. Marks and his staff for encouraging the project, assisting me in research, making valuable suggestions and undertaking a comprehensive review of the finished manuscript;

Karen Brantley, the park curator, was particularly helpful, giving freely of her time despite a heavy work schedule; she guided me through the park's impressive study collection, assisted me in finding photographs, made space for me to work and was invariably a cheerful and informative guide;

Tom Hardy, who copyedited the entire manuscript and in the process greatly improved its clarity and readability.

In addition, thanks are due the following individuals for their excellent critiques of various portions of the manuscript: Louise Hinchliffe, National Park Service: geography and climate; Robert Butterfield,

National Park Service: plant and animal distribution; Donald Keller, Museum of Northern Arizona: prehistoric peoples: Robert C. Euler, National Park Service: prehistoric peoples; Karen Brantley, National Park Service: history; T.J. Priehs, Grand Canyon Natural History Association: tourist information (Mr. Priehs also coordinated the manuscript review); Joe Wiesczyk, National Park Service: hiking and trails; Mark Sinclair, National Park Service: hiking and trails; John C. O'Brien, National Park Service: geology; Arthur Phillips III, Museum of Northern Arizona: plants; Nick Czaplewski, Northern Arizona University: mammals; Stewart Aitchison: mammals; Bryan T. Brown, National Park Service: birds; Kathy Butterfield, National Park Service: reptiles, amphibians and fish; Larry Stevens, Northern Arizona University: butterflies; in addition to reviewing the chapter, Mr. Stevens also contributed substantially to its revision.

The efforts of the above reviewers greatly improved the clarity, accuracy and readability of this handbook. Whatever factual errors may remain, however, are solely the author's responsibility.

Thanks also are due the staff of the Special Collections Division of the Northern Arizona University Library for assisting me to obtain photographs.

In writing the species descriptions, the author borrowed freely from other sources for information regarding the physical description, relative abundance and distribution of various plants and animals. The following works were particularly useful: *Birds of the Grand Canyon Region: An Annotated Checklist*, by Bryan T. Brown, et al.; *Butterflies of Grand Canyon National Park*, by John S. Garth; *Grand Canyon Amphibians and Reptiles Field Check List*, by D. S. Tomko; *Grand Canyon Wildflowers*, by W. B. McDougall; *Grand Canyon Wildflowers*, by Arthur Phillips III; *Mammals of the Grand Canyon*, by Donald F. Hoffmeister; *Seed Plants of Northern Arizona*, by W. B. McDougall; *Shrubs and Trees of the Southwest Uplands*, by Francis H. Elmore.

Finally, thanks to my wife for her support and patience during the preparation of this book.

—STEPHEN WHITNEY

SEATTLE, WASHINGTON

CONTENTS

INTRODUCTION

On first viewing the Grand Canyon, few visitors are immediately able to grasp and appreciate the scene spread before them. The forms are unfamiliar, the scale too outrageous. The landscape is so unlike any other that it suggests, if not an alien world, at least the very edge of the one we know. In some sense the spectacle simply doesn't register in the brain. The eye records, but the mind looks away. The geologist Clarence Dutton, writing in the late nineteenth century, called the Grand Canyon "a great innovation in modern ideas of scenery" and said that "its full appreciation is a special culture, requiring time, patience and long familiarity for its consummation." This handbook is offered as an aid to acquiring that special culture.

This volume is first and foremost a field guide, a handy, compact reference for the person who wants to identify and learn something about the rocks, landforms, plants and animals of the Grand Canyon. Part I, The Grandest Canyon, also provides information on geography, climate, history, trails and tourist facilities. The geographic area covered by this guide includes the canyon and its adjacent rims from Nankoweap Valley west to Grand Wash Cliffs.

Parts II, III and IV cover geology, plants and animals, respectively. Part II contains information on the rock formations, fossils, landforms and geological history of the Grand Canyon. The chapter on rocks and fossils (Chapter 11) describes the basic rock types exposed in the canyon, provides observers untrained in geology with a means of identifying the principal formations, tells how they originated, and includes illustrations of some of the common fossils found in the strata. The chapter on formation of the Grand Canyon (Chapter 12) discusses river cutting and erosion, the origin of prominent canyon landforms, and the origin of the canyon itself.

Part III contains descriptions and illustrations of numerous common ferns, wildflowers, cacti, shrubs and trees found at the Grand Canyon. Information essential to the identification of ferns is contained in the introduction to that chapter. Information on seed-bearing plants (wildflowers, cacti, shrubs and trees), which share many features in common, is found in Chapter 14. Readers are urged to familiarize themselves with the terms discussed in this chapter before attempting to identify the seed-bearing plants. The introductions to chapters 15 through 17 provide additional information on each class of plants. Though grasses, sedges, rushes and nonflowering plants other than ferns are important elements in the Grand Canyon flora, they have been excluded for reasons of space and because they are of less interest to most visitors.

Part IV covers mammals, birds, reptiles, amphibians, fish and butterflies. A few of the more common venomous arthropods—spiders, scorpions, the kissing bug—are discussed and illustrated in Chapter 10, Precautions For Hikers. Other invertebrate animals have been excluded for reasons of space.

Each account of a plant or animal begins with its common name, followed by its scientific name in italics. Many people feel uncomfortable using scientific names, which are derived from Latin and often seem difficult to pronounce. Yet common names, though pronounceable and easy to remember, pose even greater problems. Many plants and animals have several common names. Others have none at all. Two unrelated organisms may even share the same common name. Scientific names avoid such confusion because each name applies to one and only one species.

Each scientific name has two parts. The first part names the genus to which an organism belongs; the second names the species. Members of a single species are mutually fertile but are incapable of breeding with members of other species. (There are exceptions, but they need not concern us here.) Several closely related species make up a genus (plural *genera*). Several related genera comprise a family.

For example, the pine family is represented at the Grand Canyon by the following genera: *Pinus* (pine), *Abies* (fir), *Pseudotsuga* (Douglas fir) and *Picea* (spruce). The genus *Picea* is represented locally by two species: *Picea engelmannii* (Engelmann spruce) and *Picea pungens* (blue spruce).

Thus, the scientific name for a species not only separates it from all other species, but also indicates those among the others to which it is closely related.

The common names used in this guide were derived from a variety of sources and were selected, where a choice was possible, for their popularity or descriptiveness. The scientific names were taken from the following sources:

Cacti: W. B. McDougall, *Seed Plants of Northern Arizona*, 1973.

All other plants: Thomas H. Kearny and Robert H. Peebles, *Arizona Flora*, 2nd ed., with supplement, 1960.

Mammals: Donald Hoffmeister, *Mammals of the Grand Canyon*, 1971.

Birds: American Ornithologists' Union *Checklist of North American Birds*, 5th ed., 1957; 32nd supplement, 1973, and 33rd supplement, 1976.

Amphibians and Reptiles: *Standard Common and Current Scientific Names for North American Amphibians and Reptiles*, Society for the Study of Amphibians and Reptiles, 1978.

Fish: W. L. Minckley, *Fishes of Arizona*, 1973.

Butterflies: Larry Stevens, Museum of Northern Arizona.

Although the taxonomic status of some groups of plants and animals has undergone revision since the above sources were published, no attempt has been made to reflect these revisions, which are of little or no interest to the average reader.

This guide contains descriptions and illustrations of more than 500 species or genera of plants and animals. Even so, space limitations make it impossible to include every species found at the Grand Canyon. Those selected for this guide are primarily the more common and more easily identified types. Where a genus contains two or more species so similar that an untrained observer will find it difficult or impossible to separate them in the field, the genus is often represented only by the most common or widespread species. In several cases, however, two or more species are illustrated or briefly described.

Publications listed at the end of the chapters include books for general reading as well as works that supply more detailed information than could be included in this guide. Though a number of technical monographs were consulted in the preparation of this book, most are not widely available and therefore are not cited in the lists of references.

PART I

The Grandest Canyon

1. THE CANYON

Among the earth's great river gorges the Grand Canyon is unmatched in its overall vastness, topographic complexity, striking landforms and range of colors. Other canyons may equal or surpass it in one or another of these attributes, but none combines them all on such a colossal scale or in such harmonious proportion. And none is so perfectly situated for the purpose of displaying these qualities to utmost advantage. If the Grand Canyon were flanked by mountains, its impact would be diminished. As it is, the gently rolling plateaus that form its rims make the gorge appear, if possible, even deeper, wider and more rugged than it is.

The Grand Canyon is about 280 miles long. Distances across the gorge range from 4 to 15½ miles, the average being 10. From rims 6000 to 8500 feet above sea level, the canyon walls drop 3500 to 6000 feet to the Colorado River, which flows through the narrow, winding Inner Gorge within the larger chasm. The prominent horizontal rock strata exposed in the canyon walls provide dramatic counterpoint to the vertical dimension. Their various colors, ranging through the entire spectrum, combine in the eye to create the glowing red-orange hue that suffuses the canyon.

Rather than plunging directly to the river, the walls drop in a series of cliffs, slopes and terraces that reflect the varying degrees of hardness of the strata. Dissecting the walls and scalloping the rims into alternating amphitheaters and promontories are countless side canyons that branch and rebranch off the Inner Gorge like the limbs of a tree. Separating the

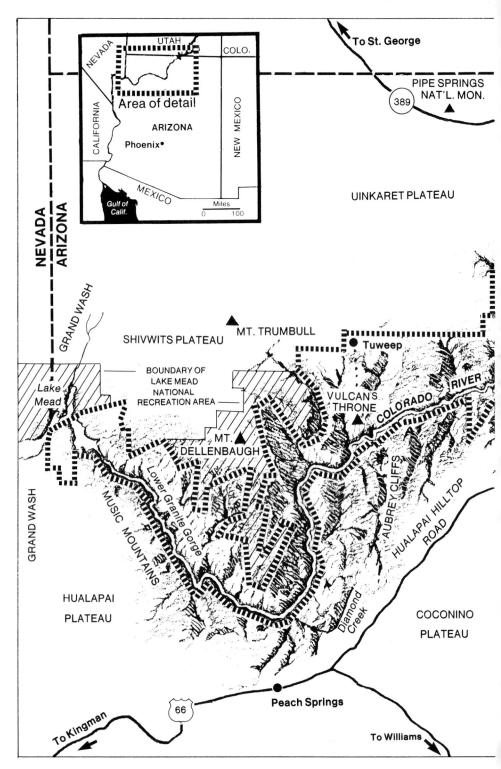

Figure 1.   The Grand Canyon of the Colorado River.

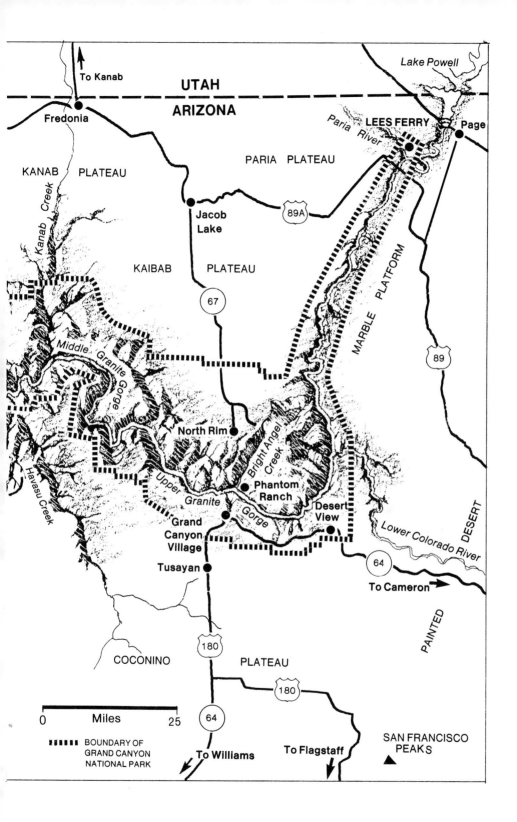

To Kanab

Lake Powell

UTAH

ARIZONA

Fredonia

LEES FERRY

Paria River

Page

PARIA PLATEAU

KANAB PLATEAU

Kanab Creek

Jacob Lake

89A

MARBLE PLATFORM

KAIBAB PLATEAU

67

89

Middle Granite Gorge

Havasu Creek

North Rim

Bright Angel Creek

Upper Granite Gorge

Phantom Ranch

Desert View

Lower Colorado River

DESERT

Grand Canyon Village

64

To Cameron

Tusayan

PAINTED

180

COCONINO PLATEAU

180

0   Miles   25

64

SAN FRANCISCO PEAKS

BOUNDARY OF GRAND CANYON NATIONAL PARK

To Williams

To Flagstaff

canyons are ridges eroded into lines of mesas, buttes and pinnacles that elsewhere would be major peaks, but in the Grand Canyon are nearly lost in the surrounding immensity.

The upper portion of the Grand Canyon—known as Marble Canyon—begins at Lees Ferry, where the Colorado River leaves the younger rocks of Glen Canyon to plunge into the older strata of the Marble Platform. Although this nearly level desert plateau is 2000 to 3000 feet lower than the Kaibab Plateau to the west, the two are formed of the same sequence of rocks, which drop from the Kaibab in a great plunging fold called the East Kaibab Monocline. Marble Canyon is a twisting corridor roughly 2000 feet deep and from less than a mile to about four miles across. Fifty miles south of Lees Ferry, just above the mouth of the Nankoweap Creek, which enters the river from the west, the canyon abruptly widens to about 8.5 miles across. Though Marble Canyon technically extends southward another 10 miles to the confluence of the Colorado and Little Colorado rivers, it is upstream at Nankoweap that the Grand Canyon first assumes the scale and grandeur for which it is famous.

For most of its length the South Rim of the Grand Canyon is formed by the Coconino Plateau, which covers about 3500 square miles. From the canyon it extends south to the base of the San Francisco Peaks and Bill Williams Mountains. From Desert View it stretches west for some 75 miles to Diamond Creek. From there west to the Grand Wash Cliffs the South Rim consists of a narrow upland called the Music Mountains. The limestone surface of the Coconino Plateau is gently undulating, with elevations ranging between 6000 and about 7500 feet above sea level. The plateau is highest near Grandview Point, east of Grand Canyon Village on the South Rim.

West of the Marble Platform, four plateaus—the Kaibab, Kanab, Uinkaret and Shivwits—form the North Rim of the Grand Canyon. The Kaibab Plateau is the highest and easternmost of the four. Elevations on the Kaibab range between 7500 and 8500 feet along the canyon rim and increase to just over 9200 feet a few miles north. Its limestone surface has eroded into gentle ridges and shallow basins and draws.

On the west the Kaibab drops about 1000 feet to the Kanab Plateau, which is cut in half by the huge gorge of Kanab Creek. This stream is the only tributary of the Colorado River to have cut through the high plateaus from sources to the north.

The Kanab is separated from the Uinkaret Plateau on the west by the lava-filled Toroweap Valley, which once extended down to the Colorado River, but now ends abruptly at the brink of the Inner Gorge, some 3000 feet above. Perched on the brink at the foot of the valley is the picturesque cinder cone called Vulcan's Throne.

This portion of the Grand Canyon has a different profile from that of the more familiar eastern section. Near Toroweap, the outer cliffs are steeper, less broken by slopes, than is the case below Grand Canyon Village. They drop 2000 feet to a broad inner terrace called the Esplanade, which is five to six miles across. The Inner Gorge, which cuts through the Esplanade, is less than a mile across, but features vertical cliffs 3000 feet high.

West of the Toroweap Valley the Uinkaret Plateau attains a general elevation of about 6000 feet, but its surface is covered by numerous cinder cones and lava flows. The highest cone is Mt. Trumbull, which rises to more than 8000 feet above sea level.

On the west the Uinkaret drops to the Shivwits Plateau, the lowest and westernmost step on the North Rim staircase. Like the Uinkaret, the Shivwits Plateau is crowned by scattered volcanic cones, the highest of which is 6690-foot Mt. Dellenbaugh. The Shivwits ends on the west at the Grand Wash Cliffs, which overlook Lake Mead and the Mohave Desert.

2. THE REGION

The Grand Canyon plateaus are located at the southwestern corner of the Colorado Plateau Province, which covers some 130,000 square miles in northern Arizona, northwestern New Mexico, western Colorado and eastern Utah. The province is bounded on the east by the Rocky Mountains, on the north by the Uinta Range, on the west by the Wasatch Mountains, Great Basin and Mohave Desert, and on the south by the Sonoran Desert, White Mountains and ranges of western New Mexico.

Elevations on the Colorado Plateau range from 5000 feet to about 12,700 feet above sea level. Its surface has been dissected by rivers ancient and modern into a maze of plateaus and gorges. Here and there, mountain ranges rise abruptly from the plateaus. Scattered throughout the province are isolated buttes and mesas, plus the oddest assortment of landforms found anywhere on the planet. No section of the country can boast of more outstanding scenery. In the province, in addition to the Grand Canyon, are found Zion Canyon, Bryce Canyon, Cedar Breaks, Glen Canyon, Monument Valley, Rainbow Bridge, the Canyonlands, Capitol Reef, Arches, Four Corners, Mesa Verde, Petrified Forest, the Painted Desert, San Francisco Peaks, Oak Creek Canyon and a host of other wonders.

Most of the Colorado Plateau Province is underlain by accumulations of sedimentary rocks that form sequences of nearly horizontal strata. Most of these rocks originated as sediments deposited in ancient seas that

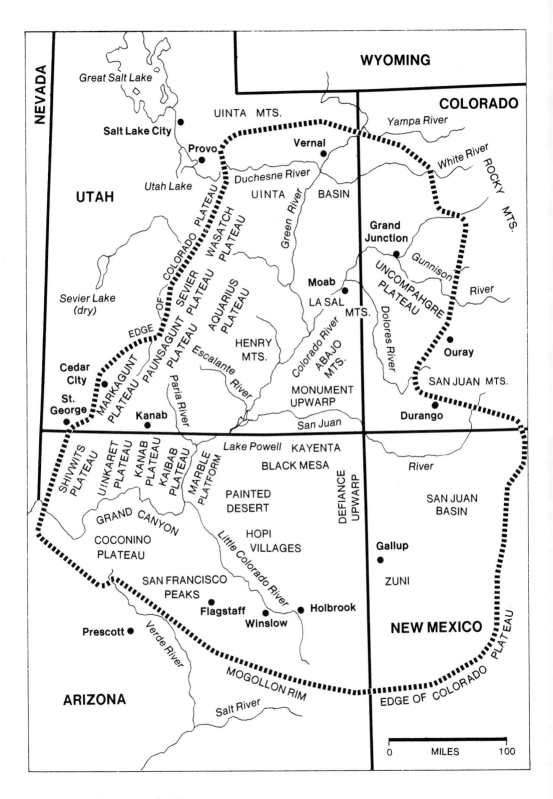

Figure 2. The Colorado Plateau.

repeatedly advanced and retreated over the region. Later the strata were uplifted thousands of feet along geological faults. In the process the rocks were often broken, bowed upward or gently folded, but their original sequence was rarely disturbed. Today, the rocks are laid open to view by the deep canyons that dissect the region and by the relative sparseness of soil cover and vegetation. As a result, the Colorado Plateau provides geologists with an unsurpassed record of much of the earth's history.

North of the Grand Canyon the strata have been eroded into a giant staircase of cliffs and tablelands culminating in the Markagunt and Paunsagunt plateaus of southern Utah, both of which top 11,000 feet elevation. The Vermilion Cliffs extend along the Utah–Arizona border from the Kanab Plateau east to near Lees Ferry. They continue beyond the river under the name of the Echo Cliffs, which curve southward to parallel the course of Marble Canyon.

Sixty miles south of Lees Ferry, the Little Colorado enters from the southeast through a narrow, steep-walled gorge cut through the Painted Desert. The desert ends abruptly at the sheer cliffs flanking the eastern end of the Grand Canyon. From Desert View north to the Little Colorado River these cliffs form the Palisades of the Desert. Northward to Nankoweap Canyon they are called the Desert Facade.

About 50 miles south of Desert View rise the lofty San Francisco Peaks, which culminate in 12,670-foot Humphreys Peak. This ancient volcano is the highest point in Arizona and one of the highest in all the Colorado Plateau Province. The mountains rise more than 5000 feet above the surrounding lands, where lava flows cover more than 3000 square miles. From the San Francisco Peaks, the Colorado Plateau extends southward to the Mogollon Rim, which cuts across central Arizona into western New Mexico.

3. THE RIVER

The Colorado River, as originally named, began in southeastern Utah at the confluence of the Grand and Green rivers. The Green originates in the Wind River Range of Wyoming, the Grand at Middle Park in the Colorado Rockies. In 1921, at the request of the Colorado state legislature, Congress redesignated the Grand River the Colorado. The Green River, a coequal partner in the Colorado River system, was thereby reduced to the status of mere tributary. But that's politics, not geography.

The Colorado River—both Grand and Green—is the major river of the American Southwest and one of the great rivers on the continent. From its headwaters in the middle and southern Rockies it flows 1440 miles to the Gulf of California. Along the way it has cut through more mountain barriers—among them the Grand Canyon plateaus—than any other river in North America. It drains about 250,000 square miles in the states of Wyoming, Colorado, Utah, Arizona, New Mexico, Nevada and California. Its major tributaries are the Yampa, White, Gunnison, Dolores, San Juan and Gila rivers.

The Colorado was once a great muddy rasp of a river, its waters stained reddish-brown by the tremendous loads of sediments swept downstream. For this reason it was called the *Rio Colorado*, or "red river," by the Spanish. Today, a visitor to the Grand Canyon is as likely to see a clear, cold, blue-green river deprived of its sediment by Glen Canyon Dam. Located near Page, Arizona, upstream from the Grand Canyon, the controversial dam was completed in 1963. Before then, the river carried an average of 500,000 tons of sediment daily through the Grand Canyon. Now, sediments originating upstream from the Grand Canyon collect at the bottom of Lake Powell, behind Glen Canyon Dam, filling the once glorious Glen Canyon with a thick layer of muck. The dam has also eliminated the great seasonal floods that once swept through the Grand Canyon. These not only scoured the Inner Gorge, but as the waters receded, laid down beaches along the river. With the loss of these floods, the river's discharge below the dam has dropped from 86,000 to 26,000 cubic feet of water per second, and the beaches are rapidly disappearing.

At the opposite end of the Grand Canyon the waters of Lake Mead drown the Colorado River at Separation Rapids, now gone, about 35 miles upstream from Grand Wash Cliffs. The lake began to form in 1936, following the completion of Hoover (or Boulder) Dam downstream in Black Canyon. Proposals for building two additional dams in the Grand Canyon itself were beaten back by conservationists in the mid-1960s, though political pressure to build the lower dam continues. As a result, the Colorado River remains free flowing, if regulated and diminished, in its passage through the Grand Canyon.

From Lees Ferry to Grand Wash Cliffs the river drops 2200 feet in roughly 280 miles. It alternately flows through long, deep pools and short, steep rapids. River depths vary from 6 to 110 feet, the average being about 20. The water is deepest in major pools and in holes at the foot of rapids. The rapids comprise only 10 percent of the river's length, but account for half its total drop. They are spaced an average of about one and a half miles apart and are most often located at the mouths of tributary canyons.

SELECTED REFERENCES FOR CHAPTERS 1–3

Braun, Ernest. *Grand Canyon of the Living Colorado*. San Francisco: Sierra Club/Ballantine, 1970.

Crampton, C. Gregory. *Land of Living Rock; The Grand Canyon and the High Plateaus: Arizona, Utah, Nevada*. New York: Knopf, 1972.

Euler, Robert C., et al. *The Grand Canyon up Close and Personal*. Western Montana College Foundation, 1980.

Fletcher, Colin. *The Man Who Walked Through Time*. New York: Knopf, 1968.

Hamblin, W. Kenneth, and Joseph R. Murphy. *Grand Canyon Perspectives.* Provo, UT: Brigham Young University Printing Service, 1969.

Krutch, Joseph Wood. *Grand Canyon, Today and All Its Yesterdays.* New York: William Sloan Associates, 1958.

Leydet, François. *Time and the River Flowing: Grand Canyon.* San Francisco: Sierra Club/Ballantine, 1968.

Peattie, Roderick, ed. *The Inverted Mountains: Canyons of the West.* New York: Vanguard, 1948.

Scharff, R., ed. *Grand Canyon National Park.* New York: McKay, 1967.

Simmons, George C., and David L. Gaskill. *River Runners' Guide to the Canyons of the Green and Colorado Rivers,* vol. 3, *Marble Gorge and Grand Canyon.* Flagstaff, AZ: Northland Press, 1969.

Sutton, Ann and Myron. *The Wilderness World of the Grand Canyon.* New York: Lippincott, 1970.

United States Geological Survey. *The Colorado River Region and John Wesley Powell.* Professional Paper 669–C, Washington, D.C.: Government Printing Office, 1969.

Wallace, Robert, and the editors of Time–Life Books. *The Grand Canyon.* New York: Time–Life, 1972.

Wampler, Joseph. *Havasu Canyon: Gem of the Grand Canyon.* Berkeley, CA: Joseph Wampler, 1978.

4. CLIMATE

The climate of the Grand Canyon is similar to that of Arizona as a whole. Precipitation is scant to moderate, with roughly equal amounts falling in summer and winter. Relative humidity is generally low. Clear skies are the norm. Winds are usually gentle to moderate. Air temperatures vary greatly between summer and winter, with as much as 50 fahrenheit degrees separating the seasonal extremes. Fall is usually mild and clear, with little or no precipitation. Spring also brings many clear, mild days, though snow often falls in April, sometimes in May, even on the South Rim. (See Table 1 for a summary of mean precipitation and mean daily temperatures at three locations in the Grand Canyon.)

Within this overall pattern, diverse topography and the considerable difference in elevation between the rims and the river have produced a variety of local climates. As a rule, air temperature drops and precipitation increases with elevation, so that the rims are significantly cooler and more humid than the bottom of the canyon. Since southern exposures receive more sunshine throughout the year than north-facing slopes, the former tend to be warmer and drier than the latter at any given elevation. Since climatic factors profoundly affect the habitats available to plants and animals, the local climates at the Grand Canyon are represented by corresponding changes in flora and fauna. These changes are discussed in the following chapter.

Mean Precipitation in inches	Phantom Ranch, Inner Gorge (el. 2570')	Grand Canyon Village, South Rim (el. 6950')	Bright Angel Ranger Station, North Rim (el. 8400')
January	0.68	1.35	3.05
April	0.53	1.00	1.62
July	0.87	1.50	1.88
October	0.67	1.07	1.43
Annual	8.39	14.46	22.78
Yearly Snowfall	0.2	64.9	128.7
Mean daily temperature in degrees F			
January Max.	56.3	41.4	37.8
January Min.	36.3	19.6	19.5
April Max.	82.1	60.2	52.9
April Min.	55.5	31.4	31.4
July Max.	106.1	84.7	77.1
July Min.	77.7	54.0	46.3
October Max.	84.9	64.9	58.6
October Min.	59.2	37.2	31.6

Table 1. Precipitation and Air Temperature at the Grand Canyon

(Data from Sellers and Hill: *Arizona Climate*, 1974.)

PRECIPITATION

Average annual precipitation at the Grand Canyon varies from less than 10 inches in the Inner Gorge to nearly 30 inches on the Kaibab Plateau. The latter receives considerably more precipitation in winter than summer, but the South Rim and canyon receive roughly equal amounts in each season. The average rainfall in the Inner Gorge for the period from May through October is about 4.5 inches. In 1968, Phantom Ranch recorded less than 4 inches for the entire year.

Winter storms move eastward into the Grand Canyon region from the Pacific Ocean. They typically last up to several days, bringing gentle snow showers to the rims and upper canyon, light rains to lower elevations. The amount of winter precipitation received at the Grand Canyon varies greatly from year to year in both amount and frequency of occurrence. In wet years a succession of storms may cross the region at weekly intervals.

On the Kaibab Plateau the average annual snowfall exceeds 125 inches. From early November to May, roads leading to the North Rim are usually blocked by up to several feet of snow. Grand Canyon Village, on the South Rim, is about 1500 feet lower than the North Rim Lodge and accordingly receives about half as much snow, or about 60 inches in an average year. Most snow falling on the South Rim remains on the ground for only a few days, though small patches may linger for much of the season in cool, shaded locations. Less than an inch of snow falls in the Inner Gorge during an average year.

After April, the incidence of Pacific storms drops sharply. And since summer thunderstorms usually don't commence until mid-July, May and June are normally the driest months at the Grand Canyon. Rainfall during this period ranges from about one-half inch in the Inner Gorge to one and one-half inches on the North Rim. A second, less severe season of drought occurs in the fall.

From mid-July to mid-September, thunderstorms may occur almost every afternoon over the Grand Canyon. During the summer, warm tropical air from the Gulf of Mexico enters the region from the southeast. As it moves northward across Arizona, it is forced up and over the Mogollon Rim. In the process the air cools, and its moisture condenses to form puffy cumulus clouds. Over the Grand Canyon this incoming air is borne even higher by powerful thermals rising off the sunbaked canyon walls. As a result the clouds gather, thicken and pile up to form massive thunderheads. The resulting thunderstorms tend to begin in mid-to-late afternoon and last about a half-hour or so. By shortly after sundown the clouds usually have dissipated. On rare occasions these storms may deliver an inch or more of rain, though lesser amounts are the rule. About one year in seven, tropical storms from the Gulf of California, to the southwest, move into Arizona during the summer. Often lasting several days, these storms account for the heaviest rainfall in the region.

AIR TEMPERATURE

Average daytime high temperatures during the summer range from the low to middle 70s on the Kaibab Plateau to more than 100° in the Inner Gorge. Daytime highs on the Coconino Plateau for this period are typically in the middle 80s. Average nighttime temperatures during the summer drop to the low 40s on the Kaibab Plateau, the low 50s on the Coconino Plateau and the high 70s in the Inner Gorge.

During the first two weeks in July, before the onset of summer storms, air temperatures in the Inner Gorge frequently exceed 115° F during the day. Temperatures in excess of 100° F have been recorded for every month from April through October. Beginning shortly after sunrise, the nearly black cliffs lining the gorge heat up rapidly to temperatures over 120° F. Throughout the day and continuing until well after sunset, the cliffs radiate this stored heat like the walls of a brick oven. Visitors unaccustomed to such heat are well advised to avoid the Inner Gorge during the summer.

Average daytime high temperatures during the winter range from the middle 30s to low 40s on the Kaibab Plateau, low to middle 40s on the Coconino Plateau and high 50s to low 60s in the Inner Gorge. The coldest periods come during winter snowstorms, when cold, moist Pacific air aloft overlies a layer of even colder Arctic air at the surface. The latter air mass is borne into the region from the Great Plains. At such times, nighttime lows on both rims may plummet to below zero. Normally, winter lows range in the middle teens on the Kaibab Plateau, in the high teens to middle 20s on the Coconino Plateau and in the middle 30s in the Inner Gorge.

SELECTED REFERENCES

Anderson, Bette Roda. *Weather in the West*. Palo Alto, CA: American West, 1975.
Sellers, William D., and Richard H. Hill, eds. *Arizona Climate*. Tucson: University of Arizona Press, 1974.

5.PLANT AND ANIMAL DISTRIBUTION

Plants and animals are neither randomly nor uniformly distributed. Instead, each species is limited to a certain type of habitat and to geographic areas that provide that habitat. Plant habitats are determined mainly by the physical environment, which includes climate, soil, topography and available water. Animal habitats are governed mainly by the food and shelter provided by various kinds of plants. An association of plants and animals occurring in a particular habitat is called a *community*.

Through photosynthesis, plants use the energy obtained from sunlight to manufacture carbohydrates from carbon dioxide and water. Animals derive nourishment (energy) from plants or from other animals and perform a variety of services beneficial to plants. These services include pollinating flowers, dispersing seeds, improving soil through burrowing and depositing feces, and controlling the populations of plant-eating animals through predation. Microorganisms break down the remains of both plants and animals into humus from which new plants will spring. Communities, then, are dynamic systems of mutual dependence and accommodation among their members. Biologists call them *ecosystems* (from the Greek word *oikos*, meaning "household"). Ecology is the branch of biology devoted to the study of ecosystems.

PLANT COMMUNITIES

Since plants are more easily seen than animals and remain in a fixed location, they provide the most convenient means for identifying various communities. The principal plant communities of the Grand Canyon are shown in Table 2. Most are named for their dominant plant or plants, which determine the appearance and structure of the community. Among all the plants found in each community, the dominants are the winners in the competition for resources. These are the plants best adapted for utilizing the resources found in a particular habitat. They even alter the habitat in ways that reduce the ability of some other plants to compete. Some plants may thereby be excluded from a community altogether. Plants able to coexist with the dominants are known as *associates*.

Rarely is a plant species restricted to a single community. More commonly, a species ranges through several communities, growing wherever suitable habitats exist. Moreover, the dominant species in one community may be an associate in another. A community occurs where the ecological ranges of all its members overlap in response to local conditions.

When the dominant plants are removed from a community by natural or human causes (disease, fire and logging, for example), the community is replaced by another. Typically, several communities will succeed one another on a disturbed site until the former dominants become reestablished. Since the resulting community will occupy the site indefinitely, barring future disturbance, it is called a *climax* community.

Animals, like plants, are rarely restricted to a single community. Those which are tend to be small creatures with highly specialized requirements for food, shelter or both. Predators, omnivores and large herbivores usually range through several communities. Migratory animals, of which birds are the prime example, move from one place to another as seasonal climatic changes affect their food supply. Cold weather as such is seldom the reason for migration.

LIFE ZONES

In regions such as northern Arizona, where great differences in elevation occur over relatively short distances, the geographic ranges of plants and animals can be conveniently expressed in terms of elevational belts called *life zones*. These primarily reflect climatic changes that occur with increases and decreases in elevation (see Chapter 4). Each zone therefore features certain habitats, plants, animals and communities that are scarce or absent in zones above and below.

The vertical zonation of plants and animals is obvious even to the most casual observer. It is typical of all mountainous regions, including

Table 2: Grand Canyon Plant Communities

Community	Characteristic Plants and Animals
Spruce–Fir Forest (Kaibab Plateau above 8200')	Dominant plants: Engelmann Spruce, Subalpine Fir. Important associates: White Fir, Blue Spruce, Quaking Aspen. Common animals: Red Squirrel, Uinta Chipmunk, Clark's Nutcracker, Hermit Thrush.
White Fir Forest (Kaibab Plateau: warmer sites above 8250')	Dominant plant: White Fir. Important associates: Ponderosa Pine, Douglas-fir, Quaking Aspen, Greenleaf Manzanita, New Mexican Locust, Arizona Rose, Gambel Oak, Creeping Mahonia. Common animals: Mule Deer, Kaibab Squirrel, Uinta Chipmunk, Porcupine, Hermit Thrush, Steller's Jay.
Mountain Grassland (Kaibab Plateau: shallow basins above 8400')	Dominant plants: various perennial bunchgrasses. Common wildflowers: Mountain Dandelions, Fleabanes, Owlclovers, Pygmy Lewisia, Yarrow, and many others. Common animals: Long-tailed Vole, Northern Pocket Gopher, Mountain Bluebird.
Ponderosa Pine Forest (North Rim: 7200–8250'; South Rim: above 7000')	Dominant plant: Ponderosa Pine. Important associates: Gambel Oak, New Mexican Locust, Cliff Rose, Apache Plume, Mountain Mahogany, Greenleaf Manzanita, Big Sagebrush, Fernbush, Rabbitbrush, understory grasses. Common animals: Abert and Kaibab Squirrels, Golden-mantled Ground Squirrel, Porcupine, Hairy Woodpecker, Steller's Jay, Mountain Chickadee, Gray-headed Junco.
Pinyon–Juniper Woodland (4000–7300')	Dominant plants: Pinyon, Utah Juniper. Important associates: Rabbitbrush, Big Sagebrush, Fernbush, Broom Snakeweed, Gambel Oak, Banana Yucca, Cliff Rose, Apache Plume, Serviceberry. Common animals: Pinyon Mouse, Desert Cottontail, Rock Squirrel, Cliff Chipmunk, Gray Fox, Mule Deer, Pinyon Jay, Sagebrush Lizard.
Blackbrush Scrub (3500–4500')	Dominant plant: Blackbrush. Important associates: Mormon Tea, Desert Thorn, Bursage, Utah Agave, Narrowleaf Yucca, various cacti. Common animals: Antelope Ground Squirrel, Canyon Mouse, Desert Wood Rat, Spotted Skunk, Jackrabbit, Canyon Wren, Chuckwalla, Spiny Lizard, Common Kingsnake.
Mohave Desert Scrub (Inner Gorge below 4000')	Dominant plant: Four-winged Saltbush, Creosote Bush. Important associates: Utah Agave, Yuccas, Mormon Tea, Mesquite, Ratany, Catclaw, various cacti. Common animals: Spotted Skunk, Ringtail, Pocket Mouse, Canyon Wren, Collared Lizard, Whipsnake.
Riparian Woodland (Banks of Colorado River and tributary streams)	Dominant plants: Tamarisk (river); Fremont Cottonwood (tributaries). Important associates: Seep-willow, Desert-willow, true Willows, Redbud, Netleaf Hackberry, Arizona Walnut (Havasu Canyon). Common animals: Raccoon, Ringtail, Spotted Skunk, Mallard, Spotted Sandpiper, Lucy's Warbler, Blue Grosbeak, Red-spotted Toad, Tree Lizard.

the high plateaus and deep canyons of Arizona and Utah. At the Grand Canyon, for example, belts of desert scrub, woodland and forest are stacked one upon the other like the rock strata striping the canyon walls.

The formal concept of life zones originated in the late nineteenth century as a result of studies carried out by the American zoologist C. Hart Merriam in the Grand Canyon region. In 1889 Merriam mapped the vegetation belts on the slopes of the San Francisco Peaks, about 50 miles south of the canyon. He attributed such zonation to changes in air temperature with elevation. He went on to suggest that to climb a mountain from desert floor to summit was comparable, in terms of climate, flora and fauna, to journeying from central Mexico to the Arctic Ocean. To express this correlation, he identified seven life zones for North America: Subtropical, Lower Sonoran, Upper Sonoran, Transition, Canadian, Hudsonian and Arctic–Alpine. The latter three were called the Boreal zones because they are best developed in the far North.

All these life zones but the Subtropical and Arctic–Alpine are represented at the Grand Canyon, and the Arctic–Alpine occurs on the summits of the nearby San Francisco Peaks. By Merriam's system, the life zones encountered on a journey from Phantom Ranch to the summit of the Kaibab Plateau are comparable to those occurring from northern Mexico to Hudson Bay.

This observation is true, however, only in a very general way. Many ecologists contend, and rightly so, that the comparison obscures the significant differences between, say, the desert scrub of the Inner Gorge and that of the Sonoran Desert, or between the spruce–fir forest of the Kaibab Plateau and the boreal forest of Canada. Today, Merriam's life zones are recognized as a pioneering attempt to explain the distribution of plants and animals according to ecological principals. At the same time, they are rather crude categories that obscure more than they illuminate. For this reason, most ecologists now prefer to think in terms of communities, a concept that more closely reflects the complexity in nature and emphasizes the dynamic interrelationship among plants, animals and their habitats.

Nevertheless, life zones do describe a phenomenon that actually exists in nature. And they provide a useful and reasonably accurate system for discussing the distribution of plants and animals in limited, well-defined areas such as the Grand Canyon or individual mountain ranges. Moreover, since Merriam conceived his sytem of life zones in northern Arizona, it applies there better perhaps than elsewhere. In this guide both life zones and plant communities are used to indicate the geographic and ecological distribution of plants and animals.

Life zones for the Grand Canyon are as follows:

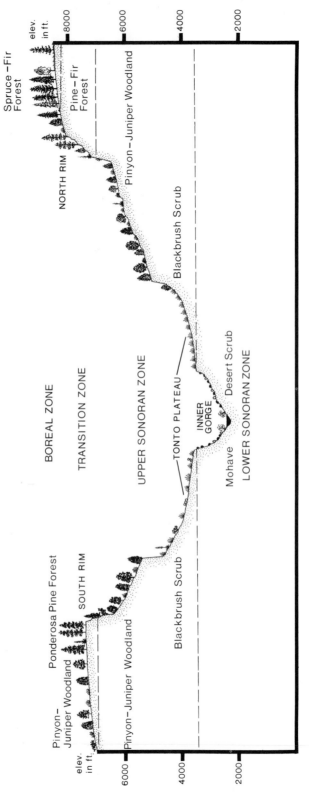

Figure 3.
Life zones and plant communities of the Grand Canyon.

1. *Lower Sonoran Zone.* Inner Gorge below 3500 to 4000 feet elevation. Desert scrub dominated by salt bush or creosote bush.
2. *Upper Sonoran Zone.* Inner Canyon and South Rim, 3500 to 7000 feet. Blackbrush scrub, sagebrush scrub, pinyon–juniper woodland.
3. *Transition Zone.* Both rims, 7000 to 8250 feet. Ponderosa pine forest.
4. *Boreal Zone.* Kaibab Plateau above 8250 feet. Canadian Zone white fir forest on warmer, drier sites; Hudsonian Zone spruce–fir forest on cooler, moister sites. The single term Boreal Zone is used here because the Canadian and Hudsonian forests on the Kaibab Plateau do not form distinct belts, but interfinger according to local topography.

The elevations given above are approximate. As a rule, life zones north of the river occur at somewhat higher elevations than the same zones south of the river. This difference exists because the north wall of the canyon faces south, toward the sun, and therefore is warmer and drier than the south wall, which faces away from the sun.

Zone boundaries do not follow neat contour lines. Instead, lower zones creep upward on hot, exposed ridges, while upper zones extend downward in cool, shady canyons and draws. Moreover, zone boundaries are seldom abrupt. Normally, the transition from one zone to the next is gradual, with certain plants becoming progressively less common while others increase in numbers. Numerous plants (and animals) occur as commonly in one zone as another. So in many places, it is difficult or impossible to assign the vegetation to one zone or the next. Recognizing life zones, however, is merely a useful way to understand the distribution of plants and animals, not an end in itself. Zones, like communities, are human inventions, convenient abstractions that only approximate actual conditions in the natural world. That nature is more complex than our notions of it is cause for celebration, not regret.

SELECTED REFERENCES

Brown, Bryan, T., et al. *Birds of the Grand Canyon Region: An Annotated Checklist.* Grand Canyon, AZ: Grand Canyon Natural History Association, 1978.

Hoffmeister, Donald F. *Mammals of Grand Canyon.* Urbana: University of Illinois Press, 1971.

Kirk, Ruth. *Desert: The American Southwest.* Boston: Houghton Mifflin, 1973.

Larson, Peggy. *A Sierra Club Naturalist's Guide: The Deserts of the Southwest.* San Francisco: Sierra Club Books, 1977.

Lowe, Charles H. *Arizona's Natural Environment.* Tucson: University of Arizona Press, 1964.

Wagner, Frederic H. *Wildlife of the Deserts.* New York: Abrams, 1980.

6. PREHISTORIC PEOPLES

The first Europeans to visit the Grand Canyon were Spanish conquistadors who were led there by Hopi guides in 1540. At that time seminomadic Paiute bands hunted and foraged on the plateaus north of the canyon. More sedentary Havasupai and Walapai peoples hunted, foraged and farmed on the South Rim and in adjacent parts of the canyon. The Hopi themselves visited the canyon from time to time but lived well to the east in the same area they occupy today. The Navajo had yet to enter the region.

The groups who lived at the Grand Canyon in 1540 were relative latecomers to the area, having arrived only a couple of centuries earlier. Before them, between A.D. 800 and 1150, Anasazi Pueblo people inhabited the eastern section of the Grand Canyon and its adjacent rims, and the Cohonina lived on the Coconino Plateau farther west.

Grand Canyon prehistory, however, begins at least 2000 years earlier. At least we as yet have no record of prior human visitation or occupation. Formal archaeological investigations in the canyon began only in this century, and while much has been learned, many details in the record remain obscure. Others are subjects of spirited debate among experts. Some may never be known with certainty. The following account is necessarily a brief outline, and the author begs the indulgence of experts for the generalizations and simplifications that such a format requires. Readers who wish to learn more should consult the sources listed at the end of this chapter. In addition, the Park Service museum at Tusayan ruins, a few miles west of Desert View, is well worth a visit.

THE EARLIEST VISITORS

The oldest human artifacts found thus far at the Grand Canyon are animal figurines fashioned from split willow twigs. These were left in caves high in the Redwall cliff between 3000 and 4000 years ago, probably by seminomadic hunters and gatherers of the Desert Culture. Similar figurines, all of about the same age, have been found in southwestern Utah, southern Nevada and southeastern California. Presumably the people who made the figurines lived in small bands and subsisted largely on hunting and foraging, the social structure and economy characteristic of hunter-gatherer peoples the world over. Perhaps they moved into the Grand Canyon region during certain seasons, but lived elsewhere during others. Or perhaps the canyon was but one of the places visited on hunting forays from home bases some distance away. In any case, the Redwall caves in which the split-willow figurines were found showed no signs of prolonged human habitation (refuse middens, fire scars or the like). Why, then, did these people make the figurines? And having done so, why did they deposit them in remote caves of difficult access?

Several of the small, artfully woven likenesses of game animals are pierced by what clearly seem to be representations of spears, suggesting that at least some of the figurines may have served as magical effigies. The hunters may have symbolically killed the figurines as a way of magically luring actual game animals to a similar fate.

Perhaps the figurine makers regarded the caves as suitable shrines where their animal effigies would be protected from the elements. Or maybe the caves served simply as temporary shelters for the artisans, places where they could leisurely construct the figurines without themselves enduring the fierce canyon heat or the buffetings of wind and rain.

Whatever their reasons and methods, the figurine makers predate the next known occupants of the Grand Canyon by about 2500 years. Precisely what happened to these hunter-artisans is unknown, though they may have been related to those Desert Culture peoples who are thought to have evolved, probably elsewhere in the region, into the Anasazi, the first people known actually to have lived in the canyon and on its rims.

THE ANASAZI

When the Navajo entered the Four Corners region, east of the Grand Canyon, around A.D. 1600, they discovered large, abandoned cliff dwellings and hundreds of smaller empty pueblos scattered throughout the region. The Navajo called the vanished people who had built these settlements the *Anasazi,* or Ancient Ones.

The Anasazi became a recognizable cultural entity different from their indigenous Desert Culture forebears sometime between 500 B.C. and A.D. 1. They inhabited much of the Colorado Plateau continuously until A.D. 1300, when drought and attendant economic and social problems forced them to abandon their settlements and seek new lands toward the south and east.

The early Anasazi are known as the Basketmakers because they made a variety of beautiful, superbly crafted baskets from grasses and plant stems woven with yucca and other fibers. They were seminomadic farmers who still depended heavily on hunting and gathering. They lived in caves or in circular houses most often constructed of poles, brush and mud. They used digging sticks to prepare the ground for crops of squash and maize, and they prepared corn meal by grinding dried kernels on basin-shaped milling stones. They foraged for wild foods such as pinyon nuts and Indian rice grass and also hunted game with throwing sticks and spears propelled by a spear-thrower *(atlatl).* Later, they also used bows and arrows.

In warm weather the men wore loin cloths; the women, aprons woven from juniper bark or yucca fibers. During the winter both sexes switched to robes fashioned from strips of fur and deerskin. They also fancied adornments such as woven belts, sashes, and jewelry made from stone, bone, seed, feather and even shell obtained through trade from coastal peoples to the southwest.

About A.D. 500 the Basketmakers added beans to their agricultural repertoire. They also learned to make fired pottery in several styles and colors. Their houses then consisted of shallow, circular pits with roofs of poles and mud mortar supported by upright poles. But by A.D. 800 this form was giving way to multiroom, above-ground structures generally located in closer proximity to agricultural fields than had been the case with earlier groups. With the advent of masonry housing, the Anasazi are known as the Pueblo Indians. Their modern descendants include the Hopi of northern Arizona and other Pueblo groups in northwestern New Mexico.

The first pueblos, as the masonry structures are called, were constructed from adobe mud and poles, with stone foundations. But by A.D. 1000 the people had begun to build multistoried dwellings of masonry laid in mud mortar. The old pit houses of their Basketmaker ancestors survived in modified form as ceremonial structures called *kivas*. Somewhat before A.D. 1000 some Pueblo groups began to construct large communal centers containing hundreds of rooms. This new type of dwelling first appeared at Chaco Canyon, in northwest New Mexico. The greatest of these was Pueblo Bonito, which had more than 800 rooms and five stories. Other large communities developed at Mesa Verde, in southwest Colorado, and at Tsegi Canyon in the Kayenta area of northern Arizona. In addition to these major centers, there were thousands of small pueblo villages and isolated dwellings linked by systems of group membership probably based primarily on kinship.

By this time the Pueblos had developed a stable economy based on agriculture combined with continued hunting of game and gathering of wild plants used for food, medicinals and the fabrication of clothing, baskets and other items. Although the Pueblos employed ditch irrigation in some areas, they mostly depended on stored soil moisture derived from winter rain and snow, supplemented by additional precipitation provided by summer thunderstorms. By the mid-eleventh century the Pueblos had also begun to grow cotton.

People from the Kayenta area began to colonize the eastern Grand Canyon about A.D. 800. They built small pueblos on the north and south rims and within the canyon. By A.D. 1100 numerous pueblos, with their associated storage structures or granaries and, occasionally, ceremonial structures, small-scale water-control systems and trails, had been located in the area. Within the canyon the most heavily populated area extended from Desert View northward to South Canyon.

Pueblo ruins below the rims are found in fertile bottomlands along the river and in various side canyons near perennial seeps and streams. The canyon provided not only more water for crops than the rims, but a longer growing season, as well as a variety of game and food plants not found at higher elevations. Presumably the people occupied the canyon mostly during the summer growing season, retreating to the rims, where firewood was plentiful, during the cold winter months. There is ample evidence, however, that many groups lived on the rims throughout the year. It is also evident from trails, way stations and other artifacts that traffic between the rims and the canyon and from rim to rim was common.

Beginning in the early 1100s, the Pueblos began to withdraw from the Grand Canyon and other outlying settlements to the larger population centers. By A.D. 1150 almost all Grand Canyon settlements had been abandoned. By A.D. 1300 even the great centers at Kayenta, Chaco Canyon and Mesa Verde lay empty. The Pueblos migrated southward and eastward to such far-flung places as the Rio Grande Valley, the Zuñi region of northwest New Mexico, and the White Mountains and Verde River Valley of Arizona.

Archaeologists have long engaged in spirited debate over the possible reasons for this initial withdrawal from outlying settlements and later exodus from the Four Corners region. Among the reasons advanced have been pressure from invading nomads, interpueblo strife and climatic change. In the Grand Canyon area, however, recent studies clearly indicate that it was the onset of prolonged drought in the twelfth century that forced the Pueblos to abandon their settlements in and around the canyon. It is also generally agreed now that drought, with its attendant stresses on the Pueblo economy and society, was responsible for the abandonment of the large centers at the close of the thirteenth century. The areas where the people resettled are characterized generally by ample arable soil and traditionally more reliable summer precipitation.

The Hopi, who today occupy mesas located about 75 miles east of the Grand Canyon, are thought to be descendants of the Anasazi. By the time the Spaniards arrived, the Hopi were already familiar with the Grand Canyon, which they periodically visited until recently for ceremonial purposes and to trade with the Havasupai. Hopi remains found in the canyon include ruins, pot sherds and clan symbols painted on rocks. In the eastern portion of the canyon the Tanner and Grandview trails follow old Hopi routes. A ceremonial salt deposit is located near the foot of the Tanner Trail. The Hopi *Sipapu*, or point of emergence from the underworld, an important element in Hopi symbolism and myth, is located deep within the gorge of the Little Colorado River not far from the Grand Canyon.

THE COHONINA

At the time of their greatest advance the Pueblos occupied the Coconino Plateau as far west as the present Grand Canyon Village. The Cohonina people, for whom the plateau is named, occupied the lands to the west. The Cohonina were hunter-gatherers and farmers who moved into the area from west-central Arizona about A.D. 600. They were strongly influenced by their Pueblo neighbors, achieving, in the words of Park Service archaeologist Robert Euler, "a veneer of Pueblo culture." They farmed much the same crops, built masonry houses and produced fired black-on-grey pottery, often with a fugitive red finish applied after firing in an attempt to mimic the true red pottery of the Pueblos. Probably, however, they retained their own religion and social structure. It is likely that changing environmental conditions caused the Cohonina, like the Pueblo, to greatly contract their range or perhaps to entirely abandon the region around A.D. 1150.

THE CERBAT

Around A.D. 1300 much of the Coconino Plateau was reoccupied by groups of a culture known as the Cerbat, who apparently entered the area from the west. It may be that these groups were related culturally to the earlier Cohonina. These people eventually occupied both the plateau and the canyon south of the river all the way east to the Little Colorado. Their modern descendents are the Havasupai ("people of the blue-green water"), whose village is located in Havasu (Cataract) Canyon, and the Walapai ("people of the pine tree"), who occupy the western section of the South Rim. The Cerbat, or Pai speakers, were primarily hunter-gatherers, but also planted crops near permanent springs and in fertile bottomlands within the canyon. Indian Gardens, located along the Bright Angel Trail below Grand Canyon Village, was farmed by the Havasupai. The Cerbat or ancestral Pai peoples lived in rock shelters or sturdy domed houses (*wikiups*) framed with branches and covered with juniper bark. Hunting implements included bow and arrow and fiber net. They were skilled at dressing hides, which they fashioned into buckskin clothing and moccasins. Important wild foods included pinyon nuts and agave stalks. They traded with the Hopi and with the Paiutes living in the region north of the canyon.

THE PAIUTES

About the time that Cerbat bands were colonizing the Coconino Plateau, ancestors of the modern Southern Paiute moved eastward from the Great Basin into the plateau country north of the Grand Canyon. The Kaibabit, Uinkaret and Shivwits Paiute were almost exclusively hunter-gatherers. During the summer they resided in the higher areas, such as the Kaibab Plateau, where game and certain wild plant foods were plentiful. With the coming of winter they moved to somewhat lower elevations, where previously stored seeds, available juniper and pinyon fuel wood and water sources supported them until the following spring. They also hunted game and gathered food plants and rock salt in the Grand Canyon, even crossing it from time to time to trade with the Havasupai, Walapai and Hopi. The Paiute made houses of branches or brush, and clothing from deerskins or the bark of juniper and cliffrose. Their tools included the grinding stone, fire drill, throwing sticks, hunting net and bows and arrows.

The Paiute Reservation is today located north of the Grand Canyon, near Pipe Springs National Monument west of Fredonia. The Havasupai were confined to their village in Havasu Canyon in 1895, but their reservation was extended to include adjacent portions of the Coconino Plateau in 1975. The Walapai Reservation covers much of the western portion of the South Rim from Peach Springs north to the Colorado River. The Navajo, whose reservation covers most of northeast Arizona and extends to the very edge of the Grand Canyon, did not arrive in the Four Corners region until around A.D. 1600 and did not enter the canyon itself until the 1860s, when they used it as a refuge from the U.S. Cavalry.

SELECTED REFERENCES

Dobyns, Henry F., and Robert C. Euler. *The Havasupai People*. Phoenix: Indian Tribal Series, 1971.

———. *The Hualapai People*. Phoenix: Indian Tribal Series, 1976.

Euler, Robert C. "The Canyon Dwellers," *American West*, May 1967, pp. 22–27, 67–71.

———. "Grand Canyon Indians," in *The Grand Canyon up Close and Personal*, pp. 35–48. Dillon, MT: Western Montana College Foundation, 1980.

———. *The Paiute People*. Phoenix: Indian Tribal Series, 1972.

———. "Willow Figurines from Arizona," *Natural History*, March 1966, pp. 62–67.

Hughes, J. Donald. *In the House of Stone and Light*. Grand Canyon, AZ: Grand Canyon Natural History Association, 1978.

Kluckholm, Clyde, and Dorothea Leighton. *The Navajo*. Cambridge, MA: Harvard University Press, 1946.

Lipe, William D. "The Southwest," in *Ancient Native Americans*, Jesse D. Jennings, ed., pp. 327–401. San Francisco: W. H. Freeman, 1978.

Longacre, W. A., ed. *Reconstructing Prehistoric Pueblo Societies*. Albuquerque: University of New Mexico Press, 1970.

Muench, David, and Donald G. Pike. *Anasazi: Ancient People of the Rock*. Palo Alto, CA: American West, 1974.

Schwartz, Douglas W., et al. *Archaeology of the Grand Canyon: The Bright Angel Site*. Santa Fe: Grand Canyon Archaeological Series, vol. 1, 1979.

———. "Grand Canyon Prehistory," in *Geology and Natural History of the Grand Canyon Region*. Four Corners Geological Society Fifth Field Conference, 1969.

Underwood, Ruth Murray. *The Navajos*. Norman: University of Oklahoma Press, 1956.

Wheat, Joe Ben. *Prehistoric People of the Northern Southwest*. Flagstaff, AZ: Grand Canyon Natural History Association Bulletin No. 12, 1959.

Wormington, Hannah Marie. *Prehistoric Indians of the Southwest*. Denver: Denver Museum of Natural History, Popular Series No. 7, 3rd ed., 1956.

Zunis, Hopis, Apaches, and Their Land; and Their Meanings to the World. Denver: Sage Books, 1962.

7. THE HISTORICAL RECORD

Space limitations do not permit a full account of all the explorers, scientists, adventurers, miners, artists, entrepreneurs and government officials who have visited and left their marks—both good and bad—at the Grand Canyon. The following account is a chronological summary for quick reference at camp or on the trail. Readers who wish to know more about human activities at the Grand Canyon are referred to *In the House of Stone and Light*, by J. Donald Hughes.

1540.   A small force of Spanish soldiers under the command of García Lopez de Cardeñas become the first Europeans to visit the Grand Canyon. Cardeñas and his men were attached to the Coronado expedition to the Seven Cities of Cibola.

1776.   Father Francisco Tomás Garcés, a Franciscan missionary with the Anza expedition, visits the Havasupai and journeys east along the South Rim to the Hopi pueblos. Garcés is the first person consistently to refer to the river of the Grand Canyon as the *Río Colorado*.

1826.   James Ohio Pattie and other trappers journey along either the north or south rim (no one knows which) of the Grand Canyon. If Pattie's account is true, he and his band were the first Americans known to have visited the canyon.

1857–1858.   An exploratory party led by Lt. Joseph Ives travels up the Colorado River by steamboat to Black Canyon, where the craft breaks up on a rock. Ives and his men travel eastward to the Coconino Plateau, descending Diamond Creek to the river and visiting the Havasupai.

1867.   Mormon settlers at Callville, Nevada, on the Colorado River, rescue James White, who claims to have journeyed through the Grand Canyon tied to his raft.

1869.   Major John Wesley Powell leads a party of nine men down the Green and Colorado rivers through the Grand Canyon. Powell's is the first party to accomplish this feat. Powell (1834–1902) was a teacher, amateur naturalist and ambitious explorer at the time he undertook this historic expedition. He was also a retired Civil War officer who lost his right arm while fighting on the side of the Union at the battle of Shiloh in 1862. Before Powell's expedition, the Grand Canyon had been visited by only a handful of Americans and was scarcely known to the rest of the populace. Powell put the Grand Canyon on the map. He was the first to explore it systematically, to understand its significance to science and to bring its wonders to the attention of the public. And though Powell did not invent the name Grand Canyon, he was the one to make it stick. After his successful expedition, Congress placed him at the helm of the Geographical and Geological Survey of the Rocky Mountain Region. In later years he helped found the U.S. Geological Survey, served as its second director, and established the Smithsonian Institution's Bureau of Ethnology to study Indian languages and customs. He was the greatest and most influential of the explorer–scientists whose work opened the West. His 1877 *Report on the Arid Regions of the United States* has been hailed as the most farsighted land-use report to emerge from the great nineteenth-century federal surveys of the West.

1870.   Powell explores the plateaus north of the Grand Canyon with Jacob Hamblin, the "Mormon Leatherstocking," a man beloved by the Indians and thoroughly familiar with the country.

1871.   Second Powell expedition overwinters at Mormon settlement of Kanab, north of the Grand Canyon.

1872.   Second Powell expedition runs the Colorado River from Lees Ferry to Kanab Creek. Powell explores the Kaibab Plateau with Henry De Motte.

1873.   Powell visits Mt. Trumbull and the Kaibab Plateau with

Figure 4.

Major John Wesley Powell. (Photo courtesy of Department of Interior, Grand Canyon National Park.)

Figure 5.

John Hance on the steps of his ranch, which was located near the head of the now abandoned Old Hance Trail. (Photo courtesy of Department of Interior, Grand Canyon National Park.)

Figure 6.

Outfitted in Flagstaff, two prospectors pause for the camera before setting off for the Grand Canyon. Although canyon mines for a time produced significant amounts of commercial-grade copper, asbestos and other ores, gold remained elusive. Despite the optimism and determination of hundreds of prospectors, no significant gold deposits have ever been located in the Grand Canyon. (Photo courtesy of Special Collections Division, Northern Arizona University Library.)

Figure 7.

  Pat Lynch, prospector and recluse. (Photo courtesy of Special Collections Division, Northern Arizona University Library.)

Figure 8.

  An abandoned mining camp. When hopes died and claims failed, prospectors typically left their gear where it lay rather than pack it back out of the canyon. (Photo courtesy of Department of Interior, Grand Canyon National Park.)

Thomas Moran, the famous landscape painter for whom Moran Point is named. Silver discovered in Havasu Canyon.

1880.   Daniel Mooney and other miners enter Havasu Canyon to work a lead–silver claim. Mooney is killed as his companions attempt to lower him by rope over the cliff next to the fall that now bears his name.

1880–1881.   Clarence Dutton, a protégé of Powell's, conducts the first full-scale geological study of the Grand Canyon for the new U.S. Geological Survey. His report, A *Tertiary History of the Grand Canyon District with Atlas*, is beautifully written and contains illustrations by Thomas Moran and another fine artist, W. W. Holmes. Dutton names the Grand Canyon buttes after oriental temples.

1882–1883.   Geologist Charles Dolittle Walcott studies Grand Canyon strata and builds the Nankoweap Trail along an old Indian route.

1883.   First stage coaches to bring tourists to the Grand Canyon journey from Peach Springs south down Diamond Canyon to the Colorado River. John Hance, hosteler, tourist guide, miner and spinner of tall tales, arrives at the canyon. In 1884 he builds his "ranch" on the South Rim east of Grandview Point. He lives there until 1906, when he moves to the new Bright Angel Lodge as an employee of the Fred Harvey Company. Hance builds the Old Hance Trail and, later, the New Hance Trail to reach his asbestos claim across the Colorado River opposite Red Canyon. Hance died in 1919.

1884.   J. H. Farlee builds a small four-room hotel on the Colorado River at the mouth of Diamond Creek. This is the first hotel at the Grand Canyon. It closed in 1889.

1889.   Robert Brewster Stanton leads a survey trip through the Grand Canyon for the purpose of establishing a railroad line along the Colorado River.

1890.   William Bass sets up camp near Havasupai Point, on the South Rim, where he lives until 1923. He locates several asbestos and copper claims in the canyon, leads tourist parties and builds the Bass and North Bass trails. He ferries tourists across the river on a boat built at the site and establishes a camp in Shinumo Canyon. Bass died in 1933.

1890.   Prospectors Peter Berry and Ralph and Niles Cameron locate the Last Chance copper claim on Horseshoe Mesa, below Grandview Point. They also widen the Bright Angel Trail, an old Havasupai route, as far as Indian Gardens.

1891.   Louis Boucher, the hermit of Hermits Rest, settles at Dripping Springs, at the head of Hermit Canyon. He builds the Boucher Trail down to his copper claim in Boucher Canyon, where he grows vegetables and plants an orchard. Boucher left the canyon in 1912.

1892.   Peter Berry builds the Grandview Trail down to Horseshoe Mesa in order to service the Last Chance Mine.

1895.   Berry and the Camerons build the Grandview Hotel, now gone, but for a time the chief hostelry at the canyon.

1896.   Construction begins on Bright Angel Lodge.

1901.   The Santa Fe railroad completes a branch line from Williams to Bright Angel Lodge on the South Rim. Grand Canyon Village grows up around the rail terminal.

1902.   Geologist and cartographer Francois Matthes begins mapping the Grand Canyon for the U.S. Geological Survey. Photographers Ellsworth and Emery Kolb set up shop at Grand Canyon Village.

1903.   President Theodore Roosevelt visits the Grand Canyon. The North Kaibab Trail is built following a route blazed by the Matthes Party. Phantom Ranch begins as a primitive trail camp.

1905.   El Tovar Hotel opens on January 14.

1906.   President Theodore Roosevelt establishes the Grand Canyon Game Reserve on the Kaibab Plateau.

1908.   Roosevelt establishes Grand Canyon National Monument, a forerunner of the national park.

1916.   A memorial monument to John Wesley Powell is erected on the South Rim.

1919.   President Woodrow Wilson signs the bill establishing Grand Canyon National Park. That year 44,000 tourists visit the canyon.

1924–1928.   The National Park Service builds the South Kaibab Trail, completes the Roaring Springs section of the North Kaibab Trail, and links the two trails with a suspension bridge across the Colorado River.

1929.   More than 200,000 people visit the Grand Canyon.

1932.   President Herbert Hoover declares a new Grand Canyon National Monument west of the national park. The Grand Canyon Natural History Association is founded.

1936.   Downstream from the Grand Canyon, Hoover (Boulder) Dam is completed in Black Canyon. The waters of Lake Mead back up into the Grand Canyon as far as Separation Rapids.

1937.   The American Museum of Natural History conducts an expedition to the "lost world" on top of Shiva Temple. More than 300,000 tourists visit the Grand Canyon.

1956.   Two airliners collide over the Grand Canyon near Temple and Chuar buttes, killing all 128 passengers. More than one million people visit the Grand Canyon.

1963.   Glen Canyon Dam is completed upstream from the Grand Canyon. Regulation of river flow through the Grand Canyon initiates profound ecological changes in and along the river. Lake Powell floods most of Glen Canyon. The U.S. Bureau of Reclamation proposes to build two dams within the Grand Canyon, at Bridge and Marble canyons. The subsequent battle between government and conservationists marks the beginning of the modern environmental movement.

1967.   Colin Fletcher—"the man who walked through time"—becomes the first person to walk the length of Grand Canyon National Park from Havasu to Nankoweap in one continuous trip. (Since then, the park has been extended west to Grand Wash and north to Lees Ferry.)

1975.   President Gerald Ford signs legislation that expands Grand Canyon National Park to 1892 square miles, twice its former size. The act also turns over to the Havasupai 185,000 acres in Havasu Canyon and on the adjacent rims.

1976.   More than three million people visit the Grand Canyon.

SELECTED REFERENCES

Babbitt, Bruce. *Grand Canyon, An Anthology*. Flagstaff, AZ: Northland Press, 1978.

Darrah, William Culp. *Powell of the Colorado*. Princeton, NJ: Princeton University Press, 1951.

Dutton, Clarence E. *Tertiary History of the Grand Canyon District with Atlas*. Washington, D.C.: Government Printing Office, 1882.

Fletcher, Colin. *The Man Who Walked Through Time*. New York: Knopf, 1968.

Fowler, Don D., et al. *John Wesley Powell and the Anthropology of the Canyon Country*. Geological Survey Professional Paper 670. Washington, D.C.: Government Printing Office, 1969; reprinted by Grand Canyon Natural History Association, 1977.

Hughes, J. Donald. *In the House of Stone and Light*. Grand Canyon, AZ: Grand Canyon Natural History Association, 1978.

———. *The Story of Man at the Grand Canyon*. Grand Canyon, AZ: Grand Canyon Natural History Association Bulletin no. 14, 1967.

Nash, Roderick, ed. *Grand Canyon of the Living Colorado*. San Francisco: Sierra Club, 1970.

Powell, John Wesley. *The Exploration of the Colorado River and Its Canyons*. Reprint of the 1895 edition entitled *Canyons of the Colorado River*. New York: Dover, 1961.

Stegner, Wallace. *Beyond the Hundredth Meridian: John Wesley Powell and the Second Opening of the West*. Cambridge, MA: Houghton Mifflin, 1954.

———. *Clarence Edward Dutton, an Appraisal*. Salt Lake City: University of Utah Press, 1936.

Watkins, T. H., and contributors. *The Grand Colorado: The Story of a River and Its Canyons*. Palo Alto, CA: American West Publishing Co., 1969.

8. VISITING THE CANYON

Most of the Grand Canyon lies within Grand Canyon National Park, which is administered by the National Park Service. Park headquarters are located at Grand Canyon Village on the South Rim. Most vacationers visit the South Rim, where complete tourist facilities are available. Far fewer people visit the North Rim, which offers similar facilities on a smaller scale. The South Rim is open to visitors year-round. The North Rim is open from mid-May to mid-October. Peak tourist season is from April 1 to October 15, though facilities are also crowded during major holidays in the off-season. At peak times lodgings are difficult or impossible to obtain without reservations.

WHERE TO GET INFORMATION ABOUT THE PARK

The National Park Service maintains public information centers on the North and South rims. Park rangers are on hand to assist visitors. Trail guides, maps, brochures and other publications are available. On arrival at the park, visitors are given a copy of the *Grand Canyon Guide*, which contains current information on all activities and facilities. Information centers on the North Rim are located in Grand Canyon

Lodge, at the North Rim entrance station and at Jacob Lake, 38 miles north of the park. The South Rim Visitor Center, at Grand Canyon Village, is open daily and features an information desk, bookstore, museum, backcountry reservation office and other facilities.

To obtain information by mail, write: **Grand Canyon National Park,** Box 129, Grand Canyon, AZ 86023.

LODGINGS

On the South Rim, lodging is available year-round at Bright Angel Lodge, El Tovar Hotel, Kachina Lodge, and Thunderbird Lodge, the Motor Lodge and Yavapai Lodge. Lodging is also available at Phantom Ranch, which is located in the canyon along Bright Angel Creek just north of the Colorado River. Reservations are required and should be made six months in advance for holidays and the peak tourist season and three months in advance for the off-season. To reach Phantom Ranch, lodgers must either hike into the canyon or sign up for a mule trip. For information and reservations, write: **Grand Canyon National Park Lodges,** P.O. Box 699, Grand Canyon, AZ 86023.

On the North Rim, lodging is available during the summer months at Grand Canyon Lodge, at Bright Angel Point. For information and reservations, write: **TWA Services,** P.O. Box TWA, Cedar City, UT 84720.

Lodging is available outside the park at Tusayan Village, just south of the park, and at Kaibab Lodge and Jacob Lake, to the north. For information, write to the park.

CAMPING

The National Park Service operates campgrounds at Grand Canyon Village and Desert View, on the South Rim, and near Bright Angel Point, on the North Rim. Campgrounds at Desert View and on the North Rim are closed during the off-season. The Mather Campground, at Grand Canyon Village, is open year-round. Space at Mather Campground is available during the summer on a reservation basis. For information, write to the park. Space at other campgrounds is available on a first-come, first-served basis. During the summer, most spaces are gone by 9 A.M. A nightly use fee is charged for all campgrounds in the park.

Outside the park, campgrounds are located on the Kaibab Plateau, at Jacob Lake and De Motte Park, and on the Coconino Plateau, 10 miles south of Grand Canyon Village, and at Valle, Arizona.

Recreational vehicle sites are available at Trailer Village, on the South Rim, For information and reservations, write Grand Canyon National Park Lodges.

HAVASU CANYON AND THE HAVASUPAI RESERVATION

The Havasupai people offer lodging in the village of Supai, in Havasu Canyon, and camping just downstream. Guided tours are available, and reservations are advisable. Hikers must pay an entrance fee to visit the canyon. For information and reservations, write: **Havasupai Tourist Enterprise,** Supai, AZ 86023.

RIVER TRIPS

River trips through the Grand Canyon ranging from three days to three weeks are offered by a number of private concessioners. Trips begin at Lees Ferry and end either at Phantom Ranch or at Pierce Ferry on Lake Mead. Reservations are essential. For a list of river-trip operators write to the park.

Five-hour, smooth-water float trips down the Colorado River from Page, Arizona, to Lees Ferry are available during the summer months. Buses to Page leave from Grand Canyon Village and the North Rim and return the same day. For information, write Grand Canyon National Park Lodges.

MULE TRIPS

One-day mule trips from Grand Canyon Village to Indian Gardens and Plateau Point and overnight trips to Phantom Ranch are conducted each day throughout the year, weather permitting. Reservations should be obtained well in advance. Trips include meals and, where applicable, lodging at Phantom Ranch. For information and reservations, write Grand Canyon National Park Lodges.

During the summer, one-day mule trips from the North Rim to Roaring Springs are conducted daily, weather permitting. For information and reservations, write: **Grand Canyon Scenic Rides,** Kanab, UT 84741.

GUIDED BUS TOURS

Tour buses leave daily throughout the year from El Tovar Hotel and Bright Angel Lodge for Hermits Rest and Desert View. For information, write Grand Canyon National Park Lodges.

SHUTTLE BUSES

From mid-May to mid-September, shuttle buses offer daily scheduled service from Grand Canyon Village to Hermits Rest. Shuttle service for Grand Canyon Village, Mather Point and Yavapai Point is available from April through October.

CAR RENTAL

Rental cars are available at Grand Canyon Airport, in Tusayan, ten miles south of the park. Reservations are advisable. For information, write Grand Canyon National Park Lodges.

OTHER FACILITIES

South Rim: restaurants, snack bars, general store, backpacking equipment sales and rental, service station, auto repair, laundry, showers, sanitary dump station, telegraph office, kennel, airport limousine, taxi service and religious services. Museums are located at the South Rim Visitor Center, Yavapai Point and Tusayan Ruins.

North Rim: restaurant and snack bar, camper store, post office, service station, showers, laundry, sanitary dump station and religious services.

TRANSPORTATION TO THE PARK

Scheduled bus and airline service is available all year to the South Rim from Flagstaff, Phoenix, Las Vegas and other western cities. Limited airline service is available to the North Rim during the summer. For information about carriers and schedules, write to the park.

9. HIKING AND
TRAILS

More than 300 miles of trails await the hiker at the Grand Canyon. Game traces and cross-country routes offer countless additional miles. Hikers of all types, from daytime strollers to seasoned backpackers, will find trails suited to their taste and level of experience. Hiking below the rims into the canyon is not for everyone, but for those with the desire and necessary stamina it is an unforgettable experience.

PERMITS AND RESERVATIONS

Backcountry permits are required for overnight hiking trips into the canyon. Campsite reservations are strongly recommended for the Indian Gardens, Bright Angel, Cottonwood and Roaring Springs campgrounds, along the Kaibab–Bright Angel trail corridor. In addition, the National Park Service has established backpacker quotas for each trailhead and campsite. All the above measures are intended to protect the canyon from overuse and to ensure hikers a degree of solitude.

For trips between March 1 and October 31, or on a holiday weekend any time of year, it is advisable to obtain permits and reservations well in advance. At other times advance reservations are usually unnecessary, except perhaps along the Kaibab–Bright Angel corridor.

When applying for a permit, be sure to specify the exact dates of your trip, the precise route you plan to follow, and the places you wish to camp each night. Also specify the number of people in your party. If possible, submit an alternative itinerary just in case your first choice is not available.

Since regulations and procedures governing the issuance of backcountry permits change from time to time, readers are advised to consult the Backcountry Reservations Office directly for detailed information. The office is located in the South Rim Visitor Center. Write **Backcountry Reservations Office,** Grand Canyon National Park, AZ 86023.

BACKCOUNTRY REGULATIONS

The following regulations are mostly plain common sense. They are intended to protect the canyon and ensure that all backpackers have safe, enjoyable trips.

1. Open campfires are not permitted. All cooking must be done on a backpacker's stove.
2. Carry out all trash, including cigarette butts, eggshells, orange peels, apple cores and other items.
3. Firearms and bows and arrows are not permitted in the canyon.
4. No dogs or other pets are permitted below the rims. Kennel service is available at Grand Canyon Village.
5. It is forbidden to cut across switchbacks. This not only increases erosion, but also can be very dangerous.
6. Do not throw or roll rocks or other objects into the canyon, as this may endanger hikers below.
7. Do not feed or tease wild animals.
8. It is unlawful to collect plants, animals, rocks or archaeological artifacts without a permit from the Park Service. Do not disturb archaeological sites or other human relics encountered in the canyon.
9. No vehicles of any type are allowed on the trails.
10. Anglers must have a valid Arizona fishing license. Fishing is not permitted in some places in the canyon.
11. A special permit is required for river crossings except over the suspension bridges on the Kaibab–Bright Angel trail corridor.

Swimming in the Colorado River is dangerous because of strong currents, deep pools and cold water.

12. Camp well away from permanent water sources. Do not toss objects into or otherwise pollute streams, pools or springs. Water is a precious commodity in the canyon.

MAPS

The Grand Canyon is covered by 7.5′ and 15′ topographic quadrangles published by the U.S. Geological Survey. A free index map of Arizona showing the sheets for the Grand Canyon is available from the USGS at the address given below. The USGS also publishes a 1:62,500 map of the eastern Grand Canyon entitled *Grand Canyon National Park and Vicinity*. This map is excellent for planning trips, but too large for use on the trail.

All USGS maps may be purchased over the counter or by mail from: Branch of Distribution, U.S. Geological Survey, Federal Center, Denver, CO 80225. When ordering, specify the series, sheet name and state for each map. USGS maps are also available at the South Rim Visitor Center or by mail from: Grand Canyon Natural History Association, P.O. Box 399, Grand Canyon, AZ 86023. Before ordering, send for a catalog listing prices and which sheets are available.

Rainbow Expeditions, of Tucson, publishes a series of recreational maps covering the Grand Canyon. As we went to press four maps were available: No. 1, *Lees Ferry*; No. 3, *Desert View*; No. 4, *Phantom Ranch* and No. 5, *Bass Canyon*. Future maps will include No. 2, *Marble Canyon*; No. 6, *Kanab Canyon* and No. 7, *Havasu Canyon*. Based on USGS 15′ topographic quads, these recreational maps show trails and principal cross-country hiking routes in red. In addition, the trails and various points of interest are briefly described on the back of each map.

Rainbow Expeditions' recreational maps may be purchased at the South Rim Visitor Center; by mail from the Grand Canyon Natural History Association; or at retail outlets throughout Arizona. Persons living outside the state may order them by mail from: Rainbow Expeditions, 915 S. Sherwood Village Drive, Tucson, AZ 85710.

The National Geographic Society publishes a full-color 1:24,000 map entitled *The Heart of the Grand Canyon*. It covers that part of the canyon below Grand Canyon Village, between Grapevine Rapids and

Travertine Canyon. In addition to showing all trails, roads and facilities, the map indicates topographic relief by means of contour lines, shading and hachures. Although its scale is suitable for trail use, the map's size may prove cumbersome. It is, however, a superb wall map and planning tool. The map is on sale at the South Rim Visitor Center.

GUIDEBOOKS

Although this chapter includes brief descriptions of the principal hiking trails at the Grand Canyon, it is not intended as a trail guide. Its purpose is merely to inform readers of the hiking opportunities available at the park. For more detailed information, consult the Backcountry Reservations Office or the following guidebooks:

• *Grand Canyon Treks* and *Grand Canyon Treks II*, by Harvey Butchart. La Siesta Press, Box 406, Glendale, CA 91209. These books, written by the dean of Grand Canyon hikers, make fascinating reading, but are difficult to use for purposes of route finding.
• *Hiking the Inner Canyon: A guide*, by the Backcountry Reservations Office and Bob Butterfield. Grand Canyon Natural History Association, P.O. Box 399, Grand Canyon, AZ 86023. This guide is easier to use on the trail than the above volumes and includes reproductions of topographic maps on which the trails have been indicated. But it does not include all the hiking possibilities in the canyon, and its descriptions, though useful, are not as complete as one might wish.

TRAILS

Trails leading into the Grand Canyon vary greatly in difficulty. Most are old miners' tracks that in places may be obscured by brush or rockslides. These trails are maintained only by hikers' boots and may require route-finding skills and a willingness to scramble. All offer excellent wilderness hikes.

Trails along the Bright Angel–Kaibab corridor are the most often used and the only ones maintained by the Park Service. They are wide, well graded and equipped with various creature comforts not found along other trails. Yet neither the Bright Angel nor Kaibab trails should be underestimated. The Bright Angel climbs more than 600 feet per mile on the average. The South Kaibab Trail is nearly 25 percent steeper and lacks both water and shade. Wilderness trails gain and lose elevation at similar rates, but are rougher.

In the following trail descriptions, hiking times are approximate and apply to average hikers in reasonable physical condition. Intended only as general guides, they may have to be adjusted for trail conditions, weather, age, physical stamina, weight of pack and other factors. Elevation figures indicate the difference between the elevation of the trailhead and that of the listed destination. They do not include ups and downs along the way.

Bright Angel Trail. Bright Angel Lodge to Indian Gardens (4.5 mi.) and the Colorado River (7.5 mi./4–5 hr. down, 7–8 hr. up/4600'). Maps: USGS quad, *Bright Angel*; Rec. Map No. 4, *Phantom Ranch*. Excellent trail. Resthouses with telephones and water 1.5 and 3 miles below rim (water unavailable Oct. 1–Apr. 30). Indian Gardens: campground, water, restrooms, ranger station. Bright Angel Campground, across river via the River Trail (see below) and Kaibab Suspension Bridge: water, ranger station. Phantom Ranch, across river beyond Bright Angel Campground: food, water, lodgings (by reservation only).

River Trail. Along river, linking the Bright Angel and South Kaibab trails (1.7 mi./1 hr. each way). Maps: see Bright Angel Trail. Excellent trail, but very hot. Hike it early or late in the day.

South Kaibab Trail. Yaki Point to Colorado River (6.3 mi./3–4 hr. down, 6–8 hr. up/4700'). Maps: see Bright Angel Trail. Good trail and fine vistas, but very steep, shadeless and without water. Not recommended for uphill direction. Chemical toilets at Cedar Ridge and the Tipoff, which also has an emergency telephone.

Hualapai (Havasupai) Trail. Hualapai Hilltop to Mooney Falls (11 mi.) and the Colorado River (17 mi./8–12 hr. down, 16–24 hr. up/3000'). Maps: USGS quads, *Supai*, *Kanab Point* and *Tuckup Canyon*. Trail maintained to Mooney Falls. A rough, precarious route from the Falls to the river. Water plentiful in Havasu Creek, which begins 6 miles below Hualapai Hilltop. Food, lodgings, campground in and near Supai village. Reservations recommended (see Chapter 8). Trailhead at end of well-graded, 63-mile dirt road leading north from Peach Springs on Highway 66.

South Bass Trail. Bass Camp to Colorado River (9 mi./5 hr. down, 9 hr. up/4000'). Maps: USGS quad, *Havasupai Point*; Rec. Map No. 5, *Bass Canyon*. Unmaintained and in places obscure, but otherwise in fairly good condition. Water from seep at base of Coconino Limestone west of Chemehuevi Point, 2 miles off the trail; otherwise dry to river. Most people cannot locate this spring. Trailhead 4 miles north of Pasture Wash Ranger Station via rough dirt road suitable only for high-clearance vehicle. Roads may be closed in winter and spring.

Hermit Trail. Hermits Rest to Hermit Camp (7 mi./4–5 hr. down, 8 hr. up/3800'). Maps: see Bright Angel Trail. Trail in fair condition; easy to follow, but requires some scrambling in Supai Formation. Water at Santa Maria Spring, 2 miles below rim, and Hermit Creek. Four-mile Spring is dry. From Hermit Camp, it's an easy 1.5-mile walk down the creekbed to the river. Chemical toilet at Hermit Creek.

Dripping Springs Trail. Hermit Trail, 1.5 miles below rim, to Dripping Springs, on the Boucher Trail (3 mi. one way/4–6 hr. round trip from Hermits Rest/800'). Maps: see Bright Angel Trail. Trail easy to follow, but precarious in places. Water at Dripping Springs (seasonal).

Boucher Trail. Dripping Springs road end to Boucher Creek, but best approached via Hermit and Dripping Springs trails (11 mi./5–6 hr. down, 9–10 hr. up/3600'). Maps: see Bright Angel Trail. One of the more difficult trails into the canyon. Slides in the Hermit Shale and Supai Group have obscured the trace and make footing treacherous, especially in winter. Water at Dripping Springs (seasonal) and Boucher Creek. From the latter, an easy 1.5-mile route leads to the river. Experienced Grand Canyon hikers only.

Grandview Trail. Grandview Point to Horseshoe Mesa (3 mi./2 hr. down, 4 hr. up/2200'). Maps: USGS quads *Grandview Point* and *Vishnu Temple*; Rec. Map No. 4, *Phantom Ranch*. Fair to good condition, but with some precarious stretches. From Horseshoe Mesa trail branches west to Cottonwood Creek, east to Hance Creek and north down to the Tonto Plateau. No water on mesa or along the trail down from Grandview Point. Water in Cottonwood Creek, Hance Creek and at a spring just off trail to Hance Creek, not far below the mesa.

New Hance (Red Canyon) Trail. South Rim, 1 mile west of Moran Point, to Colorado River (8 mi./6 hr. down, 8+ hr. up/4400'). Maps: see Grandview Trail. Trail steep, rocky, twisting, obscure in places, easy to lose in the Redwall. Trace missing from bottom of Red Canyon to river. Not recommended for an uphill trip, but a reasonable downhill route for experienced Grand Canyon backpackers. No water until river. To find trailhead, ask directions from Backcountry Reservations Office.

Tanner Trail. Lipan Point to Colorado River (9 mi./5–6 hr. down, 6–8 hr. up/4600'). Maps: USGS quad, *Vishnu Temple*; Rec. Map No. 3, *Desert View*. Trail in fair to poor condition, but negotiable. Marked in places by cairns. Little shade and no water until river.

Tonto Trail. Along the Tonto Plateau from Garnet Canyon in the west to Red Canyon in the east (72 mi./allow 1.5–2 wks., one way). Numerous ups and downs, rough or obscure in places, little or no shade or water for long distances. Used primarily as a link between trails leading in and out of the canyon. These are (from east to west): New Hance (Red Canyon) Trail, Grandview Trail, South Kaibab Trail, Bright Angel Trail, Hermit Trail, Boucher Trail and South Bass Trail. Covered by maps for these trails. Water at Boucher, Hermit, Monument, Salt, Pipe and Hance creeks, Indian Gardens, Cottonwood Creek Spring, and Colorado River at mouth of Red Canyon. Seasonal water at Garnet, Ruby, Turquoise, Slate, Cedar Springs, Horn, Boulder and Grapevine creeks (check with backcountry rangers). Emergency telephone at the Tipoff (South Kaibab Trail). Ranger station and campground at Indian Gardens.

North Kaibab Trail. Roaring Springs Canyon road end (about 2 miles by road from Grand Canyon Lodge, North Rim) to Colorado River (14 mi./6 hr. down, 10+ up/5840'). Maps: see Bright Angel Trail. Excellent trail. Water at Roaring Springs, Cottonwood Campground, Ribbon Falls, Phantom Ranch and Bright Angel Campground. Tables and chemical toilets at all campgrounds. Ranger stations at Cottonwood (open summers only) and Bright Angel campgrounds. Food and lodgings (by reservation only) at Phantom Ranch.

Clear Creek Trail. Phantom Ranch to Ottoman Amphitheater (9 mi./5 hr. each way). Maps: see Bright Angel Trail. Trail in fair condition, easy to follow. No water until Clear Creek. Beware of flash floods in creek. Hikes possible upstream to Chevaya Falls and downstream to river.

Old Kaibab Trail. End of Fuller Canyon E-2 fire road (no vehicles; a 3.2-mi. walk from the highway) to Roaring Springs (7 mi. from trailhead/5 hr. down, 10 hr. up/3600'). Maps: see Bright Angel Trail. Rocky and overgrown in places, but easy enough to follow. No water.

Tuckup Trail. Lower Toroweap Valley to Boysag Point (64 mi./allow at least 10 days). Maps: USGS quads, *Mt. Trumbull SE* and *Tuckup Canyon*. Trail indistinct in places. Water at Schmutz, June and Cottonwood springs. Experienced Grand Canyon hikers only.

Lava Falls Route. Vulcan's Throne to Colorado River (1.5 mi./2 hr. down, 4 hr. up/3000'). An extremely steep, rugged, cairned route. Water only at river.

Thunder River Trail. Monument Point to the Colorado River (10 mi./5 hr. down, 8 hr. up/5200'). Map: USGS quad, *Powell Plateau*. Trail in fair condition. No water until Thunder River; water also from Tapeats Creek and Colorado River. No camping until Tapeats Creek (watch for flash floods). Trailhead located one-half mile west of Forest Service Road 292A at eastern tip of Monument Point.

North Bass Trail. Swamp Point to the Colorado River (14 mi./3–4 days round trip/5200'). Maps: USGS quads, *Powell Plateau* and *Havasupai Point*; Rec. Map No. 5, *Bass Canyon*. Rough, obscure trail for experienced Grand Canyon backpackers only. Water at Muav Saddle Spring, White Creek above Redwall, Shinumo Creek and river.

Nankoweap Trail. End of Forest Service Road 610 (heads east from paved highway through De Motte Park) to Colorado River (14 mi./3–4 days round trip/6000'). Map: USGS quad, *Nankoweap* (trail not shown). Trail very rough, difficult, obscure and precarious. Suitable only for experienced Grand Canyon backpackers who may want to rope up in places. No water or shade until river.

DAY HIKES

Many of the above trails are also suitable for day hikes (the Tanner, Boucher, New Hance, South Bass, North Bass and Nankoweap are not).

When figuring hiking times, allot one-third of your total available walking time for hiking into the canyon, two-thirds for hiking back out. There are also a number of trails on both rims. These include the following:

1. Rim Trail. Hermits Rest to Mather Point (9 mi./4–5 hr. each way). Paved from Maricopa Point to Yavapai Point. Shuttle bus service in summer. Self-guiding nature pamphlets available.
2. Cross-country rim walks from Desert View to Zuni, Papago and Commanche points. Easy to moderate. No water but grand views and lots of solitude.
3. Desert View Nature Trail. A 15-minute walk along the rim.
4. Tusayan Ruin Walk. A 20-minute walk through prehistoric Tusayan Ruin, 4 miles west of Desert View.
5. Self-guiding nature trails at Bright Angel Point, Cape Royal and Walhalla Ruins.
6. Widforss Trail. From Bright Angel Spring to Widforss Point (5 mi./2.5 hr. each way). Easy rim-top trail with spectacular views.
7. Uncle Jim Point Trail. North Kaibab trailhead road to Uncle Jim Point (2.5 mi./1.5 hr. each way).

For other day hikes on both rims, inquire at park information centers.

GUIDED HIKES

Park rangers conduct guided hikes and nature walks each day during the peak tourist season. For information, inquire at the park visitor centers or consult the *Grand Canyon Guide* given to you on arrival. The walks and hikes are free. For information on commercial hiking tours into the canyon, write to the National Park Service.

Plate 1. Plant Communities.

Spruce–Fir Forest of the Kaibab Plateau. In the above scene young spruce grow at the edge of a meadow beneath a mature quaking aspen. If undisturbed, the spruce will eventually replace the aspen on this site.

Ponderosa Pine Forest with an understory of grasses. Some stands instead have understories composed of sagebrush and other shrubs.
(Photographs courtesy of the Department of Interior, Grand Canyon National Park)

Plate 2. Plant Communities.

Pinyon–Juniper Woodland on the South Rim. Notice the young ponderosa pines just left of center. The intermingling of Pinyon–Juniper Woodland and Ponderosa Pine Forest is typical of the area around Grand Canyon Village.

Desert Scrub of the Inner Canyon and a Fremont cottonwood typical of the Riparian Woodland along tributary streams and washes.
(Photographs courtesy of the Department of Interior, Grand Canyon National Park)

Split—twig Figurines

Anasazi Ruins, Upper Ribbon Falls

Fire Pit, Bright Angel Site

Squash Stem &
Maize Cob from Anasazi Granary

Plate 3. Prehistoric Artifacts from the Grand Canyon.

Rooms in Tusayan Ruins, S. Rim

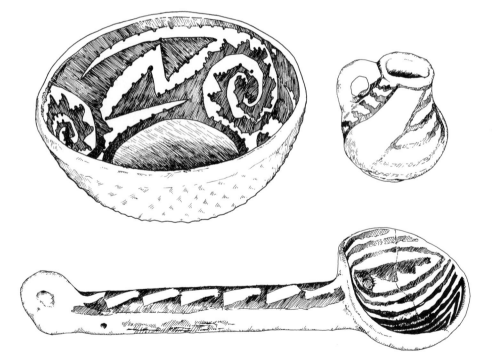

Anasazi Pottery from Tusayan Ruins

Plate 4. Prehistoric Artifacts from the Grand Canyon.

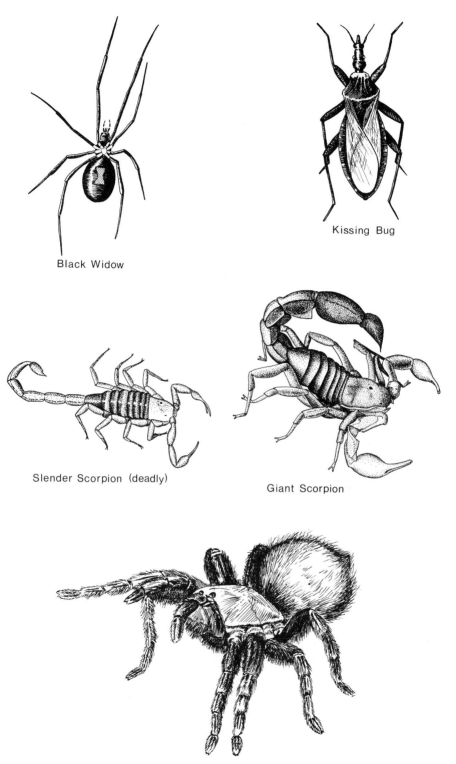

Black Widow

Kissing Bug

Slender Scorpion (deadly)

Giant Scorpion

Tarantula

Plate 5. Scorpions, Spiders and Kissing Bug.

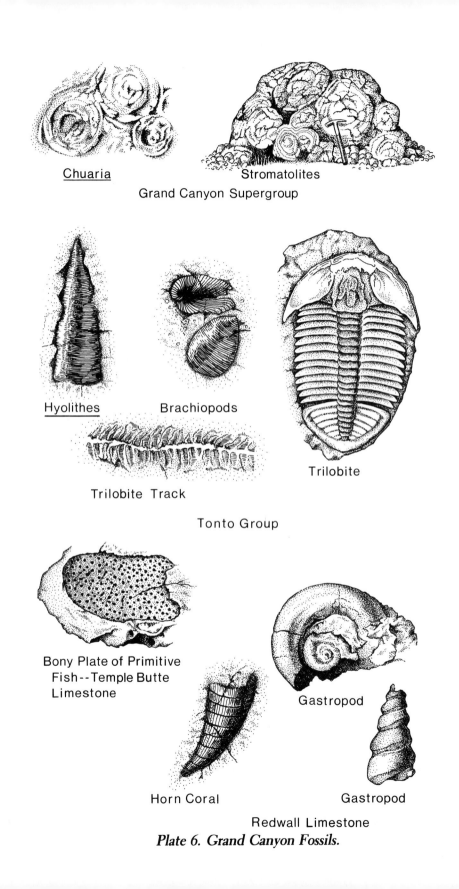

Chuaria

Stromatolites

Grand Canyon Supergroup

Hyolithes

Brachiopods

Trilobite Track

Trilobite

Tonto Group

Bony Plate of Primitive
Fish--Temple Butte
Limestone

Gastropod

Horn Coral

Gastropod

Redwall Limestone

Plate 6. Grand Canyon Fossils.

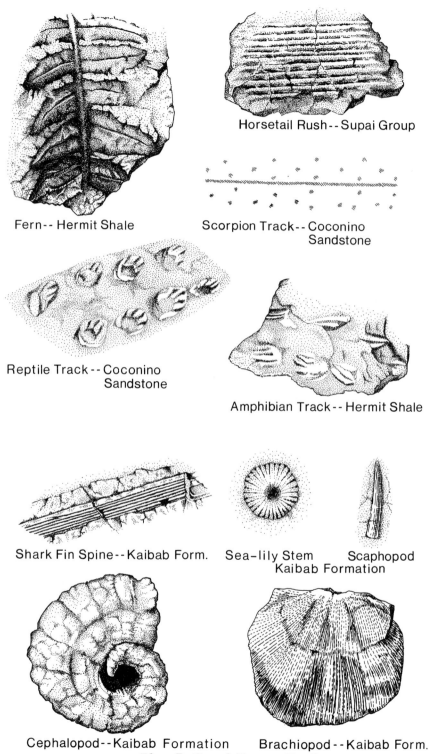

Fern-- Hermit Shale

Horsetail Rush-- Supai Group

Scorpion Track-- Coconino
Sandstone

Reptile Track-- Coconino
Sandstone

Amphibian Track-- Hermit Shale

Shark Fin Spine-- Kaibab Form.

Sea-lily Stem
Kaibab Formation

Scaphopod

Cephalopod-- Kaibab Formation

Brachiopod-- Kaibab Form.

Plate 7. Grand Canyon Fossils.

Plate 8.

A cross section of one wall of the Grand Canyon showing the Paleozoic strata and the Precambrian Grand Canyon Supergroup and Vishnu Schist. The Chuar Group and Nankoweap Formation, both members of the Grand Canyon Supergroup, are not shown. Although the overall vertical dimension is exaggerated, the relative thickness of each formation, as measured below Grand Canyon Village, is shown in proportion to those of the others. Also indicated are the approximate color and steepness of each formation. For the age of each formation, see Table 3.

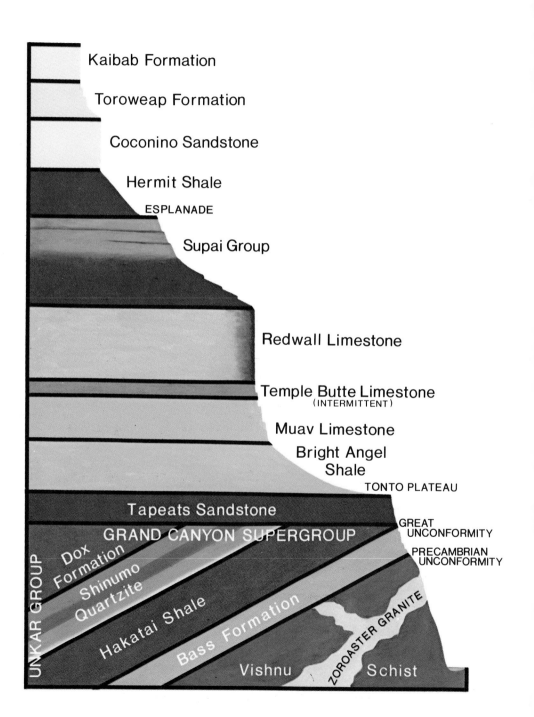

Kaibab Formation

Toroweap Formation

Coconino Sandstone

Hermit Shale

ESPLANADE

Supai Group

Redwall Limestone

Temple Butte Limestone
(INTERMITTENT)

Muav Limestone

Bright Angel
Shale

TONTO PLATEAU

Tapeats Sandstone

GRAND CANYON SUPERGROUP

GREAT
UNCONFORMITY

PRECAMBRIAN
UNCONFORMITY

UNKAR GROUP

Dox
Formation

Shinumo
Quartzite

Hakatai Shale

Bass Formation

ZOROASTER GRANITE

Vishnu   Schist

Plate 9.

The Precambrian Unconformity as it appears at the mouth of Hance Creek, below Grandview Point. The unconformity is clearly visible here as the plane of contact between the tilted strata of the Unkar Group and the dark, foliated Vishnu Schist below. Lying directly on top of the Vishnu Schist are the ledgy cliffs of the Bass Formation. Above them is the rust-red, slope-forming Hakatai Shale. The dark cliffs atop the shale are formed of Shinumo Quartzite. The Great Unconformity, which divides the Precambrian rocks from the overlying Paleozoic strata, is somewhat obscured by the angle of the photograph, but occurs here at the top of the Shinumo Quartzite, where it is overlain by the greenish, slope-forming Bright Angel Shale. In most parts of the canyon, the Great Unconformity occurs where Tapeats Sandstone rests on top of Precambrian rocks. Here, however, the Tapeats was evidently stripped away by erosion before the deposition of the Bright Angel Shale. The prominent butte in the background is Vishnu Temple, which is capped by Kaibab Limestone. Redwall Limestone forms the sheer cliff at the base of the butte.

Plate 10. Anatomy of a Fern.

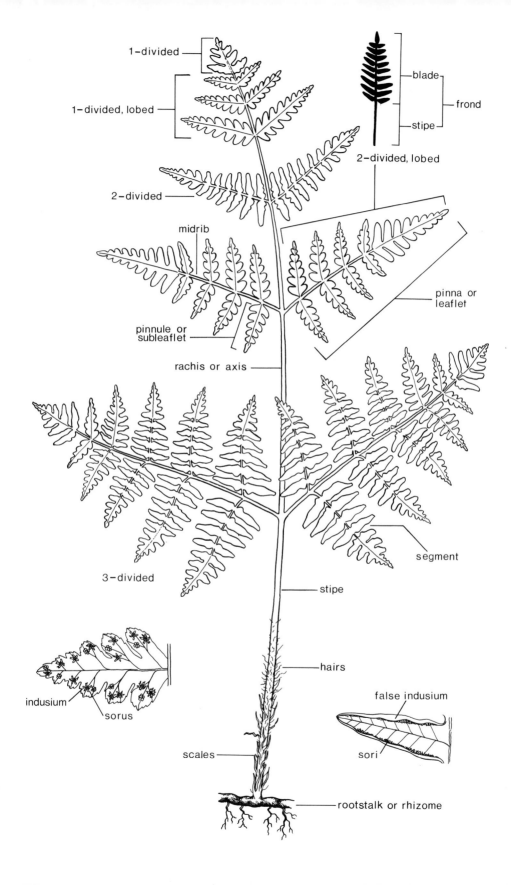

1-divided

1-divided, lobed

blade

frond

stipe

2-divided

2-divided, lobed

midrib

pinna or leaflet

pinnule or subleaflet

rachis or axis

segment

3-divided

stipe

hairs

indusium

sorus

false indusium

sori

scales

rootstalk or rhizome

Plate 11. Horsetails and Maidenhair, Woodsias and Brittle Ferns.

Horsetails or Scouring Rushes, genus Equisetum. Horsetail Family. Com. near streams, ponds, seeps and springs, and especially along Colorado River. Spores in conelike spikes at stem tips. Leaves inconspicuous, forming crownlike sheaths at stem joints. Common Scouring Rush (E. hyemale): 8–60" tall; sheaths with 2 dark bands. Smooth Scouring Rush (E. laevigatum): 12–40" tall; sheath with one dark band. Both have unbranched stems and short spore cones. Field Horsetail (E. arvense): 18" tall or less, has both branched (sterile) and unbranched (fertile) stems and longer, slimmer spore cones.

Maidenhair Fern, Adiantum capillus-veneris. Fern family. Com.– Abund., seeps and springs below 7000'. Fronds to 22" tall. Easily identified by fan-shape subleaflets and black, wiry stems.

Woodsias, genus Woodsia. Fern Family. Uncom.–Rare, moist soil in crevices, on ledges and among boulders. Two species at Grand Canyon. Mexican Woodsia (W. mexicana): fronds 3–14" long, 1–2" wide, 1–2-divided, growing in clumps; frond stems pale yellow, smooth or scaly; leaflets mostly offset or alternate, smooth or minutely glandular, toothed or lobed, with teeth ending in delicate hairs. Sori covered by spiderlike membrane. Oregon Woodsia (W. oregana): very similar to above, but stems always smooth, brown at base and paler above; leaflets mostly opposite, sometimes alternate; teeth of subleaflets do not end in hairs.

Brittle Fern, Cystopteris fragilis. Fern Family. Com. in woods, among rocks, near springs. Fronds 2-divided, delicate and thin, mostly or entirely smooth, up to 20" long, ¼–½ as wide, clustered. Sori along veins on undersides of fertile subleaflets, protected by hoodlike membranes.

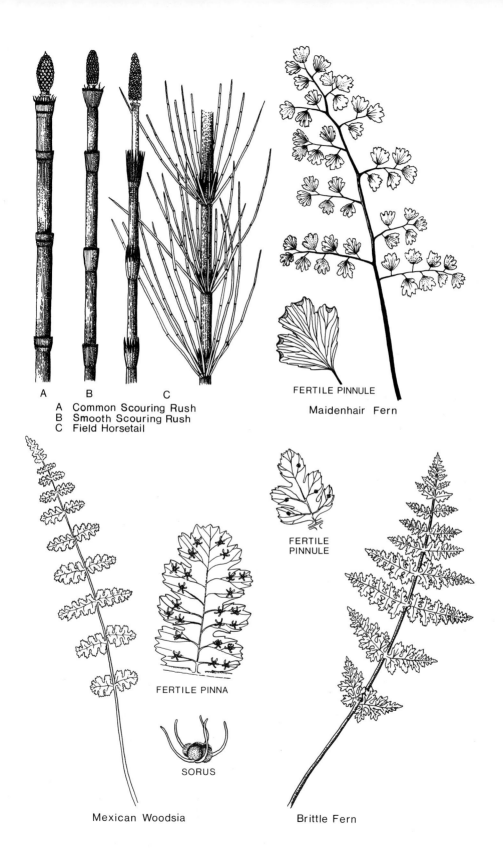

A
B
C

A Common Scouring Rush
B Smooth Scouring Rush
C Field Horsetail

FERTILE PINNULE

Maidenhair Fern

FERTILE PINNA

SORUS

Mexican Woodsia

FERTILE
PINNULE

Brittle Fern

Plate 12. Lip Ferns.

Slender Lip Fern, Cheilanthes feei. *Fern Family. Com., dry, rocky slopes and cliffs below about 7000'. Fronds to 10" long, 2–3-divided, noticeably hairy. Stems brown, scaly at base, otherwise sparsely-to-moderately white-hairy. Leaflet axes similar, sometimes lighter colored. Usually 6–12 leaflets, opposite or alternate, with long, white hairs above and brownish hairs below.*

Eaton's Lip Fern, Cheilanthes eatonii. *Fern Family. Com., crevices. Fronds to 16" long, 3-divided, with segments sometimes lobed. Stems brown, with closely pressed hairs or scales. Segments with curly white hairs above, dense, rusty hairs below. Sori covered by a single protective membrane.*

Lindheimer's Lip Fern, Cheilanthes lindheimeri. *Fern Family. Com., nonlimestone crevices. Fronds to 14" long, dark brown, with scales and woolly hairs, not clumped. Blade 3–4-divided, with white hairs above and matted rusty hairs and/or scales below. Segments beadlike.*

Parry's Lip Fern, Cheilanthes parryi. *Fern Family. Com., rocks and crevices in hot, dry places below 6500'. Fronds 3–6" long, 2-divided and lobed, so hairy they seem like fluffs of cotton. Stems chestnut brown, hairy, with few scales at base. Leaflets covered on both sides with dense hair, usually white, sometimes tan below. The most abundant dry-habitat fern in the park.*

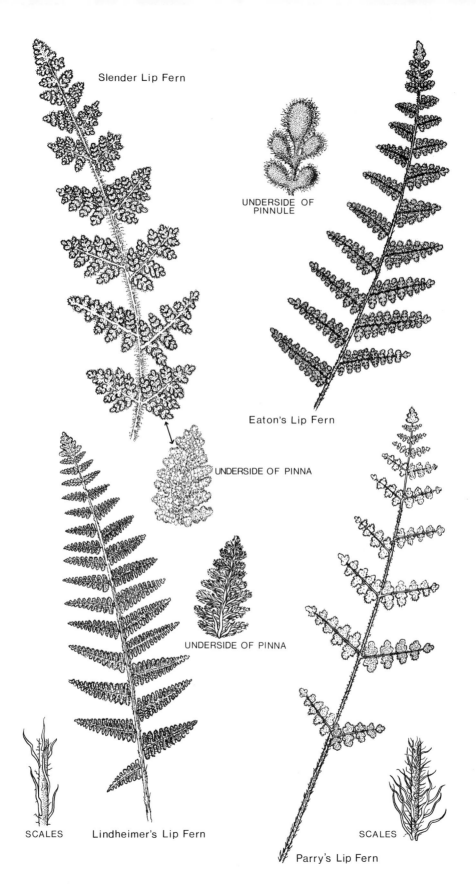

Slender Lip Fern

UNDERSIDE OF
PINNULE

Eaton's Lip Fern

UNDERSIDE OF PINNA

UNDERSIDE OF PINNA

SCALES   Lindheimer's Lip Fern

SCALES

Parry's Lip Fern

Plate 13. Bracken, Male Fern, Cloak Fern and Cliff-brake.

Bracken, Pteridium aquilinum. *Fern Family. Com., forest openings, North Rim. Fronds 20–80" long, 2–3-divided. Subleaflets smooth or slightly hairy above, densely hairy to downy below. Sori marginal, protected by rolled-over leaf margin.*

Male Fern, Dryopteris filix-mas. *Fern Family. Uncom., rocky places in cool, moist forest. Fronds 2–4' long, 6–12" wide, 1-divided, lobed. Subleaflets parallel-sided, blunt-tipped. Sori nearer midvein than margin. Indusium often has a glandular margin.*

Wavy Cloak Fern, Notholaena sinuata. *Fern Family. Com., limestone rocks below 7000'. Fronds 6–18", narrowly 1-divided, lobed. Stems white–scaly. Leaflets white-scaly above, white–brown-scaly below, with 3–6 pairs of lobes. Sori hidden by scales.*

Jones' Cliff-brake, Pellaea jonesii. *Fern Family. Uncom., limestone crevices, 3500–7000'. Fronds 2–6" long, 2-divided. Stems brown, smooth. Subleaflets smooth, with margins entire or slightly lobed. Sori covered by subleaflet margins.*

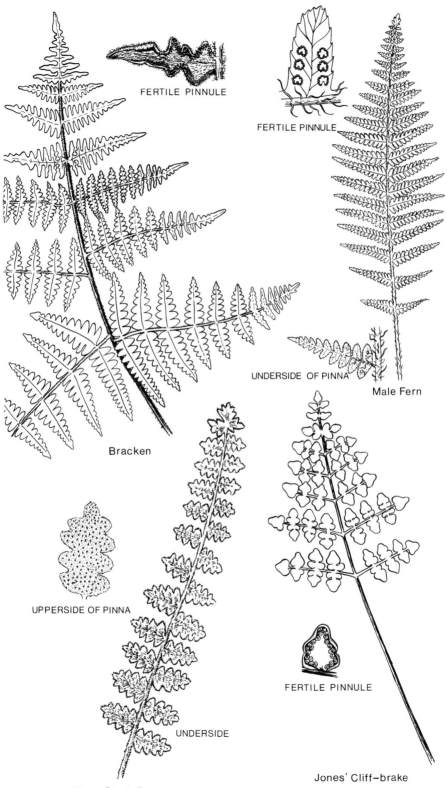

FERTILE PINNULE

FERTILE PINNULE

UNDERSIDE OF PINNA

Male Fern

Bracken

UPPERSIDE OF PINNA

UNDERSIDE

Wavy Cloak Fern

FERTILE PINNULE

Jones' Cliff-brake

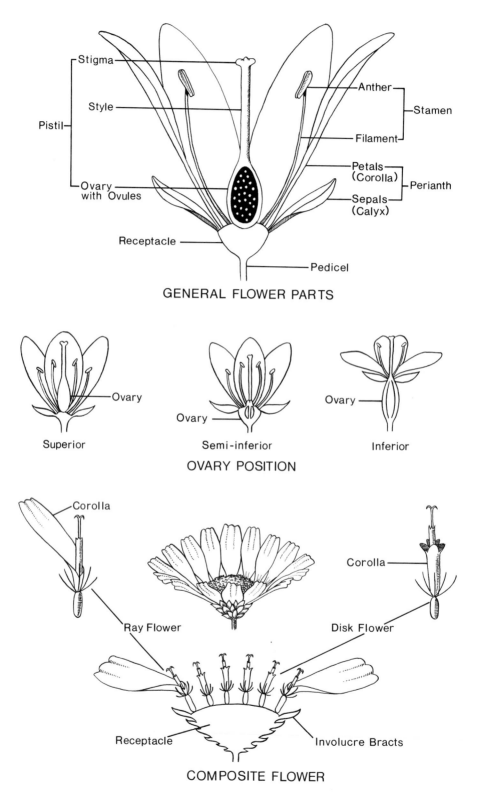

GENERAL FLOWER PARTS

Stigma

Style

Pistil

Ovary with Ovules

Receptacle

Pedicel

Anther

Stamen

Filament

Petals (Corolla)

Perianth

Sepals (Calyx)

OVARY POSITION

Ovary

Superior

Ovary

Semi-inferior

Ovary

Inferior

COMPOSITE FLOWER

Corolla

Ray Flower

Corolla

Disk Flower

Receptacle

Involucre Bracts

Plate 14. Flower Parts.

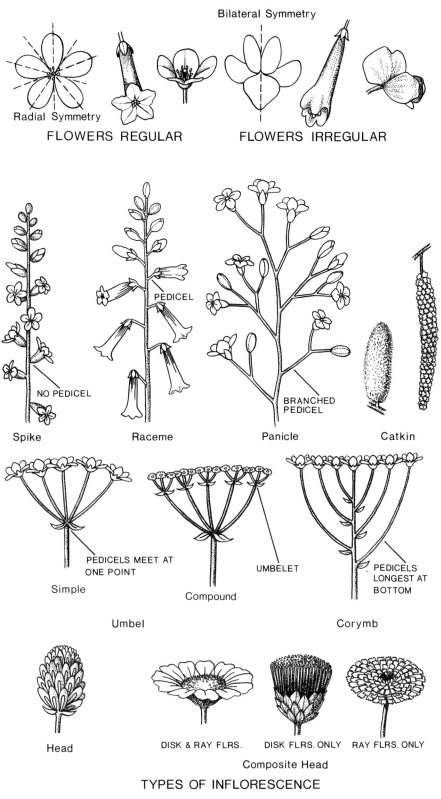

Bilateral Symmetry

Radial Symmetry

FLOWERS REGULAR   **FLOWERS IRREGULAR**

PEDICEL

NO PEDICEL

BRANCHED PEDICEL

Spike   Raceme   Panicle   Catkin

PEDICELS MEET AT ONE POINT

Simple

UMBELET

Compound

PEDICELS LONGEST AT BOTTOM

Umbel   Corymb

Head

DISK & RAY FLRS.   DISK FLRS. ONLY   RAY FLRS. ONLY

Composite Head

TYPES OF INFLORESCENCE

Plate 15. Flower and Inflorescence Types.

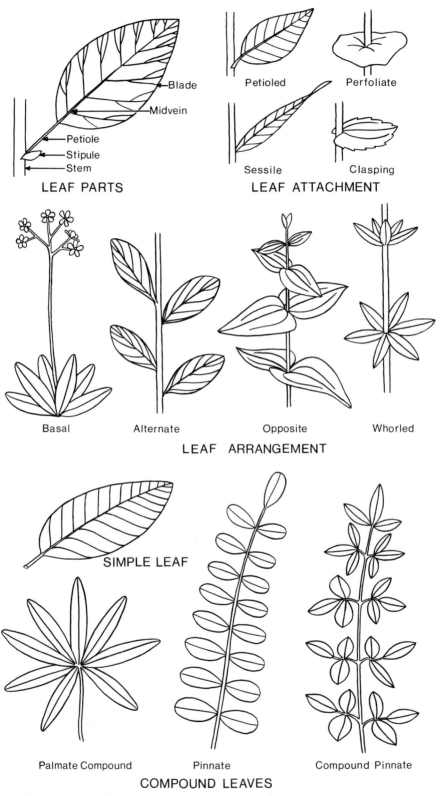

LEAF PARTS

Blade
Midvein
Petiole
Stipule
Stem

LEAF ATTACHMENT

Petioled
Perfoliate
Sessile
Clasping

Basal   Alternate   Opposite   Whorled

LEAF ARRANGEMENT

SIMPLE LEAF

Palmate Compound   Pinnate   Compound Pinnate

COMPOUND LEAVES

Plate 16. Leaf Parts, Arrangements, Attachments and Categories.

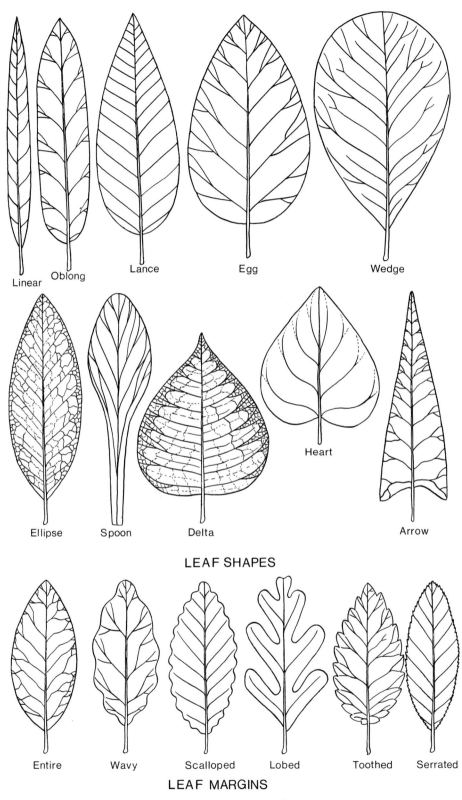

Linear
Oblong
Lance
Egg
Wedge

Ellipse
Spoon
Delta
Heart
Arrow

LEAF SHAPES

Entire
Wavy
Scalloped
Lobed
Toothed
Serrated

LEAF MARGINS

Plate 17. Leaf Shapes and Margins.

Plate 18. White Flowers.

Sego Lily, Calochortus nuttallii. *Lily Family. Com., SN Rims, dry openings, Wood. and Forest. Ht. 8–16". Lvs. linear, sparse, mostly basal. Flrs. 1–2" diam., 3 petals, sometimes lilac or yellow. May–July. Cf. Weakstem Mariposa Lily, Plate 31.*

Elegant Death-camas, Zigadenus elegans. *Lily Family. N Rim, Grass. and damp, rocky places, Forest. Ht. 8–24". Lvs. linear, basal. Flrs. partly inferior, ½" diam., 3 petals, in raceme, sometimes yellowish white with or without purple tinge. July–August.*

Snowball, Abronia elliptica. *Four O'Clock Family. CAN, mostly river beaches in dry sand. Ht. 4–20". Stems erect or trailing, sometimes sticky-downy. Lvs. opposite oblong, oval or elliptic, fleshy, ½–2½" long. Flrs. tubular, 5-lobed, fragrant, in heads 2–3" diam., night-blooming. April–November. One of 3 species of sand-verbena in CAN, others with pink or reddish flrs.*

Miners Lettuce, Montia perfoliata. *Portulaca Family. Moist, shady banks and crevices. Ht. 2–6". Lvs. basal, with 1 perfoliate leaf per stem just below the flrs. Basal lvs. variable, 2–8" long, with petioles longer than blades. Perfoliate leaf succulent, ½–2" diam. Flrs. to ¼" diam., 5 petals, in loose raceme above perfoliate leaf. January–June.*

Fendler Sandwort, Arenaria fendleri. *Pink Family. Com., N Rim Grass. Ht. 1½–12". Stems glandular-downy, at least below. Lvs. linear, stemless, opposite. Flrs. to ½" diam., 5 petals, in cyme. April–September. Other sandworts, SN Rims and CAN.*

Prickly Poppy, Argemone pleiacantha. *Poppy Family. Com., SN Rims, dry, disturbed areas and CAN along trails. Ht. to 36". Stems and leaves prickly. Lvs. stemless, lobed and spined. Flrs. to 4" across, usually 6 petals. April–September. Other, very similar species also occur in the area.*

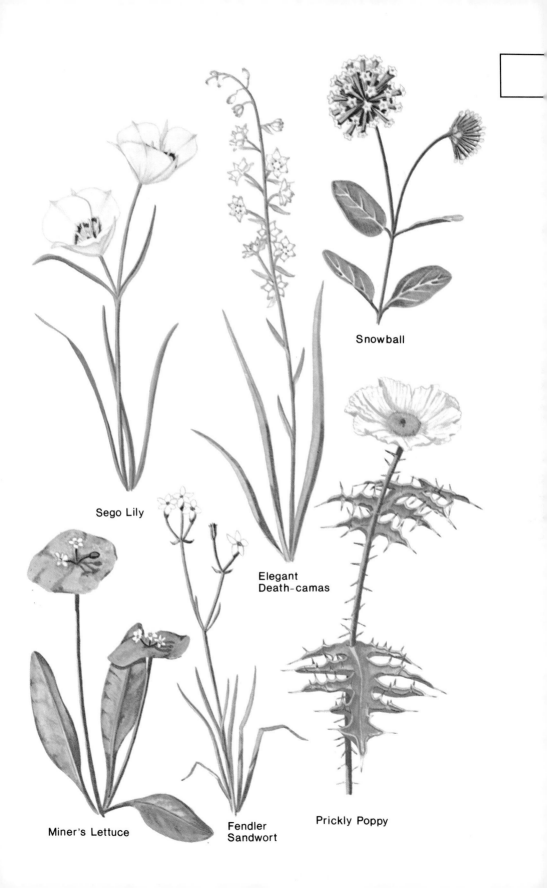

Snowball

Sego Lily

Elegant
Death-camas

Miner's Lettuce

Fendler
Sandwort

Prickly Poppy

Plate 19. White Flowers.

Watercress, Rorippa nasturtium-aquaticum. *Mustard Family. Locally com., Aquat. Stems floating, creeping or partly erect. Lvs. pinnate with oval leaflets. Flrs. tiny, 4 petals, in heads to ½" diam. April–August.*

Wild Candytuft, Thlaspi fendleri. *Mustard Family. Com., SN Rims, Wood., Forest and N Rim Grass. Ht. 6". Lvs. both basal and clasping. Basal lvs. nearly round, to ¾" long; clasping lvs. tiny, oblong. Flrs. tiny, 4 petals, in racemes. Plants often in dense clusters. March–August.*

Wild Strawberry, Fragaria ovalis. *Rose Family. Locally Com., moist shady places, N Rim Forest. Ht. to 8", erect, but with trailing runners. Lvs. palmate compound, with 3 leaflets, each mostly wedge-shape, to about 1½" long, smooth above, downy below, with coarse-toothed margins. Flrs. ½–1" across, 5 petals, in cymes on leafless stems. Fruit a tiny strawberry. May–October.*

Rock Mat, Petrophytum caespitosum. *Rose Family. Com., rocky places, SN Rims and CAN. Prostrate mat, 12–24" across. Stems woody toward base: a subshrub. Lvs. wedge- to spoon-shape, tiny, in tufts. Flrs. numerous, tiny, 5 petals, in spikes to 2" long. June–October.*

White Cranesbill, Geranium richardsonii. *Geranium Family. Com., N Rim Spruce–Fir Forest. Ht. to 36". Stems smooth or downy, upper part often glandular. Lvs. opposite, palmately lobed, to 6" diam., with stiff, flattened hairs, especially on veins. Flrs. to 1" across, 5 petals, with glandular-soft-hairy stems. April–October. Cf. Purple Cranesbill, Plate 32.*

Canada Violet, Viola canadensis. *Violet Family. Uncom., damp, shady places, Forest. Ht. 6–12". Stems slightly downy. Lvs. heart-shape, toothed, to 2" across. Flrs. ½–1", 5 petals. April–October.*

Watercress

Wild
Candytuft

Wild
Strawberry

White Cranesbill

Rock Mat

Canada Violet

Plate 20. White Flowers.

White-tufted Evening Primrose, Oenothera caespitosa. *Evening Primrose Family. Com., SN Rims, open areas and roadsides. Ht. to 8", with lvs. and flrs. all rising from root crown. Lvs. linear/lance-shape, margins wavy or cleft, to 6" long. Flrs. to 3" across, 4 petals, becoming pink with age. Each flr. blooms one night only. May–September. One of several evening primroses found in area. Cf. Tall Yellow Evening Primrose, Plate 24.*

Field Bindweed, Convolvulus arvensis. *Morning Glory Family. Com., roadsides, disturbed areas. Trailing vine with stems 8–48" long, smooth to densely downy. Lvs. variable in size or shape; usually ½–2" long, oblong. Flr. funnel-shape, ½–2" long, 5 fused petals. May–July. The related Scarlet Starglory* (Ipomoea coccinea) *has bright red flrs.*

White-veined Wintergreen, Pyrola picta. *Heath Family. N Rim, Forest. Ht. 4–10". Lvs. basal, broadly oval, sometimes finely toothed, to 2¾" long. Flrs. small, nodding, 5 petals, in raceme. July–August. One of 4 species in area.*

Bristly Hiddenflower, Cryptantha setosissima. *Borage Family. Com., SN Rims, often along roads. Ht. to 36". Stems densely covered with bristles. Lvs. linear/oblong–lance-shape, to 4" long. Lowest lvs. form basal rosette. Lvs. also along stem; lower ones with petioles; upper ones without and covered with stiff flattened hairs and bristles. Flrs. ½" diam., short-tubular, with bristly calyx, in panicle. One of 20 species of hiddenflower in the area. CAN species mostly smaller. May–September.*

Sacred Datura, Datura meteloides. *Potato Family. Com., CAN, Scrub. Ht. 20–70". Stems downy. Lvs. egg–shape, usually with asymmetric base and wavy margins, 2–12" long. Flrs. tubular, 6–10" long, 4–8" wide, night-blooming, turning purple or brown after dawn. April–October.*

Desert Tobacco, Nicotiana trigonophylla. *Potato Family. Com., CAN, especially Gorge, dry places. Ht. 8–36". Lvs. and stems glandular-downy. Lvs. variable in shape, upper ones without stems, 2–6" long, 1–4" wide. Flrs. tubular, 5-lobed. Blooms year-round. Coyote Tobacco* (N. attenuata) *is very similar and replaces the above at upper elevations in CAN and on SN Rims.*

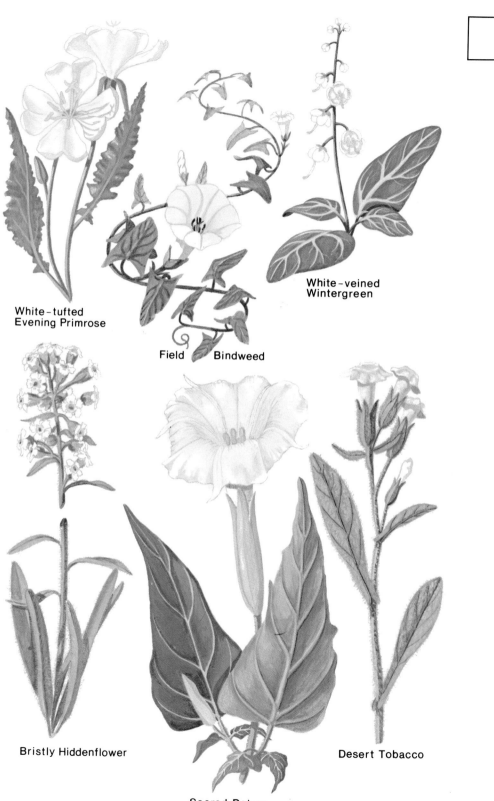

White-tufted
Evening Primrose

Field   Bindweed

White-veined
Wintergreen

Bristly Hiddenflower

Sacred Datura

Desert Tobacco

Plate 21. White Flowers.

All the wildflowers on this plate belong to the Sunflower Family.

Western Yarrow, Achillea lanulosa. *Com., sunny places, N Rim. Ht. 10–20". Stems covered with long, soft hairs. Lvs. lacy, finely dissected, 1¼–4" long, ½" wide. Flrs. composite, less than ½" diam., about 4–8 disk flowers, in dense terminal panicle. June–September.*

Baby White Aster, Aster arenosus. *Com., S Rim, Scrub and Wood. Ht. 2½–5". Stems numerous, branching from woody base, covered with stiff, flattened hairs, often glandular. Lvs. about ½" or less, linear or spoon-shape, hairy. Flrs. composite, about ½" diam. April–May, August–September. Smallest of several asters in the area. Cf. Mohave and Hoary asters, Plate 35.*

Wheeler Thistle, Cirsium wheeleri. *Com., SN Rims, Pine Forest. Ht. 16–32". Stems woolly. Lvs. deeply lobed, spiny, sparsely woolly above, densely below, to 5" long. Flrs. composite, but with disk flrs. only, usually pink or purple, sometimes white on N Rim. July–October. Cf. Carmine Thistle, Plate 30.*

Rocky Mountain Pussytoes, Antennaria aprica. *Com., SN Rims, Grass. and Forest openings. Mat-forming, 1–6" tall. Lvs. stemless, mostly basal, wedge-shape, woolly both sides, to ¾" long. Flrs. composite, but with disk flrs. only, in clustered heads at end of stem. May–August.*

Hairy Fleabane, Erigeron concinnus. *Com., SN Rims and upper elevations in CAN. Ht. 4–20". Stems and lvs. hairy, sometimes glandular. Lvs. linear, to 4" long, but usually shorter. Flrs. composite with 50–100 rays, 1–1½" diam., sometimes blue or pink. April–October. Difficult to distinguish from other fleabanes. Cf. Fleabane, Plate 35.*

Stemless Townsendia, Townsendia exscapa. *Com., SN Rims, Wood. Ht. 1–2". Plants stemless or nearly so. Lvs. basal, linear, with rolled margins, hairy, to 2" long. Flrs. composite, ½–1" diam., rays sometimes purplish. April–June.*

Western Yarrow

Baby White Aster

Wheeler
Thistle

Rocky Mtn. Pussytoes

Hairy
Fleabane

Stemless Townsendia

Plate 22. Yellow Flowers.

Desert Trumpet, Eriogonum inflatum. *Buckwheat Family. Com., CAN, rocky places and Gorge. Ht. to 30". Stems swollen at nodes. Lvs. basal, oblong to nearly round, smooth or short-haired, to 1" long. Flrs. without petals, but with petallike calyx. March–October.*

Sulfur Flower, Eriogonum umbellatum. *Buckwheat Family. SN Rims and CAN, dry, open places. Ht. 4–12". Stems woolly. Lvs. woolly, spoon-shape, basal, to 1" long. Flrs. similar to above, but in umbels. April–November.*

Golden Corydalis, Corydalis aurea. *Poppy Family. Uncom., moist places, SN Rims and CAN. Ht. 4–16". Lvs. bipinnate with dissected leaflets. Flrs. irregular, 4 petals, 2 spreading, one of these with spur at base, about ½" long. February–June.*

Utah Deervetch, Lotus utahensis. *Pea Family. Com., N Rim, sunny spots, roadsides, disturbed places; Uncom., S Rim, where it is replaced by the similar Wright's Deervetch (L. wrightii). Stems 4–12" long. Lvs. and stems downy. Lvs. pinnate or nearly palmate, stemless, with 3–7 narrow leaflets. Flrs. irregular, about ½" long, 5 united petals. June–September.*

Yellow Sweet-clover, Melilotus officinalis. *Pea Family. SN Rims, roadsides, disturbed areas; also fairly Com. in Gorge along river. Ht. to about 78". Plant bushy. Lvs. compound with 3 leaflets, each wedge-shape, ½–¾" long. Flowers irregular, 5 separate petals, ¼" long. June–October. Often grows with White Sweet-clover (M. alba), which is similar but has white flowers.*

Golden Peavine, Thermopsis pinetorum. *Pea Family. SN Rims, Pine Forest. Ht. 12–24". Stems nearly smooth to downy. Lvs. compound, with 3 leaflets, each oblong to elliptic, slightly downy, 1–3" long. Flrs. irregular, 5 united petals, ½–1" long. April–June.*

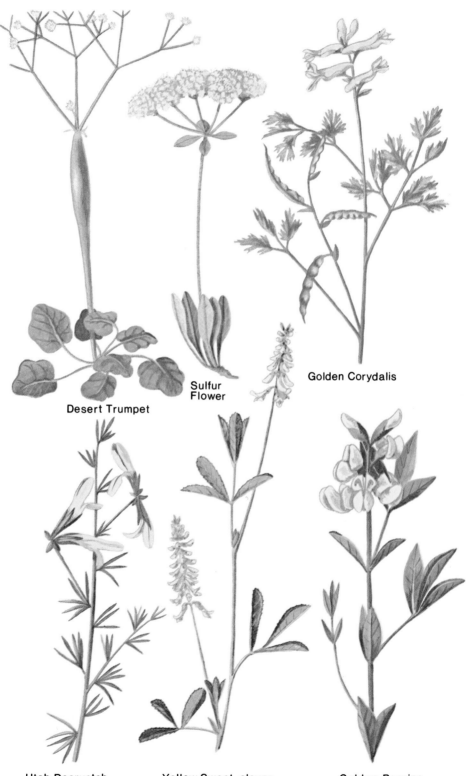

Desert Trumpet

Sulfur
Flower

Golden Corydalis

Utah Deervetch

Yellow Sweet-clover

Golden Peavine

Plate 23. Yellow Flowers.

Golden Columbine, Aquilegia chrysantha. *Buttercup Family. Com., N Rim and CAN, Ripar. and moist crevices. Ht. 12–40". Lvs. compound with 3-lobed and cleft leaflets, each smooth or slightly downy below. Flrs. regular, 2–3" long, 5 petals with spurs. April–September. Cf. Colorado Columbine, Plate 36.*

Heart-leafed Buttercup, Ranunculus cardiophyllus. *Buttercup Family. Com., N Rim, Grass.; rare, S Rim. Ht. 6–15". Plants smooth to soft-hairy. Lvs. both basal and alternate. Basal lvs. heart-shape, 1½–2½" long, with stems. Alternate lvs. stemless, with linear lobes. Flrs. ¾–1½" diam., 5 petals. One of several similar buttercups in the area. June–August.*

Western Wallflower, Erysimum capitatum. *Mustard Family. Com., SN Rims and CAN above Gorge, sunny places. Ht. to 32". Plant downy. Lvs. variable in shape and margins, 1½–6" long. Flrs. about ½" diam., 4 petals, in racemes. April–August.*

Bladderpod, Lesquerella intermedia. *Mustard Family. Com., SN Rims, open areas. Ht. ½–7½". Plants covered with star-shape hairs. Lvs. linear, mostly basal, ½–1½" long. Stem lvs. similar but smaller. Flrs. about ½" diam., 4 petals, in racemes. April–August. Cf. Purple Bladderpod, Plate 31.*

Common Monkeyflower, Mimulus guttatus. *Snapdragon Family. Un-com., limited to moist places in side canyons. Ht. 2–40". Lvs. mostly oval, opposite, usually toothed, with or without stems. Flrs. irregular, tubular, 5-lobed, about 1" long. March–September. Cf. Crimson Monkeyflower, Plate 30.*

Yellow Owl-clover, Orthocarpus luteus. *Snapdragon Family. Com., Grass. Ht. 4–15". Stems glandular-hairy. Lvs. narrow, mostly entire, less than ½" long, with glands and minute bristly hairs. Flrs. irregular, with beaklike upper lip and inflated lower lip, ½" long, in terminal spike. July–September. Cf. Purple-white Owl-clover, Plate 34.*

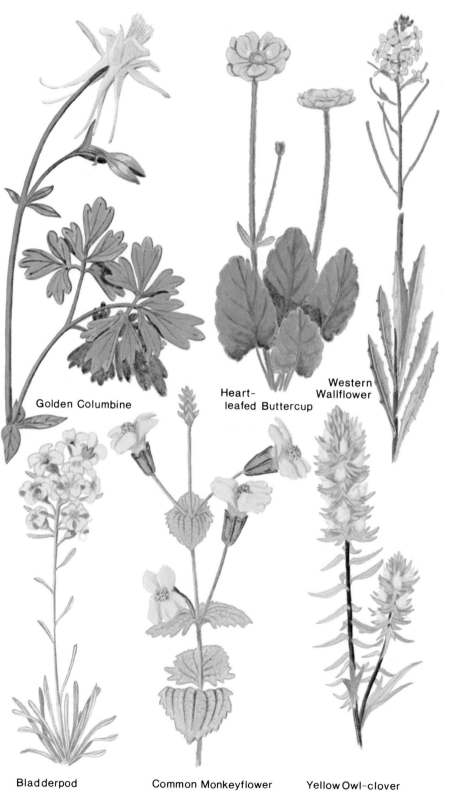

Golden Columbine

Heart-
leafed Buttercup

Western
Wallflower

Bladderpod

Common Monkeyflower

Yellow Owl-clover

Plate 24. Yellow Flowers.

Woolly Mullein, Verbascum thapsus. *Snapdragon Family. Com., SN Rims, roadsides and disturbed places, also Wood. and Forest. Ht. 1–6½'. Plant densely woolly. 1st-year lvs. basal, oblong to wedge-shape, 4–10" long. 2nd-year lvs. on flowering stem, elliptic to lance-shape, clasping, drooping. Flrs. slightly irregular, 5–6 petals, to 1" across, in terminal spike. April–September.*

Desert Plume, Stanleya pinnata. *Mustard Family. Com., steep rocky slopes, CAN. Ht. 16–60". Plant smooth or downy, with woody base. Leaves 2–6" long, lower ones deeply divided into lance-shape segments, upper ones shorter, wedge-shape, entire or divided. Flrs. about 1" diam., 4 petals with "claws," in terminal raceme 8–24" long. May–September.*

Osterhout Cinquefoil, Potentilla osterhoutii. *Rose Family. Com., SN Rims, rock crevices. Ht. 2–8". Lvs. pinnate with 5–11 glandular-hairy leaflets. Flrs. to ½" across, 5 petals. June–September. One of several species in area.*

Stickleaf, Mentzelia pumila. *Loasa Family. Com., SN Rims and CAN. Ht. 8–18". Stems rough, woody toward base, twisted, much-branched. Lvs. linear to wedge-shape, to 1½", with sandpaper texture from stiff, barbed hairs. Flrs. ¾–1½", 10 petals, solitary or a few in cymes. February–October.*

Tall Yellow Evening Primrose, Oenothera longissima. *Evening Primrose Family. Most Com., roadsides on N Rim. Ht. 3–10'. Plant with stiff hairs. Basal lvs. wedge-shape, 4–8" long; stem lvs. shorter, narrowly lance-shape. Flrs. with long floral tube and 4 petals 1¾" long. Each flr. blooms one night only, turning red toward morning. July–September. Cf. Hooker Evening Primrose, below, and White-tufted Evening Primrose, Plate 20.*

Hooker Evening Primrose, Oenothera hookeri. *Evening Primrose Family. SN Rims and CAN, moist places, incl. along river. Ht. 12–60". Stems often reddish. Plant with stiff hairs. Basal lvs. wedge- to lance-shape, margins wavy or toothed; stem lvs. lance-shape 2–5" long, nearly stemless. Flrs. similar to above species, but floral tube only 1–2" long. Each flr. blooms one night only, turning orange–red by morning. July–October. Cf. Tall Yellow Evening Primrose, above, and White-tufted Evening Primrose, Plate 20.*

Woolly Mullein   Desert Plume   Osterhout Cinquefoil

Stickleaf   Tall Yellow Evening Primrose   Hooker Evening Primrose

Plate 25. Yellow Flowers.

Rough Menodora, Menodora scabra. *Olive Family. Uncom., Grass. and Scrub, S Rim. Ht. to 14". Stems rough. Lvs. ½–1½" long, lower lvs. egg-shape, upper lvs. lance-shape, both nearly smooth and nearly stemless. Flrs. tubular, ½–¾" diam., 4-lobed. March–September.*

Many-flowered Puccoon, Lithospermum multiflorum. *Borage Family. Com., SN Rims, Pine Forest. Ht. 1–2'. Stems hairy. Lvs. linear to lance-shape, hairy, 1½–2" long. Flrs. tubular, ¼–½" long, in racemes. May–August.*

Groundcherry, Physalis crassifolia. *Nightshade Family. Com., hot, dry flats and talus slopes, Gorge. Ht. 1–2'. Stems spreading, forming a bushy plant. Lvs. egg-, delta- or heart-shape, margins entire or wavy, ½–1½" long. Flrs. bell-shape, ½" diam., petals joined. February–October.*

Orange Mountain Dandelion, Agoseris aurantiaca. *Sunflower Family. N Rim meadows. Ht. 4–24". Lvs. basal, linear, oblong, lance- or wedge-shape, entire or divided, 2–10" long. Flrs. composite, but with ray flrs. only. Heads ½–1" diam. The only orange dandelion; flrs. turn pink or purple with age. June–August. Cf. Pale Mountain Dandelion, below, and Common Dandelion (Plate 28).*

Pale Mountain Dandelion, Agoseris glauca. *Sunflower Family. Very similar to above, but flrs. are yellow. Found only on N Rim. On the S Rim it is replaced by the yellow Arizona Mountain Dandelion (A. arizonica). May–October.*

Hairy Gold-aster, Chrysopsis villosa. *Sunflower Family. Com., SN Rims and upper elevations of CAN. Ht. 4–20". Stems may be woody toward base in larger plants. Plants downy. Lvs. linear to wedge-shape, less than 1" long. Flrs. composite, heads about 1" across. May–October.*

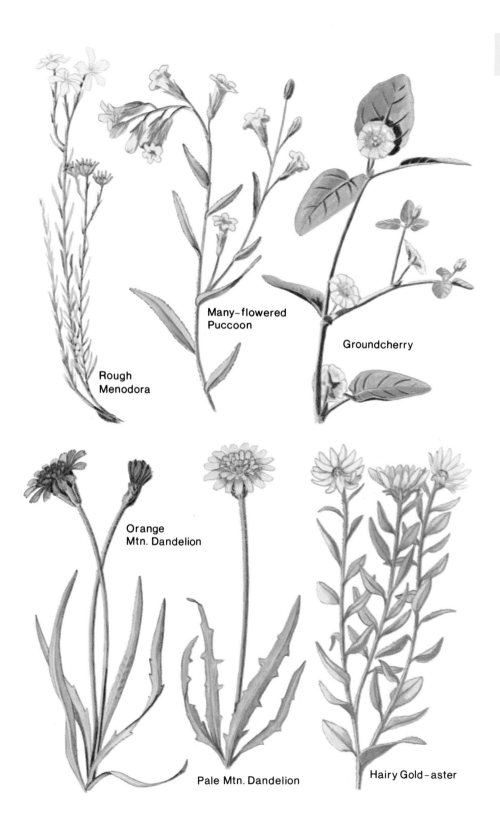

Rough
Menodora

Many-flowered
Puccoon

Groundcherry

Orange
Mtn. Dandelion

Pale Mtn. Dandelion

Hairy Gold-aster

Plate 26. Yellow Flowers.

All the wildflowers on this plate belong to the Sunflower Family.

Ragleaf, Bahia dissecta. *SN Rims and higher elevations in CAN. Ht. 4–32". Lvs. cleft 2–3 times, somewhat hairy, about 1–2¾" long. Flrs. composite, with 10–15 rays. Heads about 1" diam. with sticky hairs. June–October.*

Yellow Tackstem, Calycoseris parryi. *Tonto Plateau and Gorge, Scrub. Ht. 2–12". Stems spreading or semi-erect, with tack-shape glands on upper halves. Lvs. mostly basal, pinnately divided to entire. Flrs. composite, with ray flrs. only. Heads about 1–1½" diam. with tack-shape glands. March–May.*

Western Hawksbeard, Crepis occidentalis. *SN Rims, open areas. Ht. 3–10". Plant densely woolly, somewhat glandular. Lvs. wavy-toothed to deeply divided, with toothed lobes, mostly 4–6½" long. Flrs. composite, with 5–30 heads per stem, each head about 2" diam. June–September.*

Pinnate-leaved Blanket Flower, Gaillardia pinnatifida. *Open areas, SN Rims and CAN. Ht. 4–13¾". Plants with stiff hairs. Lvs. wedge-shape, pinnately divided or merely lobed and toothed, 1–3" long. Flrs. composite; heads about 1½" diam. April–November.*

Curlycup Gumweed, Grindelia squarrosa. *S Rim, roadsides and open areas. Ht. 6–40". Lvs. oblong to wedge-shape, 1–2¾" long, margins finely toothed or entire. Flrs. composite, with heads about 1" diam., in corymb. June–October. Rayless Gumweed* (G. aphanactis) *is similar but heads lack ray flowers.*

Broom Snakeweed, Gutierrezia sarothrae. *Com., dry, open places, SN Rims and CAN. Ht. 4–36". Stems herbaceous, but woody toward base. Plant somewhat rough-textured, with resinous glands. Lvs. linear or nearly so, smooth or hairy, about ¼" long. Flrs. composite, with 3–8 disk flrs. and like number of rays. Heads small, but numerous in clusters. July–November.* Gutierrezia microcephala *similar, but plant and flrs. smaller. Replaces* G. sarothrae *in the Gorge.*

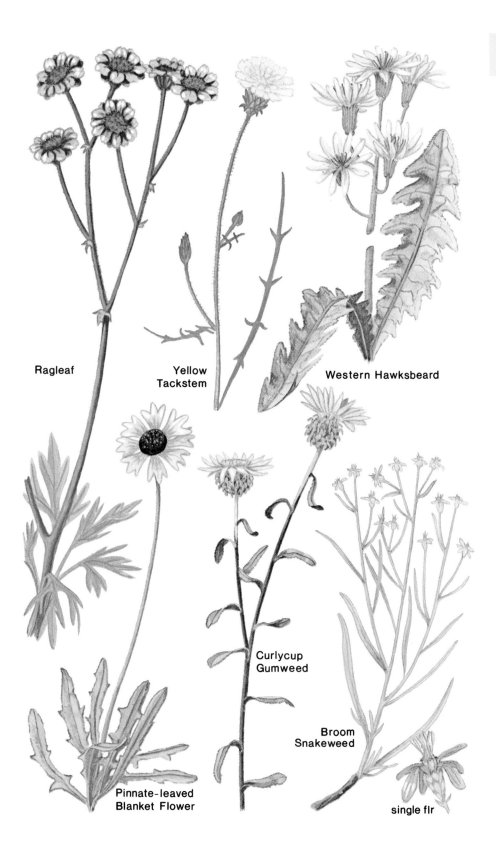

Ragleaf

Yellow
Tackstem

Western Hawksbeard

Curlycup
Gumweed

Broom
Snakeweed

Pinnate-leaved
Blanket Flower

single flr

Plate 27. Yellow Flowers.

All the wildflowers on this plate belong to the Sunflower Family.

Spiny Goldenweed, Haplopappus spinulosus. CAN, *mostly Gorge. Ht. 8–24". Stems smooth or woolly, usually glandular, sprouting from woody base. Lvs. ½–2½" long, linear or spoon-shape, smooth or woolly, margins usually with bristle-tipped teeth. Flrs. composite, ¾–2" diam., with spine-tipped bracts. One of several species of goldenweed in the area. February–May, sometimes in late summer.*

Common Sunflower, Helianthus annuus. S Rim, *roadsides and open areas. Ht. 1–6½'. Stems covered with numerous, stiff, bristly hairs. Lvs. egg-shape, 1½–8" long, entire or toothed, lower ones often heart-shape. Flrs. composite, 2–3" diam., usually solitary. March–October and August–September. The Prairie Sunflower* (H. petiolaris) *is similar but smaller.*

Hymenopappus, Hymenopappus lugens. SN Rims, *open areas. Ht. 4–20". Plants more or less woolly. Lvs. 2-divided, mostly basal, 2–3½" long. Flrs. composite, without rays. Heads less than ½" diam. May–September.*

Arizona Stemless Hymenoxys, Hymenoxys acaulis. Com. SN Rims *and upper elevations in CAN, Wood. and Forest openings. Ht. 4–12". Lvs. basal, narrowly lance-shape, nearly smooth or grey with silky hairs, glandular. Flrs. composite, about 1" diam., with white-hairy bracts. April–October.*

Greenstem Paperflower, Psilostrophe sparsiflora. CAN *above Redwall and S Rim, Wood. and Scrub. Ht. 6–14". Stems sparsely soft-haired. Lvs. mostly entire and stemless, to 2¾" long. Flrs. composite, about ½–1" diam., with small disk and a few broad, 3-lobed rays. April–August.*

Upright Prairie Coneflower, Ratibida columnaris. S Rim, *open areas. Ht. 10–32". Stems stiff-haired and glandular. Lvs. pinnately divided, stiff-haired. Flrs. composite, large and showy, with thimblelike disk and drooping rays. In some plants flowers are purplish-brown (see Plate 39). July–November.*

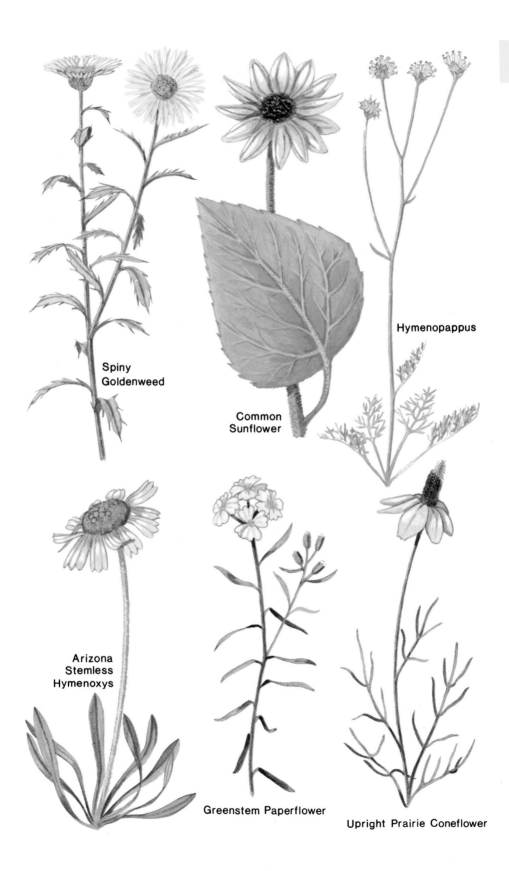

Spiny
Goldenweed

Common
Sunflower

Hymenopappus

Arizona
Stemless
Hymenoxys

Greenstem Paperflower

Upright Prairie Coneflower

Plate 28. Yellow Flowers.

All the wildflowers on this plate belong to the Sunflower Family.

Threadleaf Groundsel, Senecio longilobus. *S Rim, often along dry washes. Ht. 12–40". Plant woolly. Lvs. threadlike, some divided into threadlike lobes 1" long or more. Flrs. composite, about ½–1" diam., with drooping rays. One of several similar species in area. May–September.*

Tall Goldenrod, Solidago altissima. *SN Rims, Grass. and open areas. Ht. 2–5'. Stems downy. Lvs lance-shape, finely serrated or nearly entire, downy below, rough above, to 4¾" long. Flrs. composite, 12–15 in panicle. July–October.*

Common Dandelion, Taraxacum officinale. *Open places, SN Rims and CAN. The familiar dandelion of suburban lawns. Introduced. Ht. 2–12". Lvs. sharply lobed and toothed, stemless or nearly so, basal, to several inches long. Flrs. composite, but lack disk, about ½–2" diam. Blooms nearly all year. Cf. mountain dandelions, Plate 25, which have rather different lvs.*

Goatsbeard or Salsify, Tragopogon dubius. *SN Rims. Ht. 12–36". Lvs. linear, clasping, 1–10" long. Flrs. composite, but lack disk, with long, pointed bracts. May–August.*

Golden Crownbeard, Verbesina encelioides. *SN Rims and CAN. Ht. 12–48". Stems grey-downy. Lvs. lance- to egg-shape, 1–4" long, toothed, with stiff hairs. Flrs. composite, 1–1½" diam. April–September.*

Showy Goldeneye, Viguiera multiflora. *SN Rims, Grass. and Pine Forest. Ht. 10–40". Stems finely downy or nearly smooth. Lvs. opposite below, alternate above, linear to lance-shape. Flrs. composite, 8–12 rays, about 2" diam. May–September.*

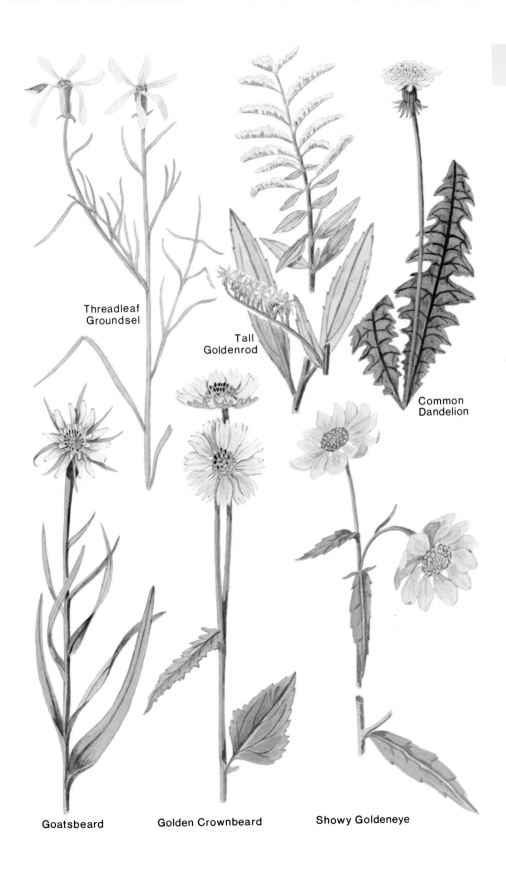

Threadleaf
Groundsel

Tall
Goldenrod

Common
Dandelion

Goatsbeard

Golden Crownbeard

Showy Goldeneye

Plate 29. Red or Orange Flowers.

Red Columbine, Aquilegia triternata. *Buttercup Family. Rare, moist places 6000–10,000 feet, notably near Ribbon Falls and in Long Jim Canyon. Ht. 8–24". Stems numerous, slender, sparsely downy, with few lvs. Lvs. mostly basal, compound, with 3-lobed and cleft leaflets at end of long petiole. Flrs. nodding, about 1½" long. July.*

Globemallow, Sphaeralcea parvifolia. *Mallow Family. Dry, open places, SN Rims and CAN, 4000–7000'. Often along roads. Stems to 40" tall, sprouting from woody crown. Lvs. 6–20" long, broadly egg-shape to nearly round, unlobed or with 3 shallow lobes, margins toothed, veins prominent. Stems and lvs. covered with grey hairs. Flrs. about 1" diam. 5 petals. May–November. One of several quite similar species in the park.*

Pinedrops, Pterospora andromedea. *Heath Family. N Rim, Forest. Ht. 8–40". Stems clammy and downy. Lvs. reduced to small scales near stem base. Flrs. to ½" diam., urn-shape, 5-lobed, nodding, in terminal raceme. Plants lack chlorophyll; probably parasitic. June–August.*

Butterfly Weed, Asclepias tuberosa. *Milkweed Family. N Rim Pine Forest openings. Ht. 12–32". Stems hairy or rough-downy. Lvs. lance-shape, stemless, margins sometimes rolled under, 1¼–4½" long. Flrs. star-shape, about ½" diam., corolla consisting of 5 petallike lobes to which are attached upright hoods, each with a small horn. Flrs. sometimes yellow or orange, in umbels about 3" diam. Of several milkweeds in area, this is the only one without milky sap. May–September. Cf. Antelopehorns, Plate 39.*

Skyrocket, Gilia aggregata. *Phlox Family. Com., N Rim; Uncom. and local, S Rim and CAN just below rim, moist Grass. and Pine Forest. Ht. 6–32". More or less sticky-hairy. Lvs. pinnately divided, 1–2" long. Flrs. tubular, with 5 pointed lobes (petals) flaring to form a star, ¾–1¾" long, color variable, including solid red, pink and white. May–September.*

Wyoming Paintbrush, Castilleja linariaefolia. *Snapdragon Family. SN Rims and CAN above Supai Formation, Wood. and Forest, dry openings and rocky places. Ht. 12–32" or more. Stems woody toward base, fine-downy to nearly smooth below, somewhat hairy near flowers. Lvs. linear, smooth or slightly downy, clasping, unlobed, ½–3" long. Flrs. irregular, tubular, beaked, 2" long, sheathed in showy, red, 3-lobed bracts in dense terminal spikes. April–October. One of four paintbrushes in park. Desert Paintbrush (C. chromosa), with 5-lobed bracts, is most common paintbrush in CAN.*

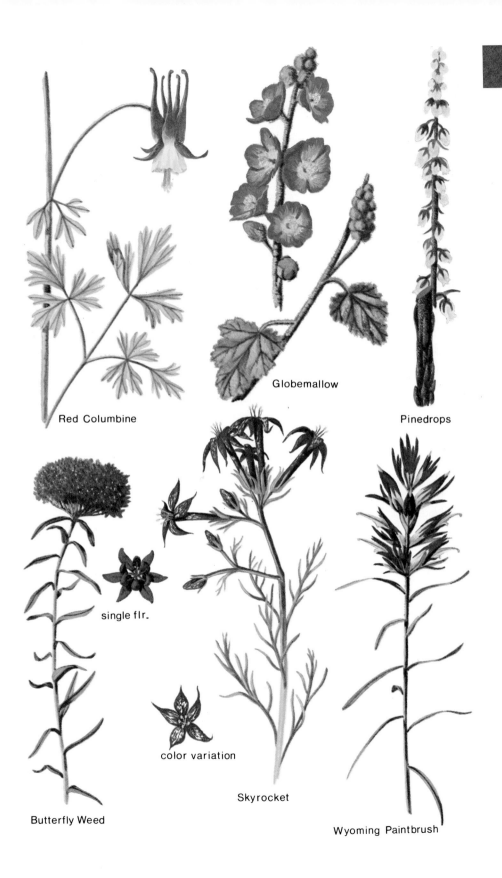

Red Columbine

Globemallow

Pinedrops

single flr.

color variation

Butterfly Weed

Skyrocket

Wyoming Paintbrush

Plate 30. Red Flowers.

Crimson Monkeyflower, Mimulus cardinalis. *Snapdragon Family. CAN, shady seeps and stream banks. Ht. 10–36". Stems erect. Lvs. oval, opposite, stemless, toothed, ¾–4½" long. Flrs. irregular, tubular, 5-lobed, about 2" long. March–October. Only bright-red monkeyflower in area. Cf. Common Monkeyflower, Plate 23.*

Utah Penstemon, Penstemon utahensis. *Snapdragon Family. CAN above Redwall, Scrub and Wood. among rocks. Ht. 6–28". Lvs. opposite, oblong to narrowly wedge-shape, ½–2" long, upper ones stemless and clasping. Flrs. nearly regular, tubular, with 5-flared petal lobes. Flrs. in panicles. April–May. Cf. two following species and other penstemons on Plates 35 and 38.*

Eaton Penstemon, Penstemon eatonii. *Snapdragon Family. CAN, rocky places. Ht. 12–39". Lvs. opposite, 1½–4"; lower ones narrowly wedge- or lance-shape; upper ones egg- or heart-shape, stemless, clasping. Flrs. irregular, tubular, with 2-lobed upper lip and 3-lobed lower lip, neither flared. Flrs. in panicles. April–July.*

Scarlet Bugler, Penstemon barbatus. *Snapdragon Family. SN Rims, Grass., Scrub, Wood. and Forest. Not in CAN. Ht. 16–55". Lvs. opposite, 1½–4" long; lower ones wedge- or spoon-shape; upper ones linear or lance-shape. Flrs. irregular, tubular, with 2-lobed, unflared upper lip and 3-lobed, flared lower lip. Flrs. in panicles. June–August.*

Cardinal Flower, Lobelia cardinalis. *Bellflower Family. CAN, moist places. Ht. 12–40". Stems smooth or sparsely downy. Lvs. linear to lance- or egg-shape, 2½–6" long, smooth or sparsely hairy. Flrs. irregular, tubular, 1–1½" long, with tube slit down one side nearly to base, with 2-lobed upper lip, 3-lobed lower lip and united stamens, in spikelike racemes. June–October.*

Carmine Thistle, Cirsium rothrockii. *Sunflower Family. SN Rims and CAN just below. Ht. 24" or more. Lvs. deeply lobed and spiny. Flrs. composite, but lacking ray flowers, with spiny bracts. Difficult to distinguish from other red thistles in area. May–October.*

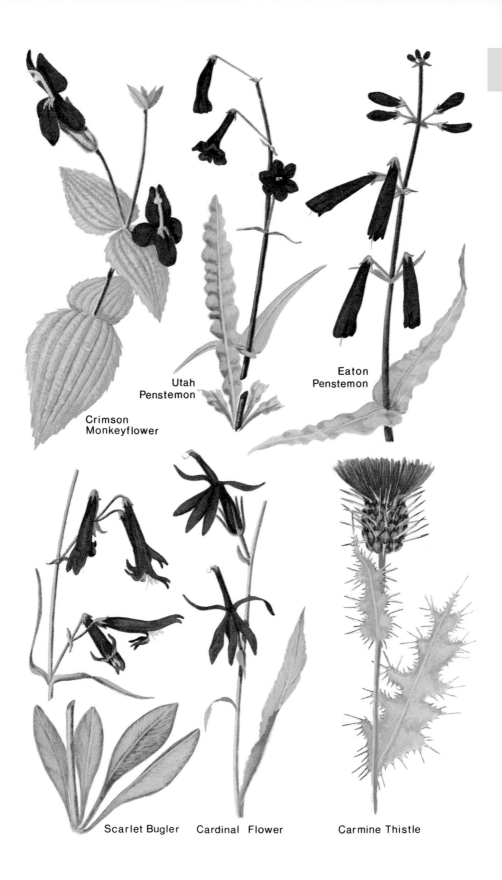

Crimson
Monkeyflower

Utah
Penstemon

Eaton
Penstemon

Scarlet Bugler   Cardinal Flower   Carmine Thistle

Plate 31. Pink or Magenta Flowers.

Weakstem Mariposa Lily, Calochortus flexuosus. *Lily Family. CAN, especially Tonto Plateau. Ht. 6–16". Stems often drooping, bent or twisted. Lvs. mostly basal, linear, to 8" long. Petals 1¼–1½" long, 3 petals, sometimes white or purple. April–June. Cf. Sego Lily, Plate 18.*

Trailing Four O'Clock, Allionia incarnata. *Four O'Clock Family. CAN, Gorge and Tonto Plateau. Stems trailing, 6–10' long, radiating out from hub of plant, covered with glandular hairs. Lvs. opposite, oval to oblong, ½–1½" long, more or less glandular-hairy. Flrs. irregular, 3 to a head, together appearing as a single regular flr. about ¾" diam., rarely white. Flrs. open before dawn, close by midday. April–September.*

Colorado Four O'Clock, Mirabilis multiflora. *Four O'Clock Family. SN Rims, roadsides, and CAN, rocky places. Ht. 12–40". Stems erect or trailing, forming clumps, sticky or nearly smooth. Lvs. opposite, numerous, broadly oval or oblong, 1–4" long, with or without hairs. Flrs. 2" long, 1" diam., 8–12 in a cluster, 5-lobed, bloom for only 1 day. April–September.*

Pygmy Lewisia, Lewisia pygmaea. *Portulaca Family. N Rim, Grass. Ht. 1–2½". Lvs. linear, basal, 1–3" long, fleshy. Flrs. 1–3 per stem. June–August.*

Perennial Rockcress, Arabis perennans. *Mustard Family. SN Rims, Wood. and CAN, rock crevices and Gorge. Ht. 6–12". Stems smooth above, covered with forked hairs below. Lvs. mostly basal, wedge- to lance-shape, toothed or entire, densely downy, upper ones stemless. Flrs. ½" diam., 4 petals, pink to purple. February–July. One of a half-dozen rockcresses in area.*

Purple Bladderpod, Lesquerella purpurea. *Mustard Family. CAN, especially Gorge. Ht. 4–20". Plant covered with star-shape hairs. Lvs. mostly basal, oblong to wedge-shape, to 4" long; stem lvs. much smaller, stemless. Flrs. nearly ½" diam., 4 petals, white streaked with purple when young, turning solid purple with age. January–May. Round seedpods distinguish this and other bladderpods from the rockcresses. Cf. Bladderpod, Plate 23.*

Weakstem Mariposa Lily

Trailing Four O'Clock

Colorado Four O'Clock

Pygmy Lewisia

Perennial Rockcress

Purple Bladderpod

Plate 32. Pink or Magenta Flowers.

Linearleaf Hedgemustard, Sisymbrium linearifolium. *Mustard Family. SN Rims, Wood. and Forest openings. Ht. 12–40". Stems sprout from somewhat woody rootstock. Lvs. mostly linear and entire ¾–3¼" long. Flrs. about 1" across, 4 petals, H-shape, sometimes fading to white or yellow. May–September.*

Rocky Mountain Bee Plant, Cleome serrulata. *Caper Family. Roadsides and open areas, S Rim. Ht. 20–40". Lvs. lance- or narrowly wedge-shape, sometimes finely toothed, ¾–3¼" long. Flrs. 1" diam., 4 petals, with long stamens, clustered in spherical racemes. June–September. Two other species, both with yellow flowers, also occur at the canyon.*

Filaree, Erodium cicutarium. *Geranium Family. Introduced. Com., roadsides, disturbed areas, SN Rims and CAN. Prostrate plant with spreading, hairy stems 4–16" long. Lvs. 2-divided, 1¼–4" long, radiating from center. Flrs. less than ½" across, 5 petals, clustered, with stems glandular-hairy. February–August.*

Purple Cranesbill, Geranium caespitosum. *Geranium Family. SN Rims, Pine Forest. Ht. 4–36". Stems downy, somewhat declining. Lvs. opposite, palmately lobed, ¾–1½" diam., covered with flattened hairs. Flrs. to 1" across, 5 petals, with downy stems. May–October. Cf. White Cranesbill, Plate 19.*

Fireweed, Epilobium angustifolium. *Evening Primrose Family. Open areas, N Rim. Ht. to 5'. Lvs. lance-shape, stemless or nearly so, 2–6" long. Flrs. about 1" across, 4 petals, in long, terminal racemes. July–September.*

Climbing Milkweed, Sarcostemma cynanchoides. *Milkweed Family. Gorge and side canyons, forming dense clumps over rocks and other plants. A vine with stems up to 6' long. Lvs. opposite, linear to oval, 1–2½" long. Flrs. ⅜" diam., 5 petals, in many-flowered umbels. April–July.*

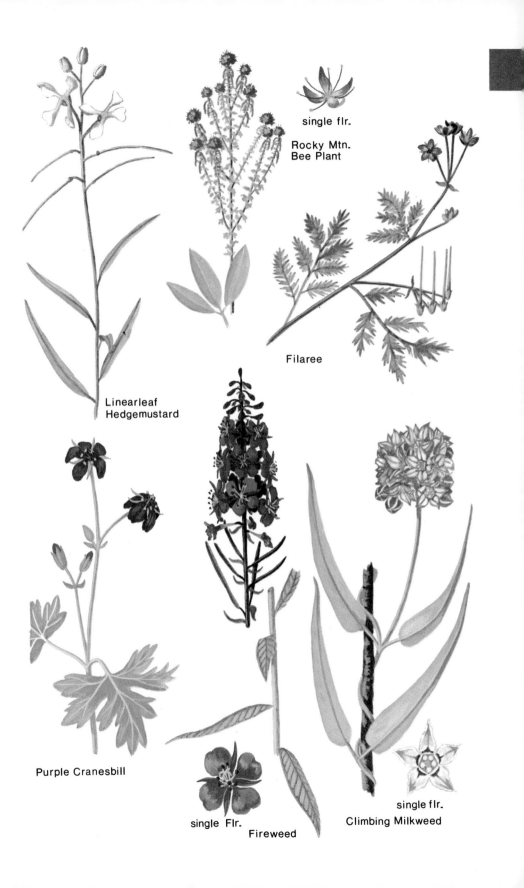

single flr.

Rocky Mtn.
Bee Plant

Filaree

Linearleaf
Hedgemustard

Purple Cranesbill

single Flr.
Fireweed

single flr.
Climbing Milkweed

Plate 33. Pink or Magenta Flowers.

Spreading Phlox, Phlox diffusa. *Phlox Family. Open, rocky places at higher elevations on N Rim. Mat or cushion plant. Lvs. needlelike, but not stiff or spine-tipped, about ½" long. Flrs. about ½" diam., often densely covering plant. Blooms shortly after snow melts. Desert Phlox (P. austromontana) similar, but with greyish green, sharp, spine-tipped lvs. It is found in CAN and on SN Rims in open, rocky places.*

Longleaf Phlox, Phlox longifolia. *Phlox Family. SN Rims and upper elevations of CAN, Wood. Ht. 2½–12". Stems vary from smooth to downy to glandular-hairy. Lvs. linear, ¾–3" long. Flrs. about ⅝–¾" diam., 5 petals, sometimes white. April–July.*

Tall Verbena, Verbena macdougalii. *Verbena Family. Com., SN Rims. Ht. 12–32". Stems downy to hairy. Lvs. elliptic to egg-shape, wrinkled above, hairy-downy on both sides, nearly stemless, 1–3" long. Flrs. tubular, tiny, in dense terminal spikes. June–September.*

Goodding Verbena, Verbena gooddingii. *Verbena Family. Dry places, CAN below 6000'. Ht. 8–18". Stems erect, branched, densely hairy. Lvs. to about 1½" long, mostly 3-cleft, hairy on both sides, tapering to a short petiole. Flrs. tubular, tiny, in dense terminal spikes. Blooms nearly all year. The similar Wright Verbena (V. wrightii) grows in the Wood. and Forest of the S. Rim.*

Cave Primrose, Primula specuicola. *Primrose Family. Wet seeps in CAN. Ht. to 4". Lvs. basal, oblong to lance-shape, to about 3" long. Flrs. tubular with 5 flared petals, in umbels, about ½" long. Note yellow flower tube. May–June.*

Alpine Shooting Star, Dodecatheon alpinum. *Primrose Family. Rare, N Rim meadows. Ht. 4–16". Lvs. basal, narrowly wedge-shape, 1–6" long. Flrs. 1" long or less, 4 petals bent backward. June–September.*

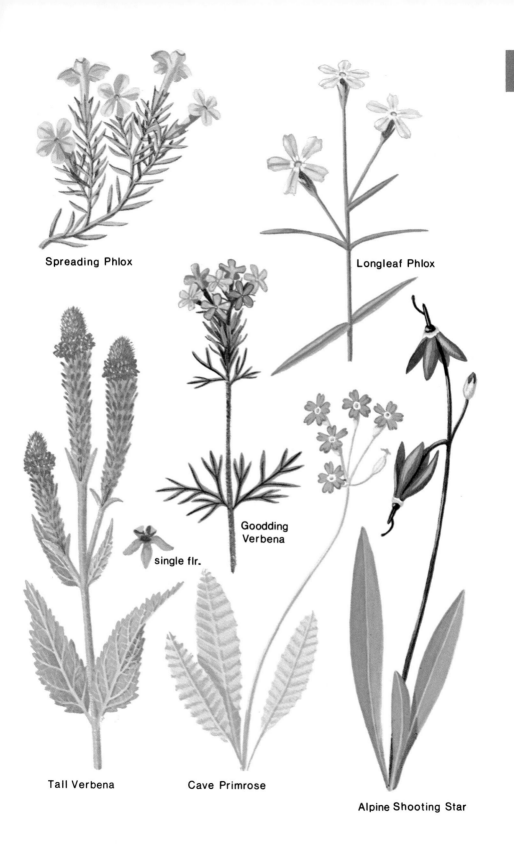

Spreading Phlox

Longleaf Phlox

Goodding
Verbena

single flr.

Tall Verbena

Cave Primrose

Alpine Shooting Star

Plate 34. Pink or Magenta Flowers.

Specklepod Locoweed, Astragalus lentiginosus. *Pea Family. Com. and widespread. Stems 4–40" long, erect, ascending or prostrate. Lvs. pinnate, to 7" long, usually with 11–27 leaflets. Flrs. irregular, to 1" long, varying from pink to purple. A highly variable species. March–August. One of numerous locoweeds in the area.*

Grassleaf Peavine, Lathyrus graminifolius. *Pea Family. SN Rims and CAN, rocky area, Wood. and Forest. A vine with stems several feet long climbing by means of tendrils. Lvs. pinnate, 1–4" long, terminating in a tendril, with 4–12 leaflets. Flrs. irregular, about ½" long. Closely related to the garden pea. April–September.*

Rocky Mountain Locoweed, Oxytropis lambertii. *Pea Family. SN Rims, Grass. and other open areas. Ht. 4–12". Lvs. pinnate, silvery-haired, with 7–17 linear to oblong leaflets. Flrs. irregular, about ½–1" long. June–September.*

Twining Snapdragon, Maurandya antirrhiniflora. *Snapdragon Family. Gorge and side canyons, often on shaded ledges. A vine with trailing or climbing stems to 6½' or more long. Lvs. delta- or arrow-shape or with 3–5 lobes, to 1" long. Flrs. irregular, about 1" long, tubular with 2-lobed upper lip and 3-lobed lower lip. March–May.*

Purple-white Owl-clover, Orthocarpus purpureo-albus. *Snapdragon Family. N Rim, Grass. Ht. 4–16". Lvs. 3-cleft, with linear lobes, stemless or nearly so, 1–6" long. Flrs. irregular, to ¾" long, upper lip beaklike, lower lip inflated, in terminal spikes with numerous leafy bracts. Resembles the paintbrushes (genus* Castilleja). *July–September. Often grows with Yellow Owl-clover (O. luteus), which has yellow flowers (see Plate 23).*

Wood Betony, Pedicularis centranthera. *Snapdragon Family. Com., SN Rims, Wood. and Forest. Ht. 1¼–6". Lvs. basal, pinnately divided with broad, toothed lobes, 2–6" long. Flrs. clustered, irregular, tubular, 2-lipped, upper lip helmet-shape, about 1½" long. April–June.*

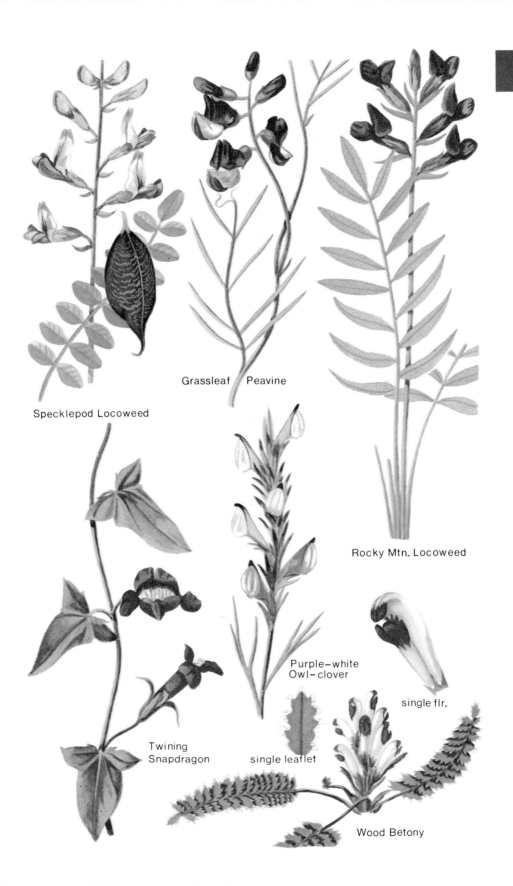

Specklepod Locoweed

Grassleaf Peavine

Rocky Mtn. Locoweed

Twining Snapdragon

Purple-white Owl-clover

single leaflet

single flr.

Wood Betony

Plate 35. Pink or Magenta Flowers.

Palmer Penstemon, Penstemon palmeri. *Snapdragon Family. SN Rims and CAN, rocky places in Scrub and Wood. Ht. 20–48". Lvs. opposite, oblong to egg-shape, 1–3" long, upper ones stemless and clasping, forming perfoliate pairs. Flrs. irregular, inflated, with 2-lobed upper lip, 3-lobed lower lip, 1–1½" long, in panicles. March–September.*

Broomrape, Orobanche fasciculata. *Broomrape Family. SN Rims and just below, Scrub and Wood. Ht. 2–8". Stems nearly leafless, with lvs. reduced to tiny, nonfunctional scales. Lacking chlorophyll. Broomrape is parasitic on the roots of sagebrush and other plants. Flrs. irregular, tubular, 2-lipped, ½–1¼" long. May–July.*

Mohave Aster, Aster abatus. *Sunflower Family. CAN below Redwall, talus slopes and dry places. Ht. 12–28". Stems slightly hairy or glandular to woolly, rising from woody base. Lvs. linear, oblong or lance-shape, hairy to woolly, stemless, 1¼–2⅜" long. Flrs. composite, 1½–2½" diam., numerous, sometimes white or blue. March–May. Cf. Hoary Aster, below, and Baby White Aster, Plate 21.*

Hoary Aster, Aster canescens. *Sunflower Family. SN Rims and CAN. Most Com. aster on S Rim. Ht. 4–16". Stems slightly hairy to nearly smooth. Lvs. linear to lance- or wedge-shape, sharply toothed, short-stemmed to nearly stemless, to 2" long. Flrs. composite, about 1" diam., numerous, with downy bracts. June–November. Cf. Mohave Aster, above, and Baby White Aster, Plate 21.*

Fleabane, Erigeron formosissimus. *Sunflower Family. N Rim, Forest, shady places. Ht. 4–16". Stems more or less glandular or hairy. Lvs. linear to spoon-shape, to 2" long, more numerous toward base, upper ones often stemless. Flrs. composite, about 1½" diam., with 75–150 rays, sometimes pale blue (see Plate 38). July–September.*

Wire Lettuce, Stephanomeria tenuifolia. *Sunflower Family. Dry places 4500–8000'. Scrub, Wood., Grass., Forest. Ht. 4–20". Stems slender, smooth, branched. Lvs. mostly erect, grasslike, lower ones more or less pinnately toothed or lobed. Flrs. composite, mostly terminal and solitary on branches, with 5 or so rays. May–September.*

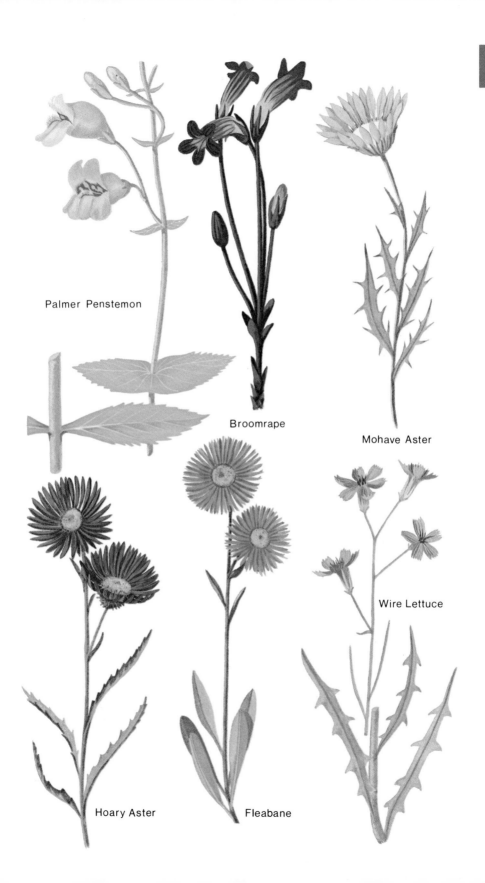

Palmer Penstemon

Broomrape

Mohave Aster

Hoary Aster

Fleabane

Wire Lettuce

Plate 36. Blue or Purple Flowers.

Colorado Columbine, Aquilegia caerulea. *Buttercup Family.* N Rim Forest and Grass., *damp places. Ht. 6–24". Lvs. mostly basal, 2–3 times palmately compound, leaflets deeply lobed. Flrs. regular, 2½–3" long and to 4" diam., 5 petals with spurs. Petallike sepals normally blue, but may be white. June–July. Cf. Golden Columbine, Plate 23 and Red Columbine, Plate 29.*

Monkshood, Aconitum columbianum. *Buttercup Family. Most streambanks above 5000'. Ht. 20" or more. Stems mostly smooth, but downy and often sticky near the flrs. Lvs. palmate with 3–5 divisions, each cleft and toothed, finely downy to nearly smooth. Flrs. irregular, to about 1½" long, in terminal raceme, sometimes white, with hood formed by sepals. June–September.*

Nelson Larkspur, Delphinium nelsoni. *Buttercup Family. SN Rims, Forest. Ht. 4–20". Stems finely haired to nearly hairless. Lvs. few, palmately lobed, with the lobes segmented, 1¼–2" diam. Flrs. irregular, with one sepal extended backward to form a spur; upper petals white, inconspicuous, largely replaced by petallike sepals. May–June.*

Barestem Larkspur, Delphinium scaposum. *Buttercup Family. SN Rims and just below, Grass., Wood. and Forest. Ht. 8–20". Stems leafless or nearly so. Lvs. mostly basal, divided 3–5 times, with divisions lobed or toothed, about 1" diam. Flrs. similar to those of Nelson Larkspur, but spur is bronze-tipped and only upper 2 petals are white. May–July.*

Blue Flax, Linum lewisii. *Flax Family. SN Rims and CAN (but not Gorge), Scrub and Wood. Ht. to 36". Lvs. linear, tiny, pressed against stem. Flrs. 1–2" diam., 5 petals. Dark blue form occurs on N Rim. March–September.*

Rocky Mountain Iris or Blue Flag, Iris missouriensis. *Iris Family. N Rim, Grass. Ht. 8–20". Lvs. basal, linear, to 18" long. Flrs. 1½–2" tall, with 3 drooping sepals or* falls, *3 upright petals or* standards *and 3 cleft, petallike styles. Ovary inferior, flower stem long, arising from juncture of 2 elongate leaflike bracts or* spathes. *May–July.*

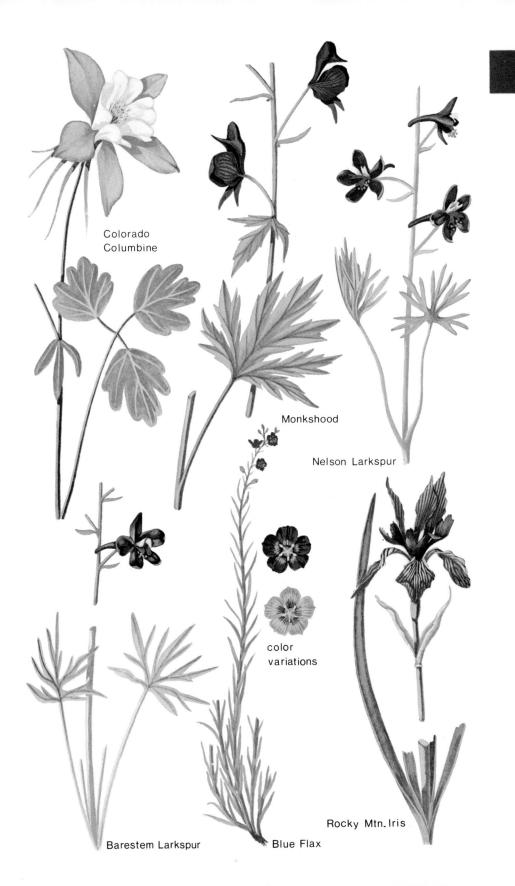

Colorado
Columbine

Monkshood

Nelson Larkspur

color
variations

Barestem Larkspur

Blue Flax

Rocky Mtn. Iris

Plate 37. Blue or Purple Flowers.

Phacelia, Phacelia corrugata. *Waterleaf Family. Rocky slopes and gravelly flats, pinyon-juniper Wood. Ht. 6–20". Stems somewhat hairy and glandular. Plant foul-smelling. Lvs. to 4" long, egg-shape to oblong, margins wavy to lobed. Flrs. small, densely packed in coiled cymes. April–September.*

Phacelia, Phacelia glechomaefolia. *Waterleaf Family. CAN, especially Gorge of western section. Ht. 4–12". Stems sticky-downy. Lvs. oblong to nearly round, entire to scalloped. Flrs. to about ½" long, varying from pale to deep blue or purple. April–September, but only when rainfall is sufficient.*

Bluebells, Mertensia franciscana. *Borage Family. Moist, shady places about 5600'; often in spruce-fir Forest above 8000'. Ht. 4–40". Lvs. elliptic, to 5" long, sometimes stemless, hairy below. Flrs. tubular, about ½" long, nodding, in cymes, pink in the bud stage. June–September.*

Parry Bellflower, Campanula parryi. *Bellflower Family. N Rim, Grass. Ht. 2½–12". Lvs. to 2½" long, lower ones spoon- to wedge-shape, upper ones, shorter, linear. Flrs. bell-shape, to 1" long, erect or nodding. July–September.*

Hill Lupine, Lupinus hillii. *Pea Family. SN Rims, Forest, Wood. and Grass. Ht. usually more than 8". Plant covered with silky hairs. Lvs. palmate-compound, 1–2" diam.; leaflets narrowly oblong. Flrs. irregular, about ¼" long, crowded in terminal raceme, sometimes white. May–September. One of numerous lupines in area. Cf. Palmer Lupine, below.*

Palmer Lupine, Lupinus palmeri. *Pea Family. SN Rims and CAN above 4000', Wood. and Forest openings. Ht. 12–18". Stems leafy, densely covered with soft hairs. Lvs. palmate-compound, with elliptic-oblanceolate leaflets about ½–1½" long. Flrs. irregular, about ½" long, in terminal raceme, but less crowded than in Hill Lupine. April–October. Cf. Hill Lupine, above.*

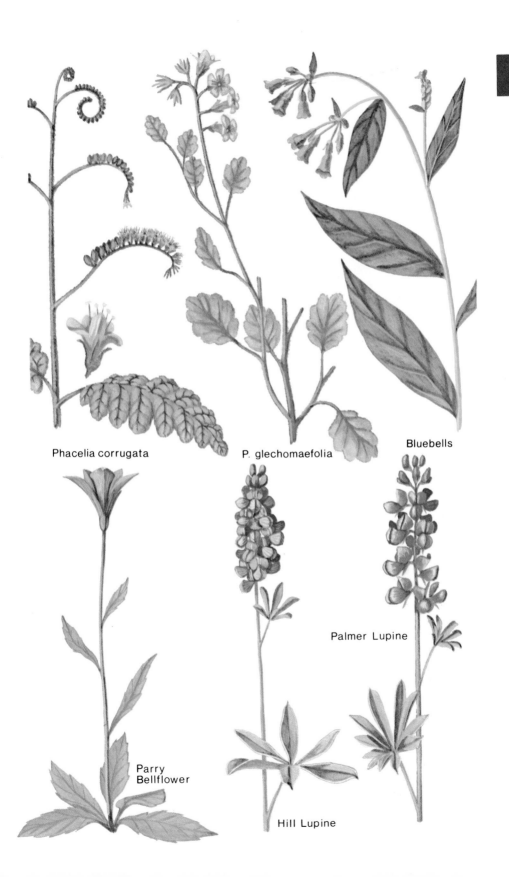

Phacelia corrugata

P. glechomaefolia

Bluebells

Parry
Bellflower

Palmer Lupine

Hill Lupine

Plate 38. Blue or Purple Flowers.

Parry Gentian, Gentiana parryi. *N Rim Grass. above 8500'. Ht. 4–16".
Stems leafy, often numerous. Lvs. opposite, stemless, egg- to lance-shape.
Flrs. bell-shape, to about 1½" long. August–September.*

Blue-eyed Mary, Collinsia parviflora. *Snapdragon Family. Rare, SN
Rims and CAN, moist places. Ht. 2–16". Stems usually covered with fine
down. Lvs. opposite, linear to egg-shape, sometimes finely toothed,
stemless or nearly so, to 2" long. Flrs. irregular, less than ½" long, with 2-
lobed upper lip and 3-lobed lower lip. February–June.*

Toadflax Penstemon, Penstemon linarioides. *Snapdragon Family. SN
Rims, Wood. and Forest. Prostrate subshrub with woody base. Stems
more or less downy. Ht. 2–14". Lvs. opposite, linear to wedge-shape,
crowded toward base of stem, to 1" long. Flrs. irregular, with short,
inflated tube, flaring upper and lower lips, about ½" long, in panicles.
June–August. Cf. Thickleaf Penstemon, below, and penstemons on Plates
30 and 35.*

Thickleaf Penstemon, Penstemon pachyphyllus. *Snapdragon Family.
Com., S Rim, Wood. and Forest. Ht. 10–26". Stems covered with fine
down. Lvs. opposite, thick, lance- to wedge-shape, about ½–3" long,
upper ones stemless. Flrs. similar to those of Toadflax Penstemon, above,
but tube less inflated. April–June. Cf. penstemons on Plates 30 and 35.*

American Speedwell, Veronica americana. *Snapdragon Family. Springs
and stream banks. Ht. 4–40". Plant somewhat succulent. Stems rising
from creeping bases. Lvs. opposite, lance- to egg-shape, short-stemmed to
3½" long, finely or minutely toothed. Flrs. slightly irregular, 4-lobed, in
racemes. June–September. The similar Water Speedwell,* Veronica
anagallis-aquatica, *has stemless lvs. and is strictly aquatic, growing along
the Colorado River and perennial sidestreams.*

Fleabane, Erigeron formosissimus. *This is the blue phase of the species
shown on Plate 35.*

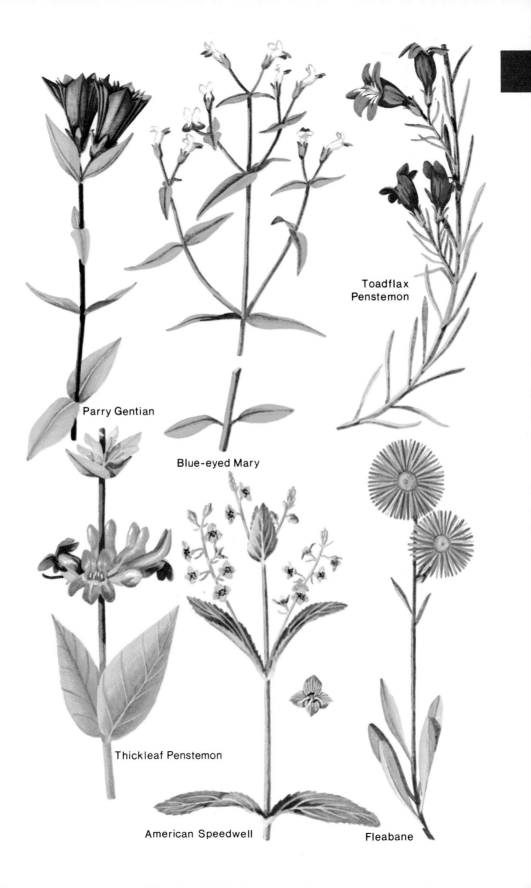

Parry Gentian

Blue-eyed Mary

Toadflax
Penstemon

Thickleaf Penstemon

American Speedwell

Fleabane

Plate 39. Greenish or Brownish Flowers.

Spotted Mountain Bells, Fritillaria atropurpurea. *Lily Family. SN Rims, Forest. Ht. 6–24". Upper half of stem leafy. Lvs. narrow, linear, more or less whorled, 1–4" long. Flrs. nodding, to ¾" long, 3 petals. April–June.*

Spotted Coralroot, Corallorhiza maculata. *Orchid Family. Forest. Ht. 8–24". Lvs. reduced to a few, tiny sheaths on stem. Flrs. irregular, about ¾" diam., distinctly orchidlike. June–July.*

Stream Orchid or Giant Helleborine, Epipactis gigantea. *Orchid Family. Seeps, springs, streams and other moist places. Ht. 8–40". Stems sparsely covered with downy hairs. Lvs. lance- to egg-shape, clasping, to 8". Flrs. irregular, about 1½" diam., distinctly orchidlike. April–July.*

Utah Green-gentian, Swertia utahensis. *Gentian Family. CAN and SN Rims, 4000–7500'. Ht. to 42". Lvs. opposite, stemless, linear to wedge-shape, white-margined, to 4" long. Flrs. to ¾" diam., 4 petals, with 1 fringed gland on each petal. June–September. Desert Green-gentian (S. albomarginata), nearly identical but with whorled lvs., often found in pinyon-juniper woodland.*

Monument Plant, Swertia radiata. *Gentian Family. SN Rims, Forest. Ht. 12–60". Stem solitary, smooth or finely downy. Similar to above species, but stem lvs. in whorls of 3–7 and corolla lobes have 2 fringed glands. June–September.*

Upright Prairie-coneflower, Ratibida columnaris. *Sunflower Family. This is the brown phase of the species shown on Plate 27.*

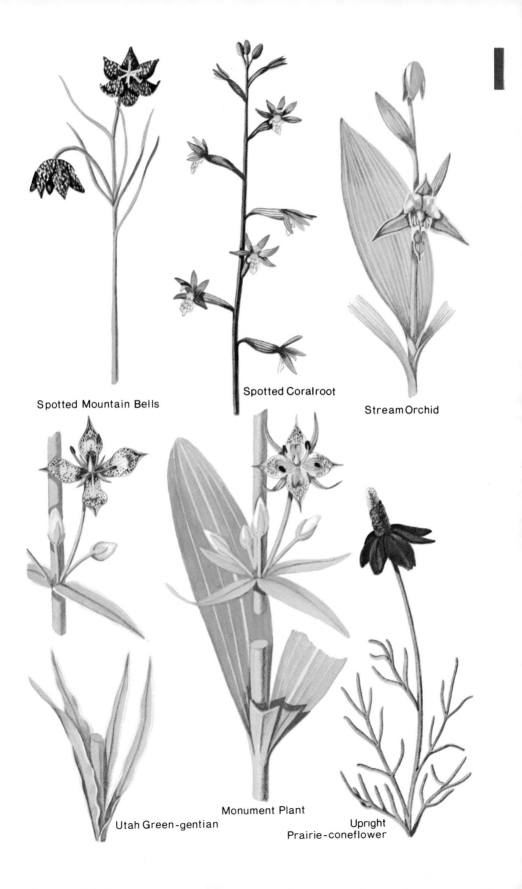

Spotted Mountain Bells

Spotted Coralroot

Stream Orchid

Utah Green-gentian

Monument Plant

Upright
Prairie-coneflower

Plate 40. Anatomy of a Cactus.

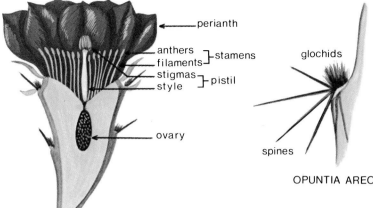

perianth

anthers ⎤ stamens
filaments ⎦

glochids

stigmas ⎤ pistil
style ⎦

spines

ovary

OPUNTIA AREOLE

GENERAL FLOWER PARTS

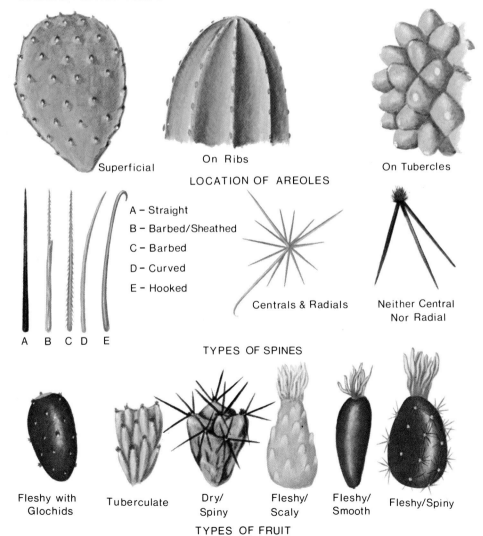

Superficial

On Ribs

On Tubercles

LOCATION OF AREOLES

A – Straight
B – Barbed/Sheathed
C – Barbed
D – Curved
E – Hooked

Centrals & Radials

Neither Central
Nor Radial

A B C D E

TYPES OF SPINES

Fleshy with
Glochids

Tuberculate

Dry/
Spiny

Fleshy/
Scaly

Fleshy/
Smooth

Fleshy/Spiny

TYPES OF FRUIT

Plate 41. Cacti.

Cushion Cactus, Coryphanta vivipara. *SN Rims and upper elevations in CAN, Wood. and Forest openings. Stems unbranched, spherical or melon-shape, to 6½" tall and 3¼" diam., solitary or clumped, with nipplelike bumps grooved on upper side. Spines straight and stiff: 3–6 central to ¾" long, turned up and down; 15–20 radial, to about ¾", spreading. Flowers to 2½" diam., pink to magenta. Fruit smooth, to 1" long. May–June.*

Cottontop Cactus, Echinocactus polycephalus *var.* xeranthemoides. *Rocky places, especially on limestone, below 7000'. Stems 1–12, unbranched, melon-shape, to nearly 24" tall and 12" thick, with 10–20 ribs, clumped. Central spines curved; radials straight, flattened, stiff and downy: 3–4 central to 3" long; 6–8 radial, smaller. Flowers about 2" diam., with woolly, scaled tube. Fruit egg-shape, to 1½" long, woolly, dry, spineless. February–June.*

Engelmann's Hedgehog Cactus, Echinocereus engelmannii. *Gorge and Tonto Plateau. Stems unbranched, melon- or barrel-shape, to 12" tall and 3¼" diam., usually with 10–13 ribs, clumped. Spines needlelike, usually flattened at base, curved or twisted, flexible: 2–6 central to 3½" long; 6–12 radial, smaller. Flowers 2" diam., several per stem. Fruit egg-shape, about 1⅜" long, spiny until mature, edible and fleshy. February–May.*

Fendler's Hedgehog Cactus, Echinocereus fendleri. *Upper CAN and SN Rims, Scrub, Wood. and Pine Forest, in openings. Stems unbranched, egg-shape, to 6" diam., with 9 or 10 ribs, solitary or in small clumps. Spines slightly up-curved, rigid: 1 central and 9–11 shorter radial spines. Flowers to 2¾" diam. Fruit egg-shape, about 1¼" long, with interlocking spines until mature, edible and fleshy. May–June.*

Claret Cup Hedgehog Cactus, Echinocereus triglochidiatus *var.* melanacanthus. *SN Rims and CAN, sandy or rocky places above 4000'. Stems unbranched, melon-shape, to 6" tall and 3¼" diam., with 5–8 ribs and dense spines; up to 50 stems per clump. Spines straight, stiff: 1–4 central to 3" long; 5–20 radial, shorter. Flowers about 1¼" diam. Fruit nearly cylindrical, edible and fleshy, more or less spiny, to 1¼" long. April–June.*

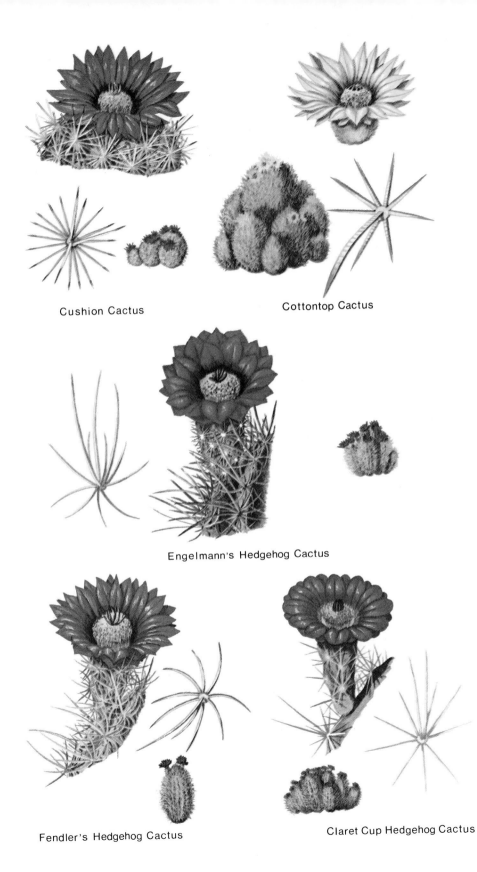

Cushion Cactus

Cottontop Cactus

Engelmann's Hedgehog Cactus

Fendler's Hedgehog Cactus

Claret Cup Hedgehog Cactus

Plate 42. Cacti.

Barrel Cactus, Ferocactus acanthodes. *Lower CAN and Gorge. Stems 1–3, unbranched, columnar, 1–3' tall and to 16" diam., with 20–30 ribs. Central spines 4, more or less flexible and twisted, the lower one often curved downward, 2–3" long; radial spines 15–25. Flowers to nearly 2½" diam. Fruit globular, about 1" diam., fleshy, scaly. April–May.*

Fishhook Cactus, Mammillaria tetrancistra. *Gorge. Stems unbranched, oblong, 4–10" tall, 2–3" diam., with nipplelike bumps; solitary or sometimes clumped. Central spines 1–4, hooked and at least some curved; radial spines straight, slender, about ½" diam. Flowers about 1" diam., often forming a wreath at crown of stem. Fruit smooth, to 1" long and ½" diam. Seeds black with a distinct brown, corky base.* Mammillaria microcarpa *is at least as common in Gorge.*

Beavertail Cactus, Opuntia basilaris. *Gorge and Tonto Plateau. Stems low and spreading, jointed, branched at joints. Pads flattened, about 3–6" long, 2–5" wide, spineless, but with tufts of glochids in areoles. Flowers 2–3" diam. Fruit about 1¼" long, egg-shape, dry and spineless. March–May.*

Pancake Pear, Opuntia chlorotica. *Rocky walls and ledges, 2000–6000'. Treelike, 3–8' tall, with stout trunk and ascending, jointed branches. Joints or pads flattened, round to broadly egg-shape, 4–8" diam. Areoles prominent, bristled and tufted with 3–7 main spines and 15–40 spinelets. Main spines to 1½" long, turned downward. Flowers to 2½" diam. Fruit fleshy, nearly globular, to 2" long and 1½" diam., not spiny. April–June.*

Grizzly Bear Cactus, Opuntia erinacea. *CAN, especially Tonto Plateau and Esplanade. Stems clumped, to about 6" tall, with erect or ascending, 2–4-jointed branches. Joints or pads flattened, round or oval, to 4" long, densely spiny. Spines 5–8 per areole, longest 1–4", flexible, straight or curved. Flowers to 2½" diam., clustered at tip of older stems, pink, magenta or yellow. Fruit dry, spiny, melon-shape, to 1¼" long. May–June.*

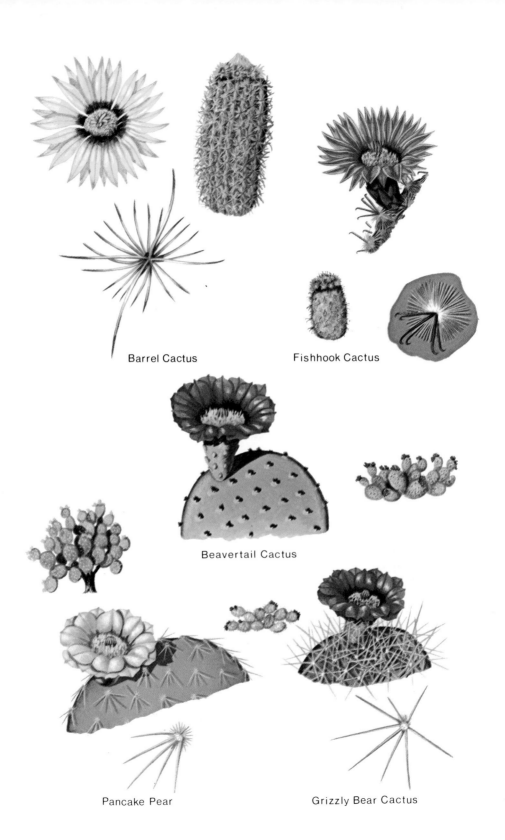

Barrel Cactus

Fishhook Cactus

Beavertail Cactus

Pancake Pear

Grizzly Bear Cactus

Plate 43. Cacti.

Engelmann's Prickly Pear, Opuntia phaeacantha. CAN, *mostly on Esplanade and below. Large, spreading cactus with branches of 10 or more joints forming clumps 2–10' diam. Without a central trunk but growing 2–3 joints high. Joints or pads flattened, egg-shape, to 10" long, often on edge along the ground. Spines 1–2" long, usually 3 per areole, missing from lower part of pads. Flowers to 3¼" diam., sometimes red or pink. Fruit edible, fleshy, spineless, egg- or club-shape, to 2" long. April–June.*

Plains Prickly Pear, Opuntia polyacantha. Wood. and Pine Forest. *Low, spreading cactus forming mats to 12" high and 12" diam. Joints or pads flattened, oval, to 4" long. Spines to 3" long, 3–10 per areole, mostly curved downward. Flowers 2–3" diam., sometimes magenta. Fruit dry, spiny, about ¾" long. May–July.*

Whipple Cholla, Opuntia whipplei. CAN. *Usually mat-forming, to 18" high. Stems jointed, cylindrical, 3–6" long, to ¾" diam., covered with nipplelike bumps. Spines 7–14, to 1" long, sheathed. Flowers about 1" diam. Fruit fleshy, spineless, bumpy, to 1¼" long. June–July. Opuntia acanthocarpa is the common cholla in the Gorge of the western canyon. Also, O. bigelovii is scattered in the Gorge.*

Simpson's Hedgehog Cactus, Pediocactus simpsonii. *Rare, Wood. and Forest above 6000'. Stems solitary or few-clumped, unbranched, nearly spherical, 1–8" diam., with nipplelike bumps. Spines straight and spreading, to ¾" long: 5–8 or more central spines; 15–30 radial spines, shorter. Flowers sometimes yellow. Fruit dry, smooth, spineless. May –July.*

Pineapple Cactus, Sclerocactus whipplei. CAN, 5000–6000', *especially on the Esplanade. Stems usually solitary, but sometimes branching to simulate small clusters, barrel-shape, to 7" tall, and 3" diam., with 13–15 ribs crowned with nipplelike bumps. Central spines usually 4, at least one hooked, surrounded by 8–10 radial spines. Flowers to 2" diam., greenish-yellow to purple or lavender. Fruit to ⁹⁄₁₆" long, scaly with tiny hairs.*

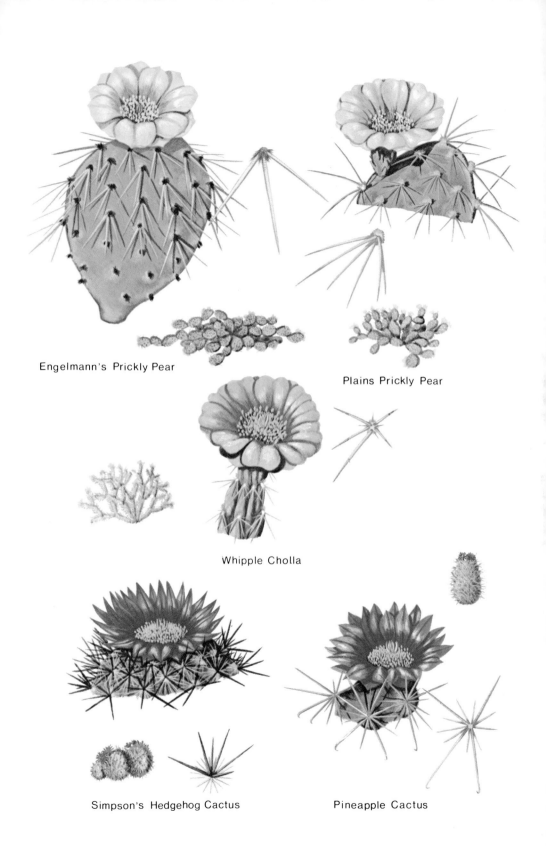

Engelmann's Prickly Pear

Plains Prickly Pear

Whipple Cholla

Simpson's Hedgehog Cactus

Pineapple Cactus

Plate 44. Lvs. Awl-shape or Needlelike.

White Fir, Abies concolor. *Pine Family. Com., N Rim, Tran. & Bor. zones; local, S Rim, just below rim. Tree to 100'. Lvs. 2-sided, 1½–3" long. Cones to 5½" long, erect on upper branches.*

Corkbark Fir, Abies lasiocarpa, *var.* arizonica. *Pine Family. Com., N Rim, Bor. zone. Tree to 90'. Lvs. similar to those of White Fir. Bark with numerous resin blisters. Cone 2–4" long, erect on upper branches. Branches horizontal or drooping, foliage often extending to the ground.*

Engelmann Spruce, Picea engelmannii. *Pine Family. Com., N Rim, Bor. zone. Tree to 100'. Lvs. 4-sided, stiff, pointed but not sharply so, to 1" long. Cones 1" long, with thin papery scales without prickles. Branches often touch ground. Stems of young trees have minute hairs.*

Blue Spruce, Picea pungens. *Pine Family. Rare, N Rim, Bor. zone. Tree to 70' or more. Similar to above, but needles are sharply pointed, bark is more furrowed, cones are larger (to 4" long) and stems of young trees are hairless.*

Douglas Fir, Pseudotsuga menziesii. *Pine Family. Not a true fir of the genus* Abies. *Com., N Rim, Tran. and Bor. zones; local, S Rim, just below rim. Tree to 80'. Lvs. ¾–1½" long, 2-sided, twisted at base. Stems look like bottle brushes. Cones usually 2–3" long, hanging rather than upright, with 3-pronged bracts protruding from between the scales.*

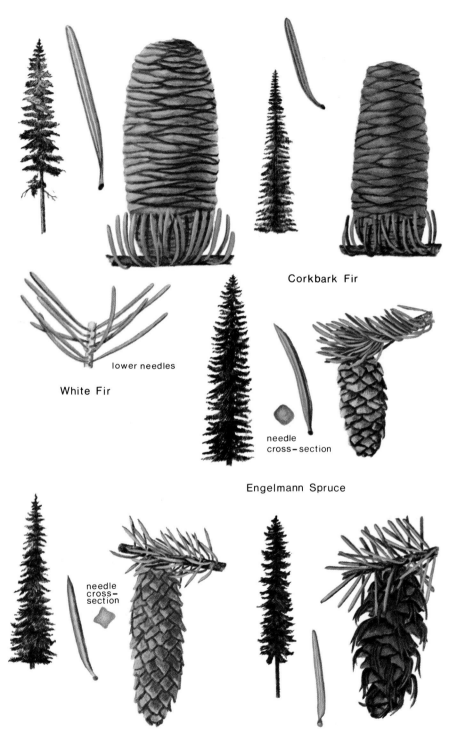

Corkbark Fir

lower needles

White Fir

needle
cross-section

Engelmann Spruce

needle
cross-
section

Blue Spruce

Douglas Fir

Plate 45. L vs. Awl-shape or Scalelike.

Ponderosa or Western Yellow Pine, Pinus ponderosa. *Pine Family. Com., SN Rims, Tran. zone. Tree to 100' or more, with open crown of huge, bent branches. Lvs. 5–11" long, in bundles of 3. Cones to 5½" long, armed with out-turned prickles. Bark of mature trees reddish to golden, divided into large vertical plates.*

Colorado Pinyon, Pinus edulis. *Pine Family. Com., SN Rims and CAN, U Son. & Trans. zones, 4000–7000'. Tree to 45', sometimes shrubby. Lvs. to 2" long, in bundles of 2. Cones 2–5" long, with edible seeds. Bark reddish, not plated. Crown usually rounded. Singleleaf Pinyon (P. monophylla) similar but needles mostly single and cones somewhat larger. Rare and local in eastern Grand Canyon, but replaces P. edulis west of Shivwits Plateau.*

Common or Dwarf Juniper, Juniperus communis. *Cypress Family. Com., N Rim, Bor. zone, Forest. Sprawling or prostrate shrub forming clumps less than 3' high. Lvs. to 1" long, awl-shape, rather than scalelike as in other local junipers. Cones berrylike, about ¼" diam.*

Utah Juniper, Juniperus osteosperma. *Cypress Family. SN Rims and CAN, 4500–7500', U Son. & Trans. zones, Wood. & Forest. Tree to 20', often shrubby but usually with a single trunk. Lvs. scalelike, tightly pressed to stems in alternately opposite pairs, margins entire. Cones berrylike, less than ¼" diam. One-seeded Juniper (J. monosperma) similar. In addition, Utah Juniper has mealy, 1–2-seeded fruit; One-seeded Juniper, smaller, fleshy, 1-seeded fruit. Fruit of both species blue with whitish bloom when fresh, but with age that of Utah Juniper turns reddish-brown while that of One-seeded Juniper becomes copper-colored. Rocky Mountain Juniper (J. scopulorum) similar to above, but lvs. smaller and have a small glandular pit; small branches often drooping. It is confined to the extremities of N Rim promontories.*

Tamarisk or Salt-cedar, Tamarix pentandra. *Tamarisk Family. Com., Ripar. Woodland along Colorado River. Lvs. scalelike, less than ⅛" long, densely clustered along stem. Foliage appears feathery. Branches somewhat drooping. Branchlets deciduous in winter. Flrs. tiny, densely clustered in showy terminal spikes. March–August.*

Colorado Pinyon

Singleleaf
Pinyon

Ponderosa Pine

leaf arrangement

Common Juniper

single flower

leaf
arrangements

Utah Juniper

Tamarisk

Plate 46. Lvs. Simple, Alternate and Lobed.

Gambel Oak, Quercus gambelii. *Beech Family. SN Rims, Tran. zone, Pine Forest. Shrub or small tree to 30', often forming thickets. Lvs. deciduous, variable, but mostly to 6" long, oblong, with deep, rounded lobes, smooth above, more or less downy below. Male and female flrs. in separate catkins on same plant. Acorns about 1" long, with cup enclosing half or more of nut. Cf. Grey Oak, Plate 51.*

Wax Currant, Ribes cereum. *Saxifrage Family. SN Rims and CAN, U Son. through Bor. zones, Wood. and Forest. Shrub to 6'. Stems spineless. Lvs. deciduous, usually less than 2" diam., with shallow lobes. Berries red. Sticky Currant* (R. viscosissimum) *is similar but lvs. more than 2" diam., with deep lobes, and berries black. May–August. Gooseberry Currant* (R. montigenum) *has 3 straight spines at each stem node, bristly purplish flrs. and bristly berries that are easily removed from stems. Whitestem Gooseberry* (R. inerme) *similar to R. montigenum, but flrs. white or pink and berries difficult to remove. Desert Gooseberry* (R. velutinum) *has yellow berries and Trumpet Gooseberry* (R. leptanthum), *black berries.*

Cliff Rose, Cowania mexicana. *Rose Family. Com., SN Rims and CAN, U Son. and Tran. zones, Wood., Pine Forest and rocky places. Large shrub or small tree to 25'. Lvs. hairless, to ½" long. Flrs. showy, about ½" diam. Fruit an akene with a white, feathery tail. April–June. Cf. Apache Plume, below.*

Apache Plume, Fallugia paradoxa. *Rose Family. Dry washes and open places, U Son. and Tran. zones, 3500–8000'. Shrub to 5', with numerous basal stems. Lvs. hairy, to ½" long. Fruit similar, but with a purple, feathery tail. April–June, also early fall.*

Canyon Grape, Vitis arizonica. *Grape Family. CAN, Ripar., in side canyons and near seeps and springs. Vine, sometimes bushy. Stems woolly when young, with shredded bark when mature. Lvs. deciduous, to 3" long, with a tendril opposite each leaf. Flowers in panicles to 2" long. Grapes black at maturity, edible but tart.*

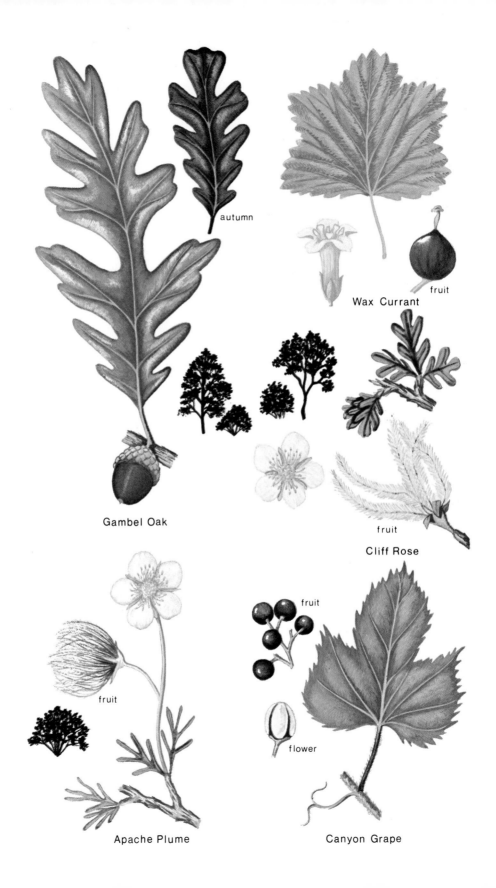

autumn

Wax Currant

fruit

Gambel Oak

fruit

Cliff Rose

fruit

flower

Apache Plume

Canyon Grape

Plate 47. Lvs. Simple, Alternate and Entire.

Arroyo Willow, Salix lasiolepis. *Willow Family. CAN, Ripar., and in moist places in arroyos on rims. Usually a shrub, sometimes a small tree to 30'. Lvs. deciduous, to 4" long, entire or nearly so, dark and smooth above, pale and smooth or downy or with whitish bloom below. Male and female flrs. in erect catkins less than 1" long. Bebb Willow* (S. bebbiana) *mostly on N Rim, with lvs. hairy on both sides. Scouler Willow* (S. scouleriana) *similar to Arroyo, but lvs. broadest toward tip and catkins more than 1" long. Coyote Willow* (S. exigua), *the most common species along the river, has entirely smooth, narrow entire lvs. Red Willow and Goodding Willow have entirely smooth, toothed lvs. (see Plate 50).*

Four-winged Saltbush, Atriplex canescens. *Goosefoot Family. SN Rims and CAN, Scrub, often in saline habitats. Shrub to 2'. Lvs. thick, usually stemless, to 2" long. Flrs. tiny, in leafy spikes or panicles. Fruit a 4-winged akene.*

Winter Fat, Eurotia lanata. *Goosefoot Family. S Rim and CAN, Scrub, L & U Son. zones. Lvs. and leaf stems densely woolly. Lvs. linear, to 2" long, sometimes in bundles. Flrs. mostly in male and female spikes on separate plants. Seed heads cottony.*

Littleleaf Mountain mahogany, Cercocarpus intricatus. *Rose Family. Com., SN Rims and just below, rock crevices. Intricately branched shrub to 5'. Lvs. to ½" long with strongly rolled margins. Flrs. tiny, profuse. Fruit an akene with a feathery tail to nearly 3" long. The less common Curl-leaf Mountain Mahogany* (C. ledifolius), *a pine forest shrub, has broader, less tightly rolled lvs. that are woolly below. True Mountain Mahogany (cf. Plate 51),* C. montanus, *has flat, partly toothed lvs.*

Lvs. always simple and alternate, but sometimes entire: Quaking Aspen, Plate 50; Grey Oak, Netleaf Hackberry, Plate 51, Seep-willow, Plate 52 and Desert-willow, Plate 54.

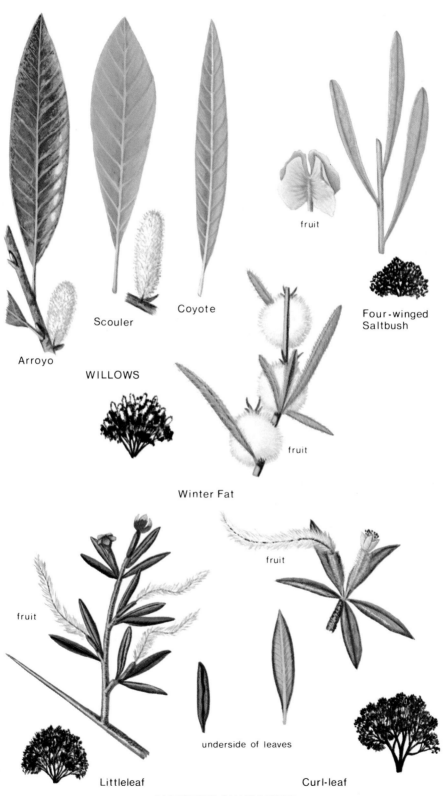

Arroyo

Scouler

Coyote

WILLOWS

fruit

Four-winged
Saltbush

Winter Fat

fruit

fruit

fruit

underside of leaves

Littleleaf

Curl-leaf

MOUNTAIN MAHOGANIES

Plate 48. Lvs. Simple, Alternate and Entire.

Western Rosebud, Cercis occidentalis. Pea Family. CAN, Ripar., also near seeps and springs. Shrub or tree to 12'. Lvs. deciduous, glossy, to nearly 4" diam. Flrs. showy, irregular, to ½" long, appearing before the lvs. Seeds in pealike pods persisting through winter. March–April.

Greasebush, Glossopetalon nevadensis. Bittersweet Family. Wood. below the rims. Shrub to 6½'. Stems spiny. Lvs. to ½" long. Flrs. to ⅛" long. March–June.

Buckbrush, Ceanothus fendleri. Buckthorn Family. SN Rims and upper elevations of CAN, Wood. and Pine Forest. Shrub to 3', often forming thickets. Branches spiny. Lvs. downy and whitish below, nearly smooth above, ½–1" long. Flrs. about ½" long, in dense racemes. Fruit a small capsule. April–November. Desert Ceanothus (C. greggii) has thicker, opposite lvs. Martin Ceanothus (C. martini) lacks spines and is found only on N Rim.

Buffaloberry, Shepherdia rotundifolia. Oleaster Family. SN Rims, rocky points. Evergreen shrub to 3'. Young twigs scaly. Lvs. to 1" long, thick, cupped downward, scaly, woolly below. Flrs. tiny, petalless, but with scaly, petallike calyx. Fruit berrylike, sweet and watery, with pale yellow juice when ripe. May–June.

Greenleaf Manzanita, Arctostaphylos patula. Heath Family. N Rim, Tran. and Bor. zones, Forest. Bark shiny, with peeling or shredding strips. Lvs. to 1½" long and diam., often held vertically. Flrs. urn-shape, nodding, in panicles with sticky-downy branches. Fruit berrylike. May––June. The similar Pointleaf Manzanita (A. pungens) is equally common, but on S Rim.

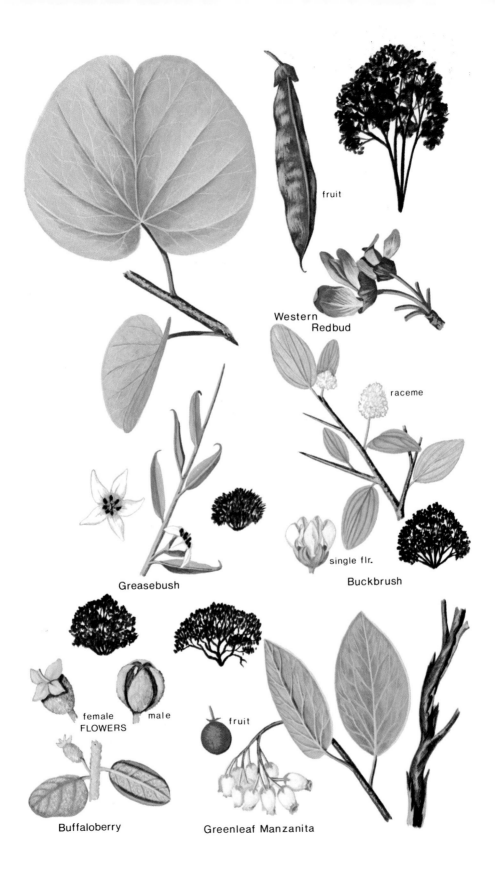

fruit

Western
Redbud

raceme

single flr.

Greasebush

Buckbrush

female
FLOWERS   male

fruit

Buffaloberry

Greenleaf Manzanita

Plate 49. Lvs. Simple, Alternate and Entire.

Desert Thorn or Pale Wolfberry, Lycium pallidum. *Nightshade Family. S Rim and CAN, Scrub and Wood., U Son. zone. Shrub to 6'. Branches spiny, sometimes downy. Lvs. to 1½" long. Flrs. to nearly 1" long. Fruits resemble small cherry tomatoes, edible but bitter. April–June. Torrey Wolfberry* (L. torreyi) *and Anderson Desert Thorn* (L. andersonii), *the common species of the Gorge, are similar, but have yellow flrs. with lavender lobes.*

Rubber Rabbitbush, Chrysothamnus nauseosus. *Sunflower Family. SN Rims and CAN, open places below 8000'. Along river only in Marble Canyon. Shrub usually to 7', often forming thickets. Twigs densely covered with feltlike hairs. Bark sometimes shredded. Lvs. smooth to woolly, to 2¾" long, aromatic, soon deciduous. Flrs. composite, in densely clustered heads, each about ¼" diam. Parry Rabbitbush* (C. parryi) *is very similar, but has flr. heads in leafy terminal racemes. Dwarf Rabbitbush* (C. depressus) *is usually less than 1' high, with twigs downy, but not covered with feltlike hairs. Greene Rabbitbush* (C. greenei) *and Douglas Rabbitbush* (C. viscidiflorus) *are both white-barked shrubs with persistent dark green lvs. and very difficult to separate.*

Brittlebush, Encelia farinosa. *Sunflower Family. Com., Gorge. Rounded shrub to 3'. Lvs. to 3", occasionally toothed, densely silver-haired, often deciduous in dry periods. Flrs. composite, with 1" heads in panicles rising above the leaves. Bush Encelia* (E. frutescens) *has solitary heads and hairy flower stalks.*

Trixis, Trixis californica. *Sunflower Family. CAN, rocky places below 5000', especially Gorge. Shrub to about 3'. Lvs. to 2", sometimes toothed, margins slightly rolled under. Flrs. composite, 9–14 per head, 2-petaled. February–June, also other times.*

Arrowweed, Pluchea servicea. *Sunflower Family. Gorge, along river and side streams, especially on sand dunes. Willowlike shrub to 16'. Lvs. to 2" long, silky-haired. Flrs. composite with heads in terminal clusters. March–July.*

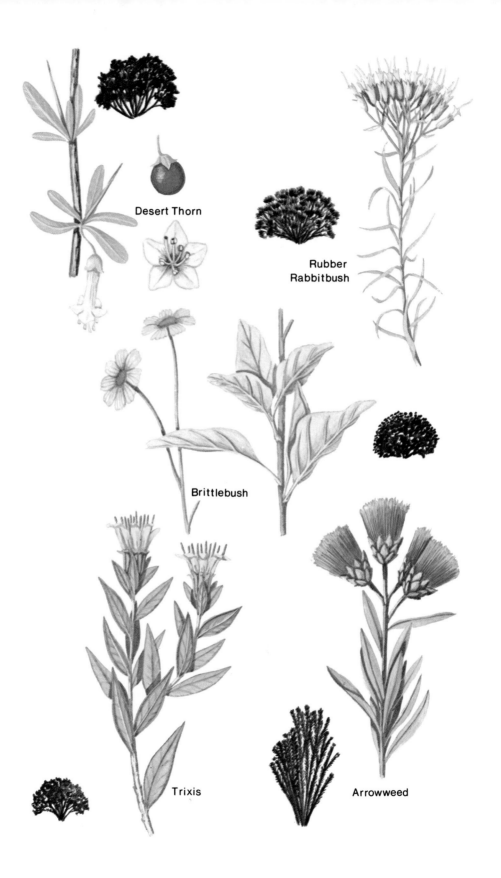

Desert Thorn

Rubber
Rabbitbush

Brittlebush

Trixis

Arrowweed

Plate 50. Lvs. Simple, Alternate, with Toothed or Scalloped Margins.

Fremont Cottonwood, Populus fremontii. *Willow Family. CAN, Ripar.,
along permanent or seasonal tributary streams, but rarely the river. Tree
to 50'. Trunk unbranched for half its length or more, branches large and
spreading. Bark deeply furrowed on old trees. Lvs. deciduous, to 3" long.
Flrs. in drooping male and female catkins.*

Quaking Aspen, Populus tremuloides. *Willow Family. Com., N Rim,
mostly Bor. zone, Forest and edge of Grass.; rare and local on S Rim.
Tree to 40'. Bark white with black stretch marks and warty patches,
becoming dark grey and furrowed at base on older trees. Lvs. deciduous,
to 2" long, sometimes nearly entire, with flat, twisted stems, causing lvs.
to quake or tremble in the slightest breeze.*

Red Willow, Salix laevigata. *Willow Family. Ripar. below 7000', mostly
CAN. Tree to near 40'. Bark rough, twigs smooth, yellowish- or reddish-
brown. Lvs. deciduous, to 5" long, so finely toothed as to sometimes seem
entire, with whitish bloom below. Flrs. in erect male and female catkins
that appear with lvs. Goodding Willow (S. gooddingii) is similar, but lvs.
with glandular margins and without whitish bloom below. Cf. willows,
Plate 47.*

Water Birch, Betula occidentalis. *Birch Family. N Rim, near Bright
Angel Spring, Roaring Springs and in Big Spring Canyon. Shrub or tree
to 30'. Lvs. deciduous, to 1½" long. Flrs. in drooping male and upright
female catkins. Fruit woody and conelike.*

Hop-hornbeam, Ostrya knowltoni. *Birch Family. CAN, U Son. zone,
Com. along trails. Shrub or tree to 25'. Lvs. deciduous, to 2" long, finely
haired below. Flrs. in drooping male and upturned female catkins. Fruit
a papery sack containing a single nut.*

*Lvs. always simple, alternate, but sometimes with toothed or scalloped
margins: See Arroyo Willow and Golden Wild Buckwheat, Plate 47, and
Brittlebush, Plate 49.*

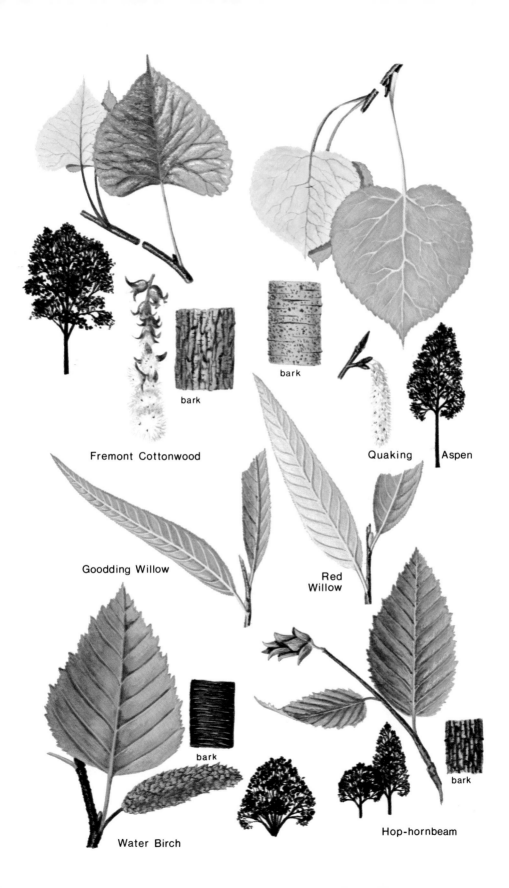

Fremont Cottonwood

bark

bark

Quaking Aspen

Goodding Willow

Red Willow

Water Birch

bark

Hop-hornbeam

bark

Plate 51. Lvs. Simple, Alternate, with Toothed or Scalloped Margins.

Grey Oak, Quercus grisea. Beech Family. Uncom., mostly in side canyons. Tree to 65'. Lvs. entire or partly toothed, finely haired below. Male flrs. in drooping catkins; female flrs. in clusters in leaf axils. Acorns to ¾" long. The more common Shrub Live Oak (Q. turbinella), always shrubby and with hollylike lvs., is dominant on the Esplanade and the rims of the western Grand Canyon. Wavyleaf Oak (Q. undulata), a 6' shrub, has wavy toothed lvs. and is confined to the CAN, mostly north of the river and west of Bright Angel Canyon. Especially common in the Esplanade woodland.

Netleaf Hackberry, Celtis reticulata. Elm Family. CAN, Ripar. Shrub or tree to 30'. Lvs. deciduous, to 2½" long, rough above. Older bark warty. Flrs. small, hairy, solitary or in small clusters. Fruit berrylike, pea-size, edible but astringent.

Utah Serviceberry, Amelánchier utahensis. Rose Family. Com. SN Rims and Wood. below rims. Shrub or tree to 15'. Twigs and buds usually downy. Lvs. to 1¼" long, entire toward base. Flrs. in racemes about 1" long, appearing in spring before lvs., fragrant. Fruit blueberrylike, slightly sweet and edible. April–June.

True Mountain Mahogany, Cercocarpus montanus. Rose Family. SN Rims and CAN, Wood. and Forest. Shrub to 10'. Lvs. flat, margins not rolled under, to 1" long or more, more or less hairy on both sides. Cf. Littleleaf Mountain Mahogany, Plate 47.

Rock Spiraea, Holodiscus dumosus. Rose Family. SN Rims, Wood. and Forest. Shrub to 10'. Lvs. to 2" long, velvety below. Bark on older branches red, later grey and peeling in thin strips. Flrs. clustered in feathery terminal racemes or panicles. June–September.

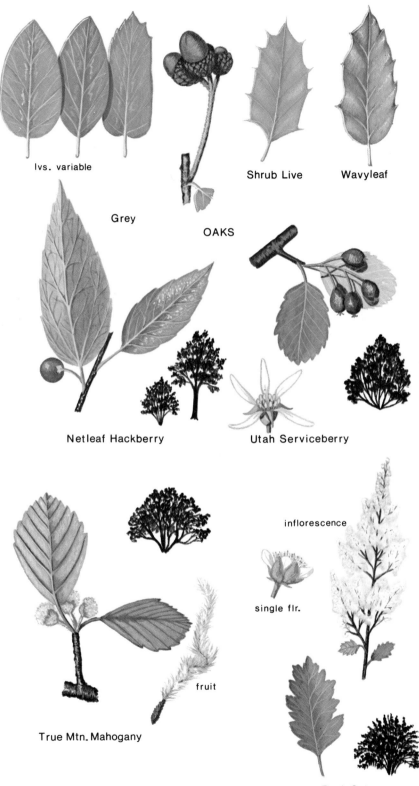

lvs. variable

Shrub Live

Wavyleaf

Grey

OAKS

Netleaf Hackberry

Utah Serviceberry

True Mtn. Mahogany

inflorescence

single flr.

fruit

Rock Spiraea

Plate 52. Lvs. Simple, Alternate, with Toothed or Scalloped Margins.

Chokecherry, Prunus virginiana. *Rose Family. N Rim, Forest. Shrub or tree to 15' or more. Lvs. to 4" long. Flrs. about ½" diam., in racemes to 4" long. Fruit very bitter. April–June. Desert Almond (P. fasciculata) is a spiny shrub of the Gorge.*

Birchleaf Buckthorn, Rhamnus betulaefolia. *Buckthorn Family. SN Rims and CAN, Ripar. and other damp places, U Son. and Trans. zones. Shrub to 8'. Lvs. to 5" long. Flrs. tiny. Fruit a 3-seeded, berrylike drupe, bitter but edible.*

Big Sagebrush, Artemisia tridentata. *Sunflower Family. Com., SN Rims and CAN above 5000', Scrub, Wood. and Pine Forest. Shrub to 4', rarely more. Lvs. mostly 3-toothed at tip, to 1½" long, silver-hairy, aromatic. Flrs. small, composite, heads in panicles. Black Sagebrush (A. arbuscula subspecies nova) and Bigelow Sagebrush (A. bigelovii) are much smaller shrubs (to 16") with silver-hairy twigs.*

Seep-willow, Baccharis glutinosa. *Sunflower Family. Com., CAN, Ripar. Shrub to 10' or more, often forming thickets along river. Lvs. to 3½" long, slightly sticky, 3-veined. Flrs. composite, heads clustered in compact terminal panicles. Fruits are fuzzy tufts of silky-haired akenes.*

Desert Brickellbush, Brickellia atractyloides. *Sunflower Family. CAN, mostly rocky places of Gorge. Shrub to 12" tall, intricately branched, with shredding bark. Lvs. stiff, to ⅝" long. Flrs. tiny, composite, about 50 in heads about ½" diam. One of 8 Brickellia species in canyon.*

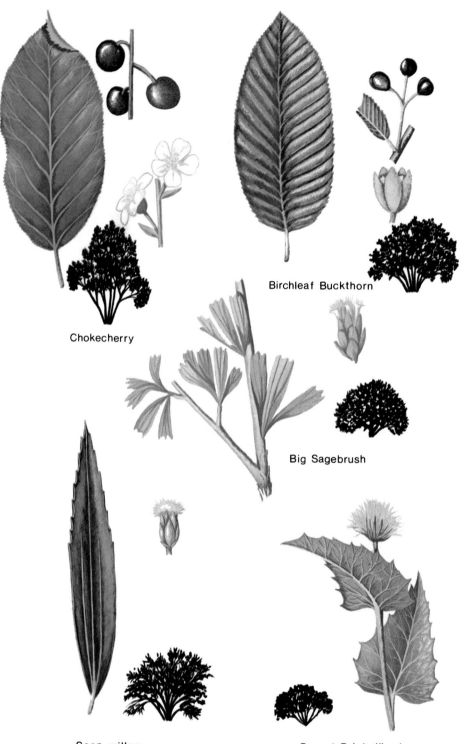

Chokecherry

Birchleaf Buckthorn

Big Sagebrush

Seep-willow

Desert Brickellbush

Plate 53. Lvs. Simple, Opposite.

Fendlerbush, Fendlera rupicola. *Saxifrage Family. Uncom., SN Rims, Com., CAN above Gorge, Scrub and Wood. Shrub to 9'. Stems smooth to downy, becoming grey with shredding bark. Lvs. to 1½" long, smooth or stiff-hairy on both sides, margins sometimes rolled under. Flrs. showy, about 1" diam. Fruit a 3-parted, persistent woody capsule. March–July.*

Fendlerella, Fendlerella utahensis. *Saxifrage Family. SN Rims and CAN, U Son. and Tran. zones, mostly open Wood. Shrub to 40". Twigs covered with stiff hairs. Lvs. numerous, sometimes bundled, to ⅝" long, 3-veined. Flrs. tiny, in sparse clusters at ends of branches, 5 petals. June–September.*

Mock Orange, Philadelphus microphyllus. *Saxifrage Family. SN Rims and CAN, dry rocky slopes. Shrub to 7'. Bark reddish-brown or tan, peeling. Lvs. about 1" long, downy below. Flrs. fragrant, about 1" across, 4 petals. May–July.*

Bigtooth Maple, Acer grandidentatum. *Maple Family. Moist, shady places just below rims, especially N Rim. Shrub or tree to 30'. Lvs. deciduous, to 4" long, with a few blunt teeth on margins. Flrs. inconspicuous. Fruit a winged samara. Cf. Boxelder, Plate 56.*

Rocky Mountain Maple, Acer glabrum. *Maple Family. Uncom., N Rim, sunny places in Forest. Shrub or tree to 30'. Lvs. deciduous, to 3" long and wide, 3–5 lobed, with numerous sharp teeth. Fruit a winged samara. Cf. Boxelder, Plate 56.*

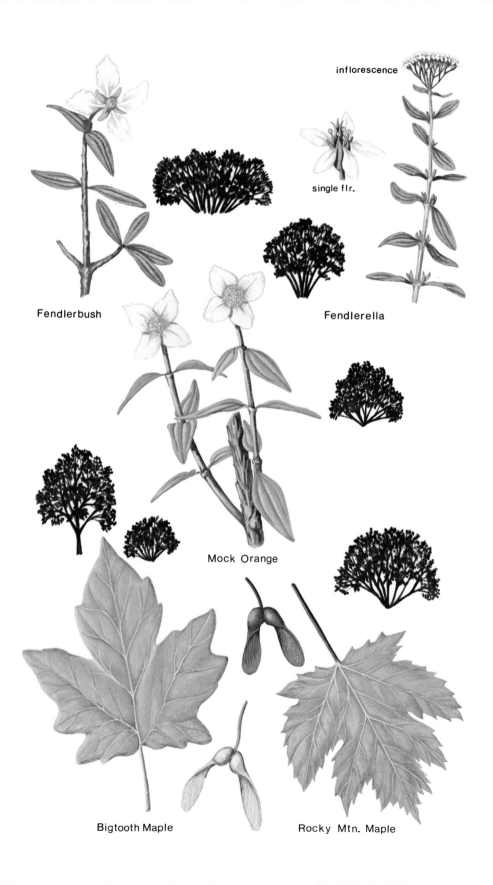

inflorescence

single flr.

Fendlerbush

Fendlerella

Mock Orange

Bigtooth Maple

Rocky Mtn. Maple

Plate 54. Lvs. Simple, Opposite.

Blackbrush, Coleogyne ramosissima. *Rose Family. CAN, Scrub, forming nearly pure stands on Tonto Plateau. Shrub to 6'. Branches tangled, often spine-tipped. Lvs. to ½", with rolled margins, in bundles. Flrs. ½" diam., solitary, with petallike sepals. March–May.*

Yellowleaf Silktassel, Garrya flavescens. *Dogwood Family. CAN, dry, rocky places in Wood. Shrub to 12'. Lvs. entire, to 2½" long. Male and female catkins on separate plants. Fruit berrylike, about ½" long, in long, drooping clusters. Lvs., flr. bracts and fruit covered with silky hairs. January–April. Wright Silktassel (G. wrightii) lacks hairs on fruit and mature lvs.*

Singleleaf Ash, Fraxinus anomala. *Olive Family. U Son. and lower Tran. zones, SN Rims and CAN. Shrub or tree to 26'. Lvs. simple or sometimes compound with 3 or more leaflets, entire or scalloped, to 2" long. Flrs. inconspicuous, in panicles. Fruit a winged akene.*

Desert-willow, Chilopsis linearis. *Bignonia Family. CAN, Ripar. below 5000'. Shrub or tree to 30'. Alternate and opposite lvs. on same plant, latter toward base, former above. Lvs. deciduous, entire, to about 5" long. Flrs. about 1" long, showy, in racemes at ends of leafy branches. Fruit a podlike capsule to 10" long. April–August.*

Longflower Snowberry, Symphoricarpos longiflorus. *Honeysuckle Family. Wood. and Forest, SN Rims and upper elevations of CAN. Shrub to 4'. Lvs. lance-shape to elliptical, entire, smooth or sparsely downy. Flrs. tubular, to ½" long or more, single or in pairs in upper leaf axils. Older stems grey and shredding; younger stems brown. Fruit white, waxy, berrylike. Mountain Snowberry (S. oreophilus) is similar, but lvs. broader, sometimes toothed, and older stems brown. Roundleaf Snowberry (S. rotundifolius) has nearly round, downy lvs. and downy young stems. Utah Snowberry (S. utahensis) and Parish Snowberry (S. parishii) have bell-shape flrs.*

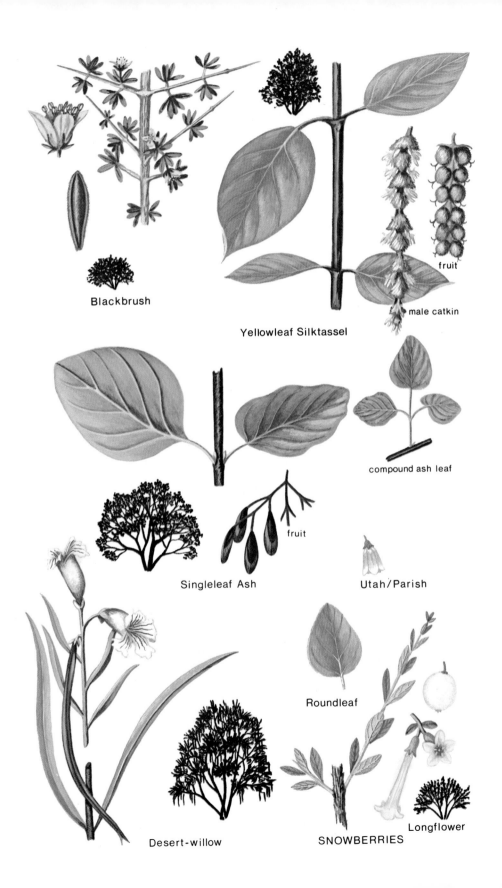

Blackbrush

Yellowleaf Silktassel

fruit

male catkin

compound ash leaf

Singleleaf Ash

fruit

Utah/Parish

Roundleaf

Desert-willow

SNOWBERRIES

Longflower

Plate 55. Lvs. Compound.

Arizona Walnut, Juglans major. Walnut Family. Havasu Canyon, Ripar. Tree to 50'. Lvs. alternate, pinnate, to 12" long with 9–13 leaflets, each toothed and to 4" long. Male flrs. in drooping catkins. Female flrs. solitary or few in a cluster. Nuts about 1" diam.

Creeping Mahonia or Barberry, Berberis repens. Barberry Family. Com., N Rim Forest, mostly above 5000'; Uncom., S Rim. Prostrate shrub to 6" high, with creeping stems. Lvs. pinnate, with 3–7 hollylike leaflets to ¾" long. Flrs. tiny, clustered. Stems root where they touch the ground. Fremont Mahonia (B. fremontii), an erect shrub to 9', with dry, blue berries, is common in shady places in CAN.

Fernbush, Chamaebatiaria millefolium. Rose Family. SN Rims and CAN, Wood., Scrub and Forest, 4500–8000'. Shrub to 6'. Lvs. fernlike, aromatic, sticky-hairy. Flrs. to ½" diam., in dense panicles at branch ends. August–September.

Catclaw, Acacia greggii. Pea Family. CAN, L & U Son. zones, Ripar. Shrub or tree to 20', often forming thickets along river, streams and dry washes. Branches with curved spines ("catclaws"). Lvs. bipinnate, with numerous tiny leaflets. Young twigs and leaflet stems are minutely hairy. Flrs. tiny, in fluffy spikes to 1½" long. Pods flat and twisted, to 5" long. April–October. Cf. Mesquite, below.

Mesquite, Prosopis juliflora. Pea Family. Gorge and side canyons at or just upstream from Gorge, Ripar. and sandy bottoms. Shrub to 20'. Branches with straight thorns in pairs at leaf axils. Lvs. bipinnate, 2-stemmed, with numerous slender leaflets, but longer than those of Catclaw. Young twigs and leaflet stems are smooth. Flrs. fragrant, tiny, in fluffy spikes to 3" long. Pods rounded and straight, to 6" long. May–July. Cf. Catclaw, above.

walnut

Creeping Mahonia

mahonia
fruit

Arizona Walnut

Fernbush

Catclaw

Mesquite

Plate 56. Lvs. Compound.

New Mexico Locust, Robinia neomexicana. *Pea Family. Com., N Rim, in thickets with Gambel Oak (see Plate 46); Uncom., S Rim. Shrub or tree to 25'. Bark and twigs armed with thorns. Lvs. pinnate, leaflets entire, to ¾" long. Flrs. fragrant, about ¾" long. June, sometimes August.*

Pale Hoptree, Ptelea pallida. *Rue Family. SN Rims and CAN, U Son. zone. Branches and lvs. unpleasantly pungent. Lvs. with 3 leaflets, each thick, firm, downy or with a whitish bloom below, smooth above. Terminal leaflet seldom 3 times longer than wide. Bark of twigs straw- to olive-colored. Flrs. about ½" diam. Narrowleaf Hoptree (P. angustifolia) is similar, but bark of twigs is dark brown or purple.*

Skunkbush or Squawbush, Rhus trilobata. *Sumac Family. Brushy and rocky areas below 7500'. Shrub to 7'. Lvs. of plants on rim have 3 leaflets, each to 1" long and 3-lobed with scalloped margins. CAN plants (variety simplicifolia) have only one leaflet per leaf. Flrs. tiny, in spikelike clusters appearing before lvs. Fruit sticky-hairy. Plant ill-smelling.*

Boxelder, Acer negundo. *Maple Family. Moist sunny places, Tran. zone Forest, mostly N Rim, also Saddle Canyon in Gorge. Tree to 60'. Lvs. with 3 leaflets, each to 4" long, entire, coarsely toothed or 3-lobed. Twigs downy when young, later smooth. Flrs. either male or female, on separate trees. Fruit a 2-winged samara. Cf. maples, Plate 53.*

Creosote Bush, Larrea tridentata. *Caltrop Family. Gorge, Scrub, below 5000' and west of Havasu Canyon. Lvs. evergreen, strong-scented, with 2 leaflets fused at the base and growing in opposite pairs. Flrs. to ½" diam., with petals twisted like the vanes of a windmill. February–April.*

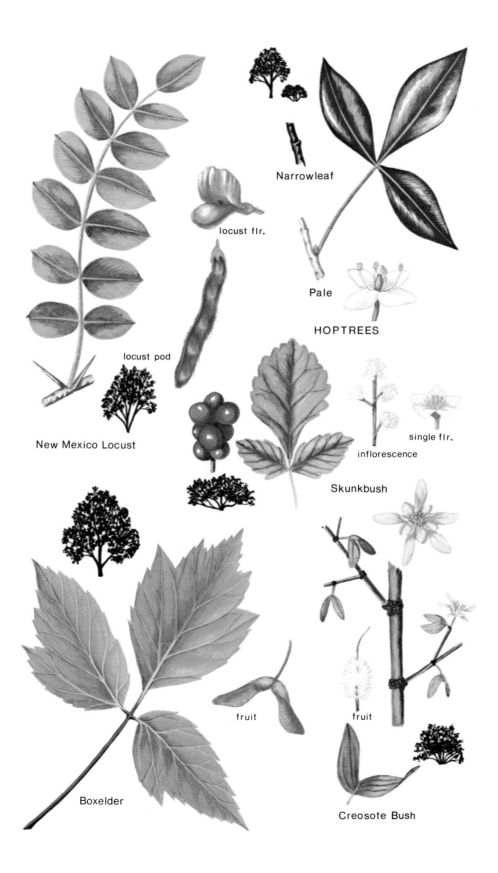

Narrowleaf

locust flr.

Pale

HOPTREES

locust pod

New Mexico Locust

Skunkbush

inflorescence

single flr.

Boxelder

fruit

fruit

Creosote Bush

Plate 57. Lvs. Basal, Inconspicuous or Absent.

Mormon Tea, Ephedra viridis. Jointfir Family. A conifer. Com., SN Rims and CAN, Scrub and Wood. below 7000' to Tonto Platform. Stems jointed, much branched to form broomlike clumps. Lvs. inconspicuous and scalelike, in opposing pairs at stem joints. Male cones have tiny flrs. on stalks emerging from between scales. Female cones stemless, on different plants from male cones. In Gorge, E. nevadensis and E. torreyana, both very similar to the above, are the more common species.

Banana or Datil Yucca, Yucca baccata. Lily Family. Wood. and Scrub, S Rim and CAN above Gorge, especially Tonto Plateau; N Rim only in dry places at canyon brink. Found along the river only in Marble Canyon. Lvs. 16–30" long, about 2" wide, with coarse fibers along margins. Flr. stalk rises from among basal lvs. and is often branched. Fruit fleshy and bananalike. April–July. Fineleaf Yucca (Y. angustissima) has much shorter, narrower lvs. with finer fibers along the margins; a mostly unbranched flr. stalk rising at or just above basal lvs.; and erect, dry seed pods for fruit. Our Lord's Candle (S. whipplei) found along the Colorado River in the western Grand Canyon, has long, narrow lvs. with serrated rather than fibrous margins and a sharp terminal spine. Its flrs., sometimes tinged purple, grow on a stalk to 12' tall.

Utah Agave or Century Plant, Agave utahensis. Amaryllis Family. SN Rims and CAN, Scrub, Wood. and Pine Forest. Shrub with rigid, fleshy, daggerlike lvs. to 15" long, with terminal spines to 2" long and shorter, curved marginal spines. Flrs. on stalk 3–14' tall, in spike covering upper ⅔ of stalk. Plants often clustered, each one blooming only once, usually after 15–25 years, thereafter dying. May–July.

Turpentine Broom, Thamnosma montana. Rue Family. CAN below Redwall. Shrub to 24". Stems much-branched, broomlike, spine-tipped, glandular. Lvs. alternate, entire, about ½" long, succulent, glandular and soon deciduous. Most of the year the plant is leafless. When crushed, it gives off a strong pungent odor not unlike citrus or turpentine. Flrs. to ⅝" long. Fruit a glandular, fleshy, 2-lobed capsule. February–April.

Ocotillo, Fouquieria splendens. Ocotillo Family. Not a cactus. Gorge, Scrub, from Havasu Canyon westward. Canelike shrub to 23'. Canes several to numerous, erect, usually leafless, mostly unbranched and crowded with thorns. Lvs. appear only for a short time following rains. They are alternate or in bundles, succulent, to 1" long. Flrs. to 1" long, in long terminal panicles. March–July.

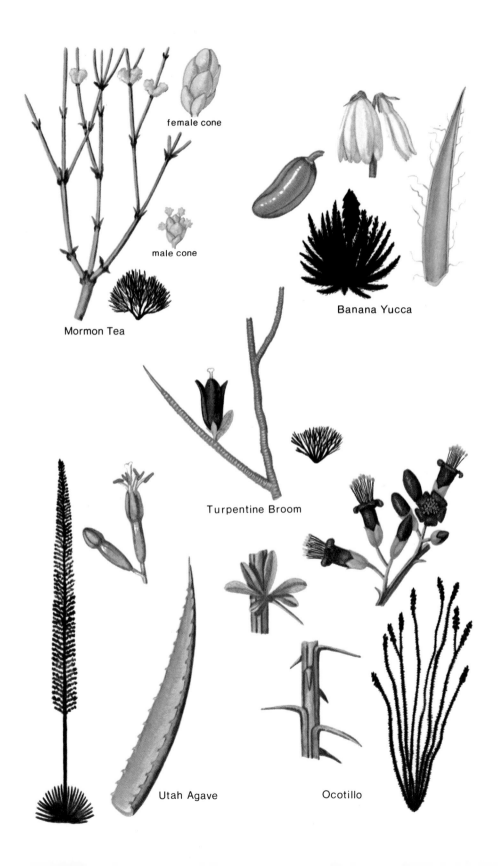

female cone

male cone

Mormon Tea

Banana Yucca

Turpentine Broom

Utah Agave

Ocotillo

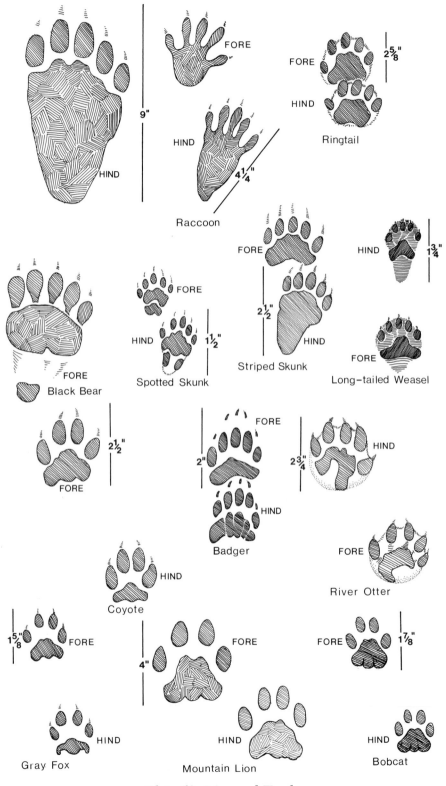

FORE

9"

HIND

HIND

4¼"

Raccoon

FORE

HIND

2⅝"

Ringtail

FORE

HIND

2½"

Striped Skunk

HIND

1¾"

FORE

Long-tailed Weasel

FORE

HIND

1½"

Spotted Skunk

FORE

Black Bear

FORE

2½"

FORE

FORE

2"

HIND

Badger

HIND

2¾"

HIND

Coyote

FORE

River Otter

1⅝"

FORE

Gray Fox

HIND

4"

FORE

HIND

Mountain Lion

FORE

1⅞"

HIND

Bobcat

Plate 58. Mammal Tracks.

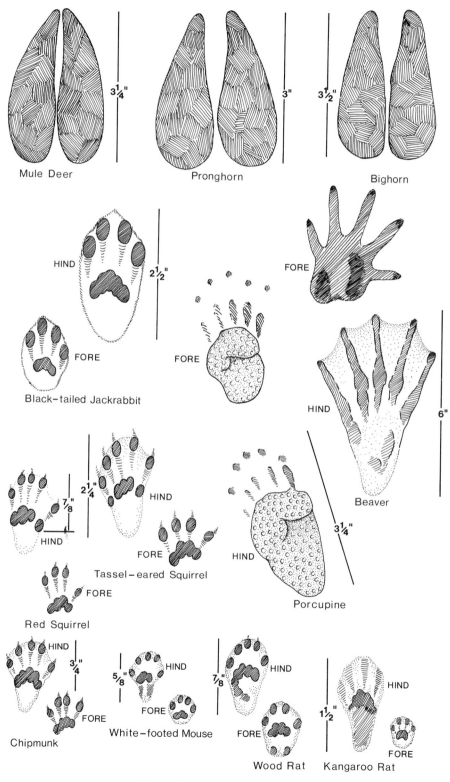

Mule Deer 3¼"

Pronghorn 3"

Bighorn 3½"

HIND · FORE 2½"
Black-tailed Jackrabbit

FORE

FORE

HIND 6"
Beaver

HIND 7/8" · HIND 2¼" · FORE
Tassel-eared Squirrel

FORE
Red Squirrel

HIND · FORE
Porcupine 3¼"

HIND · FORE 3/4"
Chipmunk

HIND · FORE 5/8"
White-footed Mouse

HIND · FORE 7/8"
Wood Rat

HIND · FORE 1½"
Kangaroo Rat

Plate 59. Mammal Tracks.

Plate 60. Carnivores.

Black Bear, Ursus americanus. *Bear Family. Lgth.: about 5'. Tail: 5".*
Black or dark brown. Uncom. to Rare, SN Rims, Grass., Wood., Forest.
Mostly nocturnal. Sign: scratch marks on trees; large black or brown
droppings.

Raccoon, Procyon lotor. *Raccoon Family. Lgth.: 33½–37½". Tail:*
11½–16¼". Grizzled grey, black mask, tail rings black and yellowish.
Uncom., CAN, Ripar. Nocturnal.

Ringtail, Bassariscus astutus. *Raccoon Family. Lgth.: 24¾–29¾". Tail:*
11¾–15". Greyish-brown, tail rings black and white. Uncom., CAN,
Ripar., Scrub, rocky places. Sign: slender, irregular droppings. Noctur-
nal.

Long-tailed Weasel, Mustela frenata. *Weasel Family. Lgth.: 11¾–14¾".*
Tail: 4–6". Brown above, orangish below, black-tipped tail, white mouth
and chin. Uncom., SN Rims; Rare, CAN, most habitats. Partly
nocturnal.

River Otter, Lutra canadensis. *Weasel Family. Lgth.: about 50". Tail:*
18". Dark brown above, lighter below, some grey on head and neck.
Uncom. to Rare, CAN, Aquat. and Ripar. Nocturnal/diurnal.

Spotted Skunk, Spilogale putorius gracilis. *Weasel Family. Lgth.:*
15¼–17⅛". Tail: 5½–6½". Black and white. Com., CAN below 4500',
all habitats. Sign: odor! Nocturnal.

Striped Skunk, Mephitis mephitis. *Weasel Family. Lgth.: 23¾–26¾".*
Tail: 10–12¾". Black and white. Com., S Rim, probable on N Rim, all
habitats. Sign: odor! Mostly nocturnal.

American Badger, Taxidea taxus. *Weasel Family. Lgth.: 23¼–31½".*
Tail: 4½–6¼". Grey tinged with yellowish-brown, undersides and tail
pale yellow, face black-and-white. Fairly Com., SN Rims, Grass.,
Wood., Forest. Sign: large burrow openings. Nocturnal/diurnal.

Long-tailed
Weasel

Raccoon

Ringtail

Spotted
Skunk

Black Bear

River Otter

American Badger

Striped Skunk

Plate 61. Carnivores and Hoofed Mammals.

Coyote, Canis latrans. *Dog Family. Lght.: 41½–49". Tail: 7–8¾". Grey or buff above, whitish below, legs rusty. Abund., SN Rims and CAN, all habitats. Sign: doglike tracks and droppings. Nocturnal/diurnal.*

Gray Fox, Urocyon cinereoargenteus. *Dog Family. Lght.: 36½–41". Tail: 15⅜–17⅜". Dark grey above, white below; sides, ears and underside of tail reddish. Com., SN Rims, status in CAN undetermined, all habitats. Sign: doglike droppings. Nocturnal/diurnal.*

Mountain Lion, Felis concolor. *Cat Family. Lght.: 6–8'. Tail: 2–3'. Tawny, slightly paler below. Uncom., SN Rims and CAN, most habitats. Sign: large catlike droppings. Nocturnal/diurnal.*

Bobcat, Lynx rufus. *Cat Family. Lgth.: 28¾–33". Tail: 5–6". Yellowish-brown or yellowish-grey above, white below, rusty spots on sides, black on legs, face, back, tail, ears and below. Com., SN Rims and CAN, most habitats. Sign: catlike droppings. Nocturnal/diurnal.*

Mule Deer, Odocoileus hemionus. *Deer Family. Lgth.: 5½–6'. Tail: about 7". Reddish in summer, grey in winter, white tail tipped in black. Com. to Abund., SN Rims; Rare, CAN, Wood. and Forest. Female lacks antlers. Usually in small bands. Sign: black, elliptical droppings to ½" long. Nocturnal/diurnal.*

Pronghorn, Antilocapra americana. *Pronghorn Family. Lgth.: about 4½'. Tail: about 6". Mostly tan, with white on rump, flanks and throat. Horn coverings shed annually. Uncom., S Rim, Scrub, Woodland. Occasional visitor from the south. Diurnal.*

Bighorn, Ovis canadensis. *Sheep and Cattle Family. Lgth.: about 5¾'. Tail: about 4". Pale brown, with creamy rump. Uncom., CAN, rocky areas and cliffs. Seldom visits rims. Sign: cylindrical droppings to ½" long, somewhat pointed at one end. Diurnal.*

Coyote

Mountain Lion

Gray Fox

Bobcat

Mule Deer

Bighorn

Pronghorn

Plate 62. Rabbits and Rodents.

Desert Cottontail, Sylvilagus audubonii. *Rabbit Family. Lgth.: 14½–16". Tail: 2–3". Grey-brown above, white below. Com., S Rim and adjacent part of CAN, Scrub and Wood. Sign: droppings—flattened pellets. Crepuscular. The very similar Nuttall Cottontail (S. nuttallii) inhabits the N Rim and adjacent CAN.*

Black-tailed Jackrabbit or Hare, Lepus californicus. *Rabbit Family. Lgth.: 20–23". Tail: 2½–4". Grey-brown with black on tip of ears and top of tail. Com., S Rim; Uncom., N Rim, Grass., Wood. and Scrub. Crepuscular.*

Porcupine, Erithizon dorsatum. *Porcupine Family. Lgth.: 26–33". Tail: 7–9". Greyish. Com., SN Rims; Rare, CAN, Wood. and Forest. Sign: conifers partly stripped of bark; tooth marks on trees. Diurnal.*

Beaver, Castor canadensis. *Beaver Family. Lgth.: 40–48". Tail: 15–21". Pale orangish-brown in the Grand Canyon. Uncom., CAN, Aquat. and Ripar. Sign: dams and lodges of brush and mud in tributary streams; gnawed or felled trees and brush. Nocturnal.*

Common Pocket Gopher, Thomomys bottae. *Pocket Gopher Family. Lgth.: 6¾–9½". Tail: 2–2¾". Brown all over. Com., S Rim and western N Rim, Grass. and Scrub. Rarely appears above ground. Sign: mounds of loose dirt piled near tunnel opening. Nocturnal/diurnal. Northern Pocket Gopher* (T. talpoides) *is similar but has white chin. It is Com. on the Kaibab Plateau, where the Common Pocket Gopher is largely absent.*

Abert Squirrel, Sciurus aberti. *Squirrel Family. Lgth.: 19–21". Tail: 7¼–9¾". Bluish-grey head, flanks and top of tail; reddish back; white on breast, belly and underside of tail; black band where flanks meet belly. Com., S Rim, Forest. Sign: globular nest of twigs placed high in pines; remains of pinecones dismantled for their seeds. Diurnal.*

Kaibab Squirrel, Sciurus kaibabensis. *Squirrel Family. Same size as above. Color similar to above, but belly dark grey and tail entirely white. Com., N Rim, Pine Forest. Unique to the Kaibab Plateau. Sign same as above. Diurnal.*

Red Squirrel, Tamiasciurus hudsonicus. *Squirrel Family. Lgth.: 12½–14". Tail: 4¾–6¼". Rusty grey above, white below, black band where flanks meet belly. Com., N Rim, Fir and Spruce–Fir Forest; Rare in Pine Forest. Sign: a feeding stump littered with nuts or dismantled pinecones. Diurnal.*

Desert Cottontail

Porcupine

Black-tailed Jackrabbit

Beaver

Common Pocket-gopher

Red Squirrel

Abert Squirrel

Kaibab Squirrel

Plate 63. Rodents: Ground Squirrels and Chipmunks.

Rock Squirrel, Spermophilus variegatus. *Squirrel Family. Lgth.:* 17½–20". *Tail: 7½–9½". Mottled grey, lower back often rusty. Com., SN Rims and CAN, rocky areas. Much larger than other Grand Canyon ground squirrels. Diurnal.*

Spotted Ground Squirrel, Spermophilus spilosoma. *Squirrel Family. Lgth.: 7½–9". Tail: 3¼". Reddish-brown and spotted above, paler below. Uncom. and local, S Rim, open sandy areas. Diurnal.*

White-tailed Antelope Ground Squirrel, Ammospermophilus leucurus. *Squirrel Family. Lgth.: 7¾–9". Tail: 2½–3½". Pale reddish- or sandy-grey above, white below and on underside of tail, 2 white back stripes not bordered with black. Fairly Com., S Rim and CAN, Scrub. Sign: burrows with radiating paths. Diurnal.*

Golden-mantled Ground Squirrel, Spermophilus lateralis. *Squirrel Family. Lgth.: 9½–11½". Tail: 3–4½". Rusty-gold with black and white stripes on back, but not head (cf. chipmunks, below); tail brown below. Sign: burrows near rocks and logs. Diurnal.*

Cliff Chipmunk, Eutamias dorsalis. *Squirrel Family. Lgth.: 7¾–9". Tail: 3⅜–4". Reddish-grey with indistinct back stripes and bolder face stripes; tail dark above and rusty below. Com., SN Rims and CAN, cliffs and rocky places. The only chipmunk on the S Rim. Diurnal.*

Least Chipmunk, Eutamias minimus. *Squirrel Family. Lgth.: 7¼–8". Tail: 3¼–3¾". Yellowish-grey above, buff below, with 9 distinct, narrow back stripes; tail yellowish below. Fairly Com., N Rim, open Wood. and Forest. Diurnal.*

Uinta Chipmunk, Eutamias umbrinus. *Squirrel Family. Lgth.: 8–9¼". Tail: 3½–4¼". Bright rusty-grey above, white below, with broad back stripes, the lowest on each side white. Com., N Rim, Forest, rocky places. Diurnal.*

Gunnison Prairie-dog, Cynomys gunnisoni. *Squirrel Family. Lgth.: 13–14½". Tail: 1¾–2¾". Buffy above, white below and on tail. Rare and local, S Rim, open sandy areas. Sign: prairie-dog "towns," with numerous burrows and radiating paths. Diurnal.*

Rock Squirrel

Spotted Ground Squirrel

White-tailed Antelope Ground Squirrel

Golden-mantled Ground Squirrel

Cliff

Least

Uinta

CHIPMUNKS

Gunnison Prairie-dog

Plate 64. Mice, Rats and Shrew.

Deer Mouse, Peromyscus maniculatus. New World Mice and Rats Family. Lgth.: 5¾–7″. Tail: 2¼–3¼″. Reddish- to yellowish-brown above, white below, tail short and furred. Abund., SN Rims, Uncom. and local in CAN. Nocturnal. One of 5 species of very similar white-footed mice in the area. The others are listed at the end of the introduction to this chapter. Distinguishing features are not provided because they are nearly impossible to make out in the field.

Bushy-tailed Wood Rat, Neotoma cinerea. New World Mice and Rats Family. Lgth.: 13¼–16⅞″. Tail: 5½–7½″. Sandy-brown above, darker on tail; feet and underside of body and tail, white. Note bushy, squirrellike tail. Sign: collections of sticks and woody debris among rocks; black cylindrical droppings. Nocturnal. One of 5 species of very similar wood rats (or pack rats) in the area. The others lack the bushy tail, however. They are listed at the end of the introduction to this chapter, but distinguishing features are not provided because they are nearly impossible to make out in the field.

Northern or Short-tailed Grasshopper Mouse, Onychomys leucogaster. New World Mice and Rats Family. Lgth.: about 6″. Tail: 1½–2⅛″. Brownish-grey above, white below and on tip of tail. SN Rims, Scrub, Wood. and rocky places. Nocturnal.

Western Harvest Mouse, Reithrodontomys megalotis. New World Mice and Rats Family. Lgth.: 5–6″. Tail: 2½–3″. Reddish-brown above, white below. Abund., SN Rims and CAN, Grass.; Uncom. in other habitats. Sign: spherical fiber nests in grass. Nocturnal.

Long-tailed Vole, Microtus longicaudus. New World Mice and Rats Family. Lgth.: 6½–7½″. Tail: 2–2½″. Dark brown above, grey below. Com., N Rim, Grass. Sign: runways in grass. Nocturnal/diurnal. Mexican Vole (M. mexicanus) similar but only found on S Rim.

Rock Pocket Mouse, Perognathus intermedius. Pocket Mouse Family. Lgth.: 6–7″. Tail: 3⅜–4″. Buff to grey above, white below. Com., CAN south of river, rocky places, Scrub.; local on S Rim. Nocturnal. Silky Pocket Mouse (P. flavus) similar but rare. Long-tailed Pocket Mouse (P. formosus) similar but only found north of river.

Ord Kangaroo Rat, Dipodomys ordii. Pocket Mouse Family. Lgth.: 9–10″. Tail: 5¼–6″. Buffy above, white below. Uncom. and local, S Rim, sandy places. Nocturnal.

Merriam Shrew, Sorex merriami. Shrew Family. Lgth.: 3½–4¼″. Tail: about 1½″. Brownish-grey above, white below. Rare, SN Rims, Grass. and Forest. One of 3 species in area, all exceedingly difficult to distinguish in the field.

Deer Mouse

Bushy-tailed Wood Rat

Western Harvest Mouse

Northern Grasshopper Mouse

Long-tailed Vole

Rock Pocket Mouse

Ord Kangaroo Rat

Merriam Shrew

Plate 65. Herons, Ducks, Sandpiper.

Herons

Great Blue Heron, Ardea herodias. *Fairly Com. Migr. and Vis. along river and near other open water. Recorded all months but June. Note large size, daggerlike bill, long legs and blue-grey plumage.*

Black-crowned Night Heron, Nycticorax nycticorax. *Uncom. Sum. Res. along river, where it nests in Ripar. A recent addition to the checklist of Grand Canyon birds. Note stocky build, white breast, black back and crown. Immatures brown with streaked breast and spotted back. Often hunt at night.*

Waterfowl

Mallard, Anas platyrhynchos. *Fairly Com. Migr. and all-year Vis. along river and on other open water. Note male's green head and white collar. Female (not shown) is mottled brown, with orangish bill, white on tail and iridescent blue wing patch (speculum).*

Common Goldeneye, Bucephala clangula. *Com. Spr. Migr. along river. Note male's striking black and white plumage, green sheen on head and white spot before the eye; female's brown head and white collar.*

Common Merganser, Mergus merganser. *Fairly Com. Migr. and all-year Vis. along river. Note male's white body and green head; female's crested, rusty head. Both have narrow, hooked, serrated bills.*

Sandpipers

Spotted Sandpiper, Actitis macularia. *Fairly Com. Sum. Res. along river. Note spotted underparts and bobbing walk. Spots absent in winter plumage. Nests on ground.*

Great Blue Heron
42-52

Black-crowned Night Heron
23-28

Mallard 20½-28   male

Spotted Sandpiper 7-8

female

Common Goldeneye 16-20

female

Common Merganser 22-27

Plate 66. Vulture, Hawks, Eagle, Falcons.

New World Vultures

Turkey Vulture, Cathartes aura. *Fairly Com. Sum. Res., L & U Son. and Trans. zones, most habitats. Usually seen soaring or perching in trees. Nests in cliff crevices, among rocks, on ground. Note naked red head and uniform black plumage.*

Hawks and Eagles

Goshawk, Accipiter gentilis. *Rare to Uncom. Res., Tran. and Bor. zones, Forest. Note light breast, grey back and red eye. Immatures (not shown) have brown backs and spotted breasts.*

Cooper's Hawk, Accipiter cooperii. *Uncom. Sum. Res., mostly Forest and Wood. Note large size and round-tipped tail (cf. Sharp-shinned Hawk, below).*

Sharp-shinned Hawk, Accipiter striatus. *Uncom. Sum. Res., mostly Forest and Wood. Note small size and notch-tipped tail (cf. Cooper's Hawk, above).*

Red-tailed Hawk, Buteo jamaicensis. *Fairly Com. Res., most habitats. Usually seen soaring or perched on tree, pole or post. Note rusty tail. Some birds darker than shown.*

Golden Eagle, Aquila chrysaetos. *Uncom. Res., U Son. through Bor. zones, most habitats. Nests on cliffs. Usually seen soaring. Note very large size and dark, uniform color.*

Falcons

Prairie Falcon, Falco mexicanus. *Rare Res. below Bor. zone, most habitats but prefers open country. Nests in cliffs. Note pale plumage, pointed wings and black in "wingpits."*

Peregrine Falcon, Falco peregrinus. *Rare Res. below Bor. zone, most habitats but prefers open country. Nests in cliffs. Note grey back, black and white head, pointed wings and absence of black in "wingpits."*

American Kestrel (formerly Sparrow Hawk), Falco sparverius. *Fairly Com. permanent Res., most habitats, but prefers open areas with shrubs or rocks for vantage points. Note small size, pointed wings, rusty coloration. Female (not shown) similar, but has rusty wings and banded tail. Most common "hawk" along river.*

Turkey Vulture
26-32

Goshawk
20-26

Sharp-shinned Hawk
10-14

Golden Eagle 30-41

Red-tailed Hawk 19-25

Cooper's Hawk
14-20

Prairie Falcon 17-20

male

Peregrine Falcon 15-21

male

American Kestrel
9-12

male

Plate 67. Owls, Nighthawk, Poor-will.

Owls

Great Horned Owl, Bubo virginianus. *Fairly Com. Res., most habitats, SN Rims and CAN. Note large size, ear tufts and barred undersides. Nests in trees, on cliffs, even on ground. Nocturnal.*

Spotted Owl, Strix occidentalis. *Rare Res., Wood. and Pine Forest. Note large size, dark eyes, round tuftless head and heavily spotted and streaked underparts. Nests in tree cavities or caves and crevices in cliffs. Nocturnal.*

Pygmy Owl, Glaucidium gnoma. *Rare Res., Tran. and Bor. zones, Wood. and Forest. Nests in tree cavities. Note songbird size, black patches at nape of neck and streaked sides. Partly diurnal.*

Saw-whet Owl, Aegolius acadicus. *Irreg. Sum. Res. and Win. Vis., Forest. Note songbird size, lack of ear tufts and streaked underparts. Immatures have white V above eyes. Nocturnal.*

Screech Owl, Otus asio. *Uncom. Res., U Son. and Tran. zones, Ripar., Wood., Forest. Note small size and ear tufts. Some birds brown or cinnamon. Nests in tree cavities. Nocturnal.*

Flammulated Owl, Otus flammeolus. *Rare Sum. Res., Forest. Note small size, dark eyes and inconspicuous ear tufts. Nests in tree cavities. Nocturnal.*

Goatsuckers

Poor-will, Phalaenoptilus nuttallii. *Fairly Com. Sum. Res., L & U Son. zones, Ripar., Grass., Scrub. Note rounded wings without white bars and short, rounded tail with white outer corners. Nocturnal. Rests during the day in shady places on or near the ground. Seldom noticed.*

Common Nighthawk, Chordeiles minor. *Fairly Com. Sum. Res., Wood., Forest. Note pointed, swept-back wings with white bar on each. Usually seen flying at twilight in the manner of swifts or swallows, but much larger. Utters a metallic peent during flight. Lesser Nighthawk (C. acutipennis) very similar, but rare.*

Poor-will 7-8$\frac{1}{2}$

Great Horned Owl
18-25

Common Nighthawk 8$\frac{1}{2}$-10

grey phase

Screech
Owl 7-10

Saw-whet Owl 7-8$\frac{1}{2}$

Spotted Owl 16$\frac{1}{2}$-19

Pygmy Owl
7-7$\frac{1}{2}$

Flammulated Owl
6 7

Plate 68. Grouse, Quail, Turkey, Roadrunner, Pigeons.

Grouse

Blue Grouse, Dendragapus obscurus. *Uncom. Res., N Rim Forest. Note chickenlike appearance and dark coloration.*

Quail and Pheasants

Chukar, Alectoris chukar. *Uncom. Res., Uinkaret Plateau and Rare Res. or Vis., Toroweap Valley. Note red legs and lack of topknot. Native to Old World. Introduced to area in 1960.*

Gambel's Quail, Lophortyx gambelli. *Uncom. Res., U Son. zone, Grass., Scrub, Wood. Note bold markings and topknot. Female (not shown) is similar. Nests on ground among brush.*

Cuckoos

Roadrunner, Geococcyx californianus. *Uncom. Res., L & U Son., Grass., Scrub, Wood. Note long tail, streaked plumage, slight crest. Feeds on lizards, snakes, insects. Nests in low trees, brush and cactus.*

Turkeys

Turkey, Meleagris gallopavo. *Fairly Com. Res., SN Rims, Pine Forest. Note bare bluish head with red wattles. Females smaller, slimmer, less iridescent. Introduced to Kaibab Plateau in 1950. Though once possibly native to region, S Rim birds may be escaped domestic birds.*

Pigeons

Band-tailed Pigeon, Columba fasciata. *Uncom. Sum. Res., Wood., Pine Forest. Similar to Rock Dove (domestic pigeon), but slimmer, with white crescent at nape of neck and light band on tail.*

Mourning Dove, Zenaida macroura. *Com. Sum. Res., Scrub, Wood., Pine Forest. Note slim build, pale plumage and long pointed tail bordered with white (especially noticeable in flight).*

Blue Grouse 15½-21

Chukar 13

Gambel's
Quail
10-11½

Roadrunner 20-24

male

Turkey 48

Band-tailed
Pigeon 14-15½

Mourning Dove 11-13

Plate 69. Woodpeckers.

Common (formerly Red-shafted) Flicker, Colaptes auratus. Com. Res., Tran. and Bor. zones, Grass. and Forest. Note red streak (absent in female) on grey cheek and orange on underside of wings and tail. Nests in tree cavities, but feeds on ground, mostly on ants.

Acorn Woodpecker, Melanerpes formicivorus. Uncom. Res., Wood., Pine Forest. Note clownlike face and black back. Feeds on acorns, which it stores in holes drilled in trees, utility poles, etc.

Lewis' Woodpecker, Melanerpes lewis. Rare Sum. Res., N. Rim, Wood., Forest. Note red face, pink underparts, green head and back.

Yellow-bellied Sapsucker, Sphyrapicus varius. Fairly Com. Sum. Res., Ripar., Wood., Forest. Note red crown and chin (partly white in females), black patch on breast, white wing patch and barred back. Feeds on sap and bark insects. Note rows of holes circling tree trunks.

Williamson's Sapsucker, Sphyrapicus thyroideus. Uncom. Sum. Res., N Rim Bor. Forest. Nests in aspens. Note black back and breast, black crown and red chin and white wing patch. Female (not shown) has brown head, barred back and wings and yellow belly.

Hairy Woodpecker, Picoides villosus. Com. Res., Forest, sometimes visiting Ripar. below Redwall. Note clear white back and large black bill. Female (not shown) lacks red on head.

Downy Woodpecker, Picoides pubescens. Rare Res., Forest, often wandering to lower elevations. Very similar to preceding species, but smaller overall and with slimmer bill. Female (not shown) lacks red on head.

Ladder-backed Woodpecker, Picoides scalaris. Rare Res., L & U Son. zones, Ripar., Grass., Wood. Note striped face and barred back. Female lacks red cap.

Northern Three-toed Woodpecker, Picoides tridactylus. Rare Res., Forest. Note yellow cap of male and barred sides of both sexes.

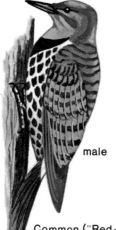

Common ("Red-
shafted") Flicker
$12\frac{1}{2}$-14

Acorn Woodpecker
8-$9\frac{1}{2}$

Lewis' Woodpecker
$10\frac{1}{2}$-$11\frac{1}{2}$

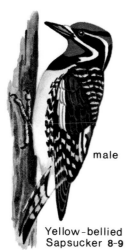

male

Yellow-bellied
Sapsucker 8-9

male

Williamson's
Sapsucker $9\frac{1}{2}$

male

Hairy Woodpecker
$8\frac{1}{2}$-$10\frac{1}{2}$

male

Downy Woodpecker
6-7

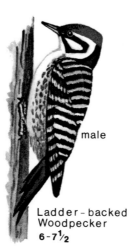

male

Ladder-backed
Woodpecker
6-$7\frac{1}{2}$

male

Northern
Three-toed
Woodpecker
8-$9\frac{1}{2}$

Plate 70. Hummingbirds, Swift, Swallows.

Hummingbirds

Black-chinned Hummingbird, Archilochus alexandri. *Fairly Com. Sum. Res., most habitats below Bor. zone. Note male's black chin, iridescent purple throat and white breast patch; female's lack of rust-colored plumage.*

Broad-tailed Hummingbird, Selasphorus platycercus. *Com. Sum. Res., Forest. Note male's rosy throat, green back and dark tail; female's rusty tail and sides.*

Rufous Hummingbird, Selasphorus rufus. *Com. Fall Migr. and Rare Spr. Migr., most habitats. Note male's rusty head, back, sides and tail. Female (not shown) is virtually identical to—but slightly smaller than— female Broad-tailed Hummingbird.*

Swifts

White-throated Swift, Aeronautes saxatalis. *Com. Sum. Res. below Bor. zone, usually seen swooping and diving over the canyon. Told from swallows by black-and-white plumage; long, narrow swept-back wings; more erratic flight; and "twinkling" wing movements in flight. Nests on cliffs, but spends most of life in the air.*

Swallows

Violet-green Swallow, Tachycineta thalassina. *Com. Sum. Res., cliffs and Forest. Note white rump patches and white around eye. Flight steadier than swift's and wings not swept back.*

Cliff Swallow, Petrochelidon pyrrhonota. *Irreg. Sum. Res., nesting on cliffs. Note pale rump, unforked tail and reddish-brown throat.*

Purple Martin, Progne subis. *Uncom. Sum. Res., Forest, nesting in tree cavities. Note uniform, dark coloration and forked tail. Female (not shown) has pale-grey breast.*

Black-chinned
Hummingbird $3\frac{1}{3}$-$3\frac{3}{4}$

male

male

Rufous
Hummingbird
$3\frac{1}{3}$-4

male

Broad-tailed Hummingbird
4-$4\frac{1}{2}$

White-throated Swift 6-7

Violet-Green Swallow 5-$5\frac{1}{2}$

male

Cliff Swallow 5-6

Purple Martin $7\frac{1}{4}$-$8\frac{1}{2}$

Plate 71. Tyrant Flycatchers.

Western Kingbird, Tyrannus verticalis. *Uncom. Sum. Res., Ripar. and Wood. Note pale breast, poorly defined white patch on throat and white border on tail. Cf. Cassin's Kingbird, below.*

Cassin's Kingbird, Tyrannus vociferans. *Uncom. Sum. Res., Ripar. and Wood. Note dark breast, well-defined white throat patch and lack of white border on tail. Cf. Western Kingbird, above.*

Ash-throated Flycatcher, Myiarchus cinerascens. *Fairly Com. Sum. Res., Ripar. and Wood. Note cinnamon wings and tail.*

Black Phoebe, Sayornis nigricans. *Uncom. Res., Ripar. Note black breast. Rarely found away from water. From perch amid or near a stream or puddle, it repeatedly sallies forth for flying insects. This habit is common to all tyrant flycatchers.*

Say's Phoebe, Sayornis saya. *Fairly Com. Sum. Res., most habitats below Bor. zone. Note rusty belly.*

Gray Flycatcher, Empidonax wrightii. *Com. Sum. Res., S Rim Wood. Note small size, two white wingbars, flycatching habit. Virtually impossible to distinguish in the field from the Willow Flycatcher (E. traillii), Rare Sum. Res., Ripar., and the Western Flycatcher (E. difficilis), a Sum. Vis. or Res. (?), Ripar., Scrub, Wood., Forest. Even experts have trouble with these and related species.*

Western Wood Pewee, Contopus sordidulus. *Fairly Com. Sum. Res., Wood. of U Son. zone. Similar to preceding species, but larger (sparrow-size), with darker back and breast, no eye ring and longer wings in proportion to body.*

Olive-sided Flycatcher, Nuttallornis borealis. *Uncom. Sum. Res., Forest. Note lack of wing bars and olive "vest" over white breast. More often heard than seen: song Hip, Three Cheers uttered from upper branches of conifers.*

Western
Kingbird
8-9½

Cassin's
Kingbird
8-9

Ash-throated
Flycatcher
7½-8½

Black Phoebe
6¼-7

Say's Phoebe
7-8

Gray Flycatcher
5½

Western
Wood Pewee
6-6½

Olive-sided
Flycatcher
7-8

Plate 72. Jays, Raven, Phainopepla.

Jays and Raven

Clark's Nutcracker, Nucifraga columbiana. *Com. Res., Bor. Forest. Wanders widely in winter. Note large, black, awl-shape bill and black-and-white wings and tail.*

Pinyon Jay, Gymnorhinus cyanocephalus. *Com. Res., Wood. and Forest. Told from following species by uniform blue-grey color. Often in flocks. Preferred food is pinyon nuts.*

Scrub Jay, Aphelocoma coerulescens. *Fairly Com. Res., Wood. Told from preceding species by white throat, dark necklace and olive-grey back. Seldom in flocks. Prefers brush and small trees to forest.*

Steller's Jay, Cyanocitta stelleri. *Com. Res., Pine Forest. Note dark-blue body and black, crested head. Nearly twice the size of the following species, the only other dark, crested bird in the area.*

Common Raven, Corvus corax. *Com. Res., most habitats, but usually seen indulging in aerial acrobatics along the rims and over the canyon. Told from Common Crow (C. brachyrhynchos, Irreg. Sum. Vis.) by large size, thick bill, shaggy throat feathers, wedge-shape tail and deeper, harsher call* (croak or cronk).

Silky Flycatchers

Phainopepla, Phainopepla nitens. *Rare Sum. Res., L & U Son. zones, Ripar. and Scrub. Note dark plumage with crest and white wing patches in flight. Note female's grey plumage and lighter wings and dark tail. Red eye of both sexes is distinctive.*

Clark's Nutcracker **12-13**

Pinyon Jay **9-11¾**

Scrub Jay **11-13**

female

Steller's Jay **12-13½**

Phainopepla **7-7¾**

Common Raven **21½-27**

Plate 73. Titmice, Nuthatches, Creeper.

Titmice

Mountain Chickadee, Parus gambeli. *Com. Res. Wood., Forest. Note black bib and white stripe over eye. Gleans insects from outer branches of conifers, often hanging upside-down in the process.*

Plain Titmouse, Parus inornatus. *Fairly Com. Res., U Son. zone, Wood. Note plain grey plumage and crest. Told from female Phainopepla (Plate 72) by dark eye, eye ring, lighter tail.*

Common Bushtit, Psaltriparus minimus. *Fairly Com. Res., U Son. Wood. and Win. Vis., Ripar. Note tiny size, long tail and brown cheek. Occurs in loose, chattering flocks.*

Nuthatches

White-breasted Nuthatch, Sitta carolinensis. *Com. Res., U Son. and Tran. zones, Ripar., Wood., Forest. Told from following species by black eye on white face. Nuthatches typically hang upside-down on branches and head-down on tree trunks.*

Red-breasted Nuthatch, Sitta canadensis. *Uncom. Res., Bor. Forest, N Rim. Note pinkish underparts and white stripe over eye. Behavior similar to that of White-breasted Nuthatch, above.*

Pygmy Nuthatch, Sitta pygmaea. *Com. Res., Pine Forest, SN Rims. Note brown cap and black eye stripe. Behavior similar to that of White-breasted Nuthatch, above.*

Creepers

Brown Creeper, Certhia familiaris. *Fairly Com. Sum. Res., Bor. Forest, N Rim. Note curved beak, rusty, pointed tail and streaked brown back. Spirals head-first up tree trunks searching for bark insects, then flies to the base of nearby tree and repeats the process. Easily overlooked.*

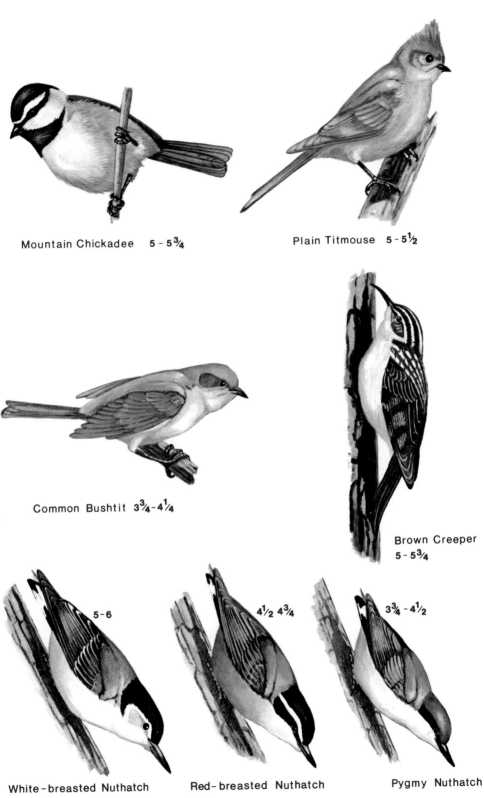

Mountain Chickadee   5 - 5¾

Plain Titmouse 5 - 5½

Common Bushtit 3¾ - 4¼

Brown Creeper
5 - 5¾

5 - 6

4½ 4¾

3¾ - 4½

White-breasted Nuthatch

Red-breasted Nuthatch

Pygmy Nuthatch

Plate 74. Wrens, Dipper, Lark, Starling, House Sparrow.

Wrens

House Wren, Troglodytes aedon. *Fairly Com. Sum. Res., N Rim Bor. Forest. Note plain grey-brown plumage and lack of eye stripe.*

Bewick's Wren, Thryomanes bewickii. *Uncom. Sum. Res., most habitats below the Forest. Note white underparts, white in tail, bold white stripe over eye and plain brown back.*

Canyon Wren, Catherpes mexicanus. *Com. Res., cliffs and canyons. Note contrasting white breast and brown belly. The song of this bird—a rich, cascading series of whistles, descending in pitch and slowing toward the end—is one of the most common sounds in the canyon.*

Rock Wren, Salpinctes obsoletus. *Com. Res., Grass., Scrub, Wood., rocky places. Note buffy corners of tail, lightly streaked breast and faint white stripe over eye.*

Dippers

Dipper or Water Ousel, Cinclus mexicanus. *Fairly Com. Res. along permanent tributaries in the canyon; fairly Com. Win. Vis. along the river. Note slate color, stubby tail and constant bobbing motion. Rarely far from running water. Feeds in stream shallows and even dives beneath the surface after insects.*

Larks

Horned Lark, Eremophila alpestris. *Com. Res., U Son. Grass. Note black bib, face patch and "horns," yellow face and pale underparts. Immatures (not shown) lack horns and show little or no black. Usually seen in flocks, feeding on open ground.*

Starlings

Starling, Sturnus vulgaris. *Uncom. Res. (?) near human habitations. Note yellow bill and short tail of breeding adult; black bill and spotted plumage of winter birds. An exotic. Cf. blackbirds, Plate 78.*

Weaver Finches

House Sparrow, Passer domesticus. *Com. Res. near human habitations. Note male's black bib and grey crown. Female (not shown) has pale-grey breast and light eye stripe. An exotic. Cf. sparrows, Plate 80.*

House Wren 4½-5¼

Bewick's Wren 5-5½

Canyon Wren 5½-5¾

Rock Wren 5-6¼

Dipper 7-8½

Horned Lark 7-8

winter

Starling 7½-8½

summer

House Sparrow 5¾-6¼

male

Plate 75. Shrike, Mockingbird, Thrushes.

Shrikes

Loggerhead Shrike, Lanius ludovicianus. *Uncom. Res., Grass. and Wood., L & U Son. zones. Note black mask and hooked, hawklike bill. A predatory songbird, feeding on small rodents and birds as well as insects. Called "butcherbird" because it impales prey on thorns for later use.*

Mimic Thrushes

Mockingbird, Mimus polyglottos. *Uncom. Sum. Res., U Son. zone, Grass., Scrub and Wood. Note conspicuous white tail margins and wing patches. An accomplished mimic of other birds, with a large repertory of songs.*

Thrushes

American Robin, Turdus migratorius. *Com. Res., Forest. Probably the best-known American bird. Note rusty breast and dark back.*

Hermit Thrush, Catharus guttata. *Com. Sum. Res., Forest. Note spotted breast, rusty tail and beautiful flutelike song. The Sage Thrasher (Oreoscoptes montanus), an Uncom. Sum. Vis., is somewhat similar, but has a longer, curved bill and longer tail.*

Western Bluebird, Sialia mexicana. *Com. Res., Wood. and Forest. Note male's bright blue head, wings and tail; rusty back and breast. Female (not shown) is similar, but far paler.*

Mountain Bluebird, Sialia currucoides. *Fairly Com. Sum. Res., Grass. and other open places in Forest. Note uniform turquoise color. Female (not shown) resembles female Western Bluebird, above, but has a grey, rather than rusty, breast.*

Townsend's Solitaire, Myadestes townsendii. *Fairly Com. Res., Wood., Forest. Note white eye ring, white tail margins and buffy wing patches.*

Loggerhead
Shrike 8 - 10

Mockingbird
9 - 11

American
Robin 9 - 11

Hermit
Thrush 6½ - 7¾

male Western
Bluebird 6½ - 7

Townsend's Solitaire
8 - 9½

male Mountain
Bluebird 6½ - 7¾

Plate 76. Gnatcatchers, Kinglets, Vireos.

Gnatcatchers and Kinglets

Blue-grey Gnatcatcher, Polioptila caerulea. *Com. Sum. Res., CAN, Ripar., Scrub, Wood.; Uncom. Sum. Res., SN Rims. Note blue-grey crown, white eye ring and predominance of white on underside of tail.*

Black-tailed Gnatcatcher, Polioptila melanura. *Occasional to Rare Res. or Vis., L Son. zone, Ripar., western Grand Canyon. Note summer male's black cap, lack of eye ring and predominance of black on underside of tail. Female and young have grey-brown head and back. Winter male duller, without black cap.*

Golden-crowned Kinglet, Regulus satrapa. *Rare Sum. Res., N Rim Bor. Forest. Note male's yellow, red and black crown. Female similar, but lacks red on crown.*

Ruby-crowned Kinglet, Regulus calendula. *Com. Sum. Res., N Rim Bor. Forest. Red crown patch of male often hidden. Female (not shown) lacks red crown patch but otherwise similar. Note lack of yellow on crown, broken eye ring, and habit of constantly fluttering its wings.*

Vireos

Bell's Vireo, Vireo bellii. *Com. Sum. Res., CAN, Ripar. Note olive color, pale yellow sides and usually 2 wingbars. Does not twitch tail, flutter wings or sally forth after flies (cf. tyrant flycatchers, Plate 71).*

Gray Vireo, Vireo vicinior. *Rare Sum. Res., U Son., Wood. Note grey color, grey or buffy sides, obscure white "spectacles" and 1 faint wingbar. Twitches tail, but doesn't flutter wings or sally forth after flies.*

Solitary Vireo, Vireo solitarius. *Com. Sum. Res., Wood., Pine Forest. Note white "spectacles," snow-white throat and 2 prominent wingbars.*

Warbling Vireo, Vireo gilvus. *Uncom. Sum. Res., Tran. and Bor. zones of N Rim (and S Rim?). Note faint eye stripe and whitish breast.*

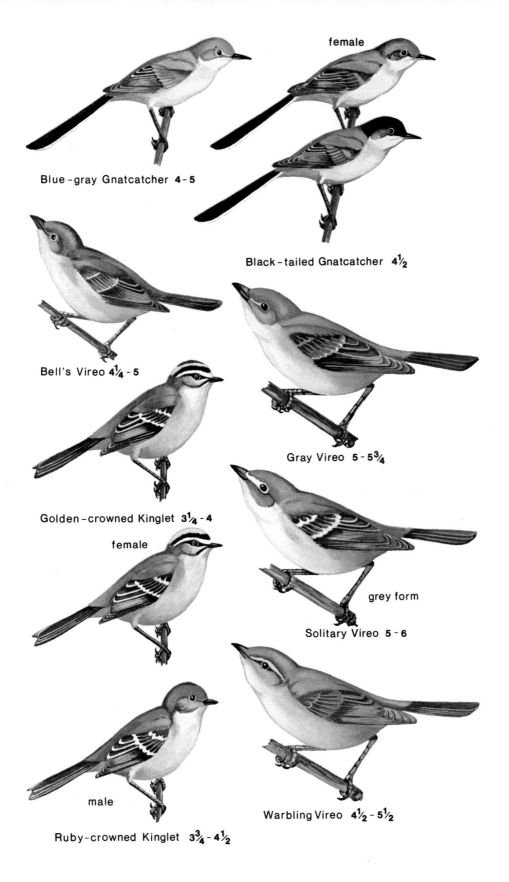

Blue-gray Gnatcatcher 4-5

female

Black-tailed Gnatcatcher 4½

Bell's Vireo 4¼-5

Gray Vireo 5-5¾

Golden-crowned Kinglet 3¼-4

female

grey form

Solitary Vireo 5-6

male

Warbling Vireo 4½-5½

Ruby-crowned Kinglet 3¾-4½

Plate 77. Wood Warblers.

Virginia's Warbler, Vermivora virginiae. *Fairly Com. Sum. Res., N Rim Forest. Note yellowish rump and breast.*

Lucy's Warbler, Vermivora luciae. *Com. Sum. Res., L & U Son. zones, Ripar., Scrub. Note reddish-brown rump and whitish breast. The most common warbler along the Colorado River.*

Yellow Warbler, Dendroica petechia. *Fairly Com. Sum. Res., L & U Son. zones, Ripar. Note yellow tail spots and rusty streaks on breast. Streaks faint or missing in female.*

Yellow-rumped Warbler (Audubon's Warbler), Dendroica coronata. *Com. Sum. Res., N Rim Forest. Note yellow throat and rump, black breast and white wing patches. In spring and summer, female (not shown) brown with two white wingbars. Winter birds brownish, streaked, white below, with yellow throats.*

Black-throated Gray Warbler, Dendroica nigrescens. *Fairly Com. Sum. Res., U Son. zone, Wood. Note black crown, cheeks and throat. Female (not shown) duller and lacks black throat patch.*

Grace's Warbler, Dendroica graciae. *Fairly Com. Sum. Res., N Rim Bor. Forest. Note striped flanks and yellow throat and breast.*

Common Yellowthroat, Geothlypis trichas. *Fairly Com. Sum. Res., L & U Son. zones, Ripar. Note male's black mask and yellow throat; female's white belly and buffy sides.*

Yellow-breasted Chat, Icteria virens. *Fairly Com. Sum. Res., L & U Son. zones, Ripar. Note large size, thick bill, yellow breast and white belly. Very unwarblerlike.*

Wilson's Warbler, Wilsonia pusilla. *Fairly Com. Migr. below Bor. zone. Note black cap of male. Female lacks cap, wingbars or other conspicuous markings.*

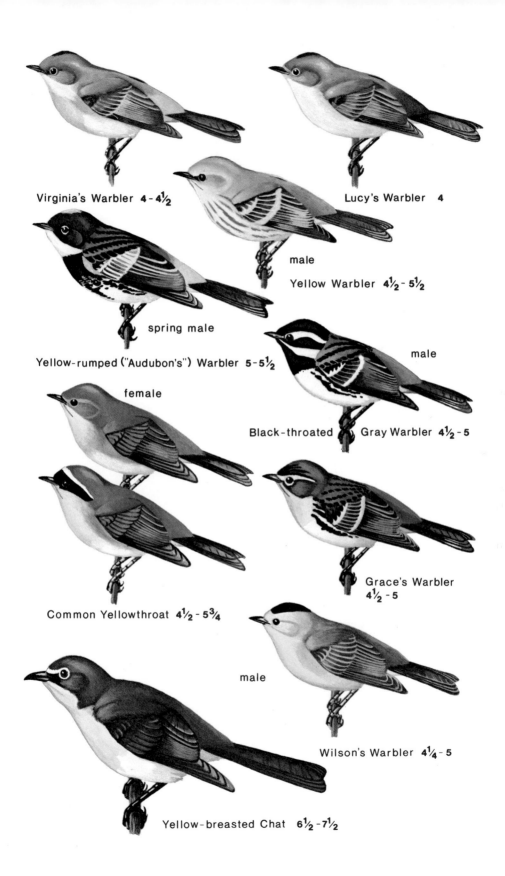

Virginia's Warbler **4-4½**

Lucy's Warbler **4**

male

Yellow Warbler **4½-5½**

spring male

Yellow-rumped ("Audubon's") Warbler **5-5½**

male

female

Black-throated Gray Warbler **4½-5**

Grace's Warbler
4½-5

Common Yellowthroat **4½-5¾**

male

Wilson's Warbler **4¼-5**

Yellow-breasted Chat **6½-7½**

Plate 78. Meadowlark, Blackbirds, Orioles, Tanagers.

New World Blackbirds and Orioles

Western Meadowlark, Sturnella neglecta. *Fairly Com. Res., U Son. zone, Grass., Scrub. Note yellow underparts and black V-shape necklace. Cf. Horned Lark, Plate 74.*

Red-winged Blackbird, Agelaius phoeniceus. *Rare Res. along river, nesting in cattails and tamarisk lining upper shoreline of Lake Mead, between Separation Rapids and Grand Wash. Note male's red shoulder patches and female's streaked underparts.*

Brewer's Blackbird, Euphagus cyanocephalus. *Fairly Com. Sum. Res., N Rim; Irreg. Sum. Res., S Rim. Nest in bush or tree; usually forages in open areas. Note male's yellow eye, dark bill and iridescent black plumage; female's grey plumage, long, pointed bill and black eye.*

Brown-headed Cowbird, Molothrus ater. *Com. Sum. Res., SN Rims, most habitats. Note male's brown head and sparrowlike bill. Female (not shown) is grey, with sparrowlike bill.*

Hooded Oriole, Icterus cucullatus. *Uncom., Sum. Res. along river. Note male's yellow-orange crown and black throat; female's yellowish underparts.*

Scott's Oriole, Icterus parisorum. *Uncom. Sum. Res., U Son. zone, Wood. Note male's lemon-yellow and black plumage, female similar to female Hooded Oriole, but underparts yellow-green and back streaked.*

Northern Oriole, Icterus galbula. *Uncom. Sum. Res., Ripar., especially cottonwoods. Note male's black crown, orange cheek and white wing patch. Female similar to female Hooded Oriole, but belly white.*

Tanagers

Western Tanager, Piranga ludoviciana. *Com. Sum. Res., Tran. and Bor. zones, Forest. Note male's red head, yellow breast and black wings and tail; female's thick bill and conspicuous wingbars.*

Summer Tanager, Piranga rubra. *Rare Sum. Res. along river. Note male's uniform rosy plumage. Female (not shown) similar to female Western Tanager, but lacks wingbars.*

female

female

Western Meadowlark
8½-11

Red-winged
Blackbird
7-9½

Brewer's
Blackbird
8-10

male

Brown-
headed
Cowbird
6-8

female

Hooded
Oriole
7-7½

male

female

Western Tanager
6¼-7½

Scott's
Oriole
7¼-8¼

male

Summer Tanager
7-7¾

male

Northern
(Bullock's)
Oriole 7-8½

Plate 79. Grosbeaks, Buntings, Finches, Towhees.

Black-headed Grosbeak, Pheucticus melanocephalus. *Com. Sum. Res., Wood., Pine Forest. Note male's black head, ocher to rusty breast and white wing spots; female's large size, striped head, thick bill.*

Blue Grosbeak, Guiraca caerulea. *Fairly Com. Sum. Res. along river. Note both sex's thick bills and tan wingbars.*

Indigo Bunting, Passerina cyanea. *Uncom. Sum. Res., CAN, along permanent tributaries; Uncom. Sum. Vis. along the river. Note male's uniform blue plumage; female's faintly streaked underparts and lack of wingbars.*

Lazuli Bunting, Passerina amoena. *Uncom. Sum. Res., CAN, along permanent tributaries. Note male's rusty breast, white belly and white wingbars; female's unstreaked underparts and white wingbars.*

Cassin's Finch, Carpodacus cassinni. *Com. Res., N Rim Bor. Forest. Note male's brownish neck and lack of side streaks.*

House Finch, Carpodacus mexicanus. *Com. Sum. Res., most habitats below Bor. zone. Note male's streaked sides. Female very similar to female Cassin's Finch. Male Purple Finch* (C. purpureus), *an Irreg. Vis. to the Bor. Forest, lacks streaked sides and brown neck. Cf. Cassin's Finch.*

Pine Siskin, Carduelis pinus. *Fairly Com. Res. N Rim Bor. Forest; Irreg. Sum. Vis. or Res., S Rim; fairly Com. Win. Vis., CAN. Note heavy streaking and yellowish wings and tail. In flocks.*

Lesser Goldfinch, Carduelis psaltria. *Fairly Com. Sum. Res. along the river and Vis. throughout the area. Note male's black back and head; female's olive-green rump.*

Green-tailed Towhee, Pipilo chlorurus. *Fairly Com. Sum. Res., N Rim Bor. zone. Note rusty cap and white throat. Call a catlike* mew.

Rufous-sided Towhee, Pipilo erythrophthalmus. *Com. Sum. Res., Tran. and Bor. Forest, and Win. Vis., U Son., Scrub, Wood. Note white underparts, rusty sides and black head, breast, back and tail. Female (not shown) similar, but with brown head and back.*

female

Black-headed
Grosbeak
$6\frac{1}{2}$-$7\frac{3}{4}$

female

Indigo Bunting
$5\frac{1}{4}$-$5\frac{3}{4}$

female

Blue Grosbeak 6-$7\frac{1}{2}$

female

Lazuli Bunting
5 - $5\frac{1}{2}$

Pine Siskin
$4\frac{1}{2}$-$5\frac{1}{4}$

female

Cassin's Finch
6 - $6\frac{1}{2}$

female

Lesser
Goldfinch
$3\frac{3}{4}$-$4\frac{1}{4}$

male

House Finch
5 - $5\frac{3}{4}$

Green-tailed
Towhee
$6\frac{1}{4}$ - 7

male

Rufous-sided
Towhee   7 - $8\frac{1}{2}$

Plate 80. Sparrows.

Vesper Sparrow, Pooecetes gramineus. *Uncom. Sum. Res., U Son. Grass., occasionally Tran. zone. Note streaked breast and white outer tail feathers.*

Lark Sparrow, Chondestes grammacus. *Uncom. Sum. Res., U Son. Grass. and Scrub; Sum. Vis. throughout area. Note bold head stripes and black spot on white breast.*

Rufous-crowned Sparrow, Aimophila ruficeps. *Uncom. Res., U Son. Scrub and Wood. Note rusty cap and black streak near bill.*

Black-throated Sparrow, Amphispiza bilineata. *Fairly Com. Sum. Res., L & U Son. zones, Grass., Scrub. Note white head stripes and black throat.*

Dark-eyed Junco (includes Oregon Junco and Slate-colored Junco), Junco hyemalis. *Com. Win. Vis. below Bor. zone, SN Rims and CAN. Oregon Junco has black or grey hood, brown back, pale brown sides. The rare Slate-colored Junco has dark grey hood, breast and back.*

Gray-headed Junco, Junco caniceps. *Com. Res., SN Rims, Forest. Note grey sides and hood and brown back.*

Chipping Sparrow, Spizella passerina. *Com. Sum. Res., SN Rims, Forest, especially open, grassy areas. Note rusty crown and white "eyebrow."*

Black-chinned Sparrow, Spizella atrogularis. *Possibly Rare Sum. Res., L & U Son. zones, Scrub and Wood. Note grey head and breast, with pink bill surrounded by black. Female lacks black chin.*

White-crowned Sparrow, Zonotrichia leucophrys. *Com. Win. Vis., most habitats throughout the region. Possible Rare Sum. Res., N Rim Bor. Forest. Note white crown, grey throat and pink bill. Immatures have striped grey and brown crowns.*

Lincoln's Sparrow, Melospiza lincolnii. *Fairly Com. Migr. throughout region. Note streaked, buffy breast.*

Vesper Sparrow
5 - 6½

Lark Sparrow
5½ - 6¾

Rufous-crowned
Sparrow 5 - 6

Black-throated
Sparrow 4¾ - 5¼

Dark-eyed Junco
("Oregon Junco") 5 - 6

Gray-headed
Junco   5½ - 6

male

Black-chinned
Sparrow   5 5½

Chipping Sparrow 5 - 5¾

White-crowned 5½ - 7
Sparrow

Lincoln's Sparrow
5 - 6

Plate 81. Amphibians and Iguanid Lizards.

Amphibians

Cloudy Tiger Salamander, Ambystoma tigrinum, *subsp.* nebulosum. *Ambystoma Family. 6–13⅜". Dark grey or olive with dusky spots on back and sides. Recently transformed adults may also have yellow blotches. Com., Tran. and Bor. zones. Breeds in ponds and "tanks," rests in crevices, decayed logs or burrows of other animals. Usually abroad only on warm nights during or after a rain.*

Great Basin Spadefoot Toad, Scaphiopus intermontanus. *1½–2". Spadefoot Toad Family. Olive or grey-green with light stripes on flanks, hump between eyes and wedge-shape "spade" on each hind foot. Com., N Rim, Tran. and Bor. zones. Breeds in ponds, pools and quiet streams. Western Spadefoot Toad (S. hammondi) of CAN and S Rim is darker and lacks hump between eyes.*

Red-spotted Toad. Bufo punctatus. *Toad Family. 1–2½". Olive-green to grey-brown, with numerous red warts. Song a high-pitched trill. Most active at twilight. Breeds in pools and streams, rests in rock crevices. Abund., CAN, near water. Woodhouse's Toad (B. woodhousei), 2½–5", also Abund., CAN, near water, has numerous dark spots on pale tan or reddish ground. Its song is a wheezy trill.*

Canyon Treefrog, Hyla arenicolor. *Treefrog Family. 1¾–2¼". Olive, tan or grey, with darker blotches. Male's throat black or grey. Note large toe pads. Breeds in streams and pools, rests in rock crevices. Com., CAN, perennial tributary streams.*

Iguanid Lizards

Chuckwalla, Sauromalus obesus. *Iguana Family. 11–16½". Male with black head, forelegs and forward part of trunk, becoming grey, yellowish or reddish toward rear. Female and young (not shown) often crossbanded. Com., CAN, Ripar. and Scrub. Rests in crevices. Diurnal, sometimes seen sunning on rocks.*

Short-horned Lizard, Phrynosoma douglassi. *Iguana Family. 2½–5⅞". Grey or brownish, with 2 rows of darker spots down back. Note flat body and prominent, reddish, horizontal spines on head. Com., U Son. and Tran. zones, Grass., Wood. and Forest. Desert Horned Lizard (P. platyrhinos), a Rare resident of Grass. and Scrub in the Son. zones, is very similar, but with somewhat longer head spines, wavy crossbands on sides of head and dark splotches on neck.*

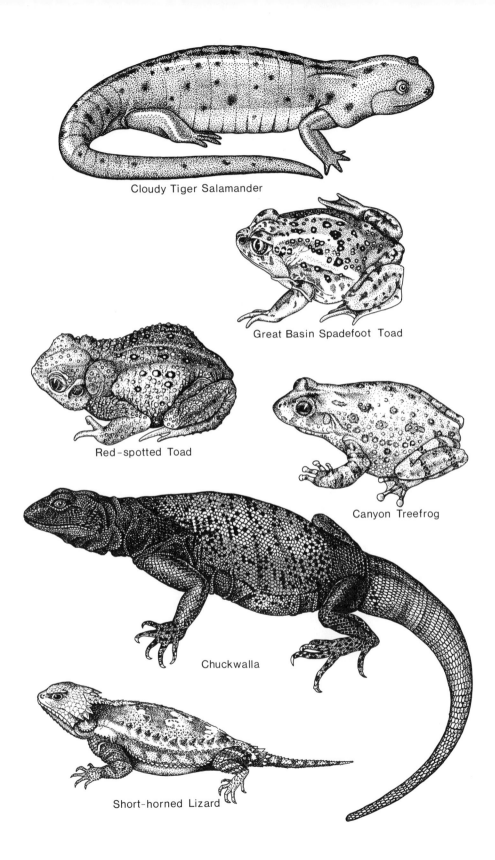

Cloudy Tiger Salamander

Great Basin Spadefoot Toad

Red-spotted Toad

Canyon Treefrog

Chuckwalla

Short-horned Lizard

Plate 82. Iguanid Lizards, Whiptail, Skink.

Western Collared Lizard, Crotaphytus collaris. *Iguana Family. 8–14".* *Note black-and-white collar, rounded tail and dark mouth lining. Body color of males mostly green. Many individuals drabber than shown. Females may have orange bands or spots on sides. Young often crossbanded. Com., L and U Son. zones, Scrub and Wood. Desert Collared Lizard* (C. insularis), *is similar, but mostly tan, with pale yellow crossbands. Throat of male blue with dark blotch. Also note flattened tail and light mouth lining. Leopard Lizard* (C. wislizenii) *lacks collar.*

Tree Lizard, Urosaurus ornatus. *Iguana Family. 4½–6¼". Com., L and U Son. zones, Ripar. Note blue, orange or yellowish throat and male's blue belly patches.*

Side-blotched Lizard, Uta stansburiana. *Iguana Family. 4–6⅜". Abund., L and U Son. zones, most habitats. Note dark blotch behind forelimb. Color and patterns variable. Mostly ground-dwelling.*

Eastern Fence Lizard, Sceloporus undulatus. *3½–7½". Iguana Family. Abund., U Son. and Tran. zones, Wood. and Forest. Prefers open, rocky areas. Note blue patch on each side of throat, yellow on back of legs and lateral striping. Sagebrush Lizard* (S. graciosus)—*Com., U Son. zone, Grass.—has entirely blue throat and white on back of legs. Desert Spiny Lizard* (S. magister)—*Abund., L and U Son. zones, most habitats—has black shoulder patches and coarse, pointed scales.*

Western Whiptail, Cnemidophorus tigris. *8–12". Whiptail Family. Abund., L and U Son. zones, most habitats. Prefers open areas. Color variable, stripes sometimes faded or replaced by mottling. Plateau Whiptail* (C. velox) *similar, but tail light blue and pale stripes separated by dark bands without spots. Tails of immatures are bright blue in both species.*

Many-lined Skink, Eumeces multivirgatus. *Skink Family. 5–7⅝". Com., Forest. Note short limbs and numerous narrow stripes. Immatures have bright blue tails. Western Skink* (E. skiltonianus) *has a broad brown stripe down the middle of the back.*

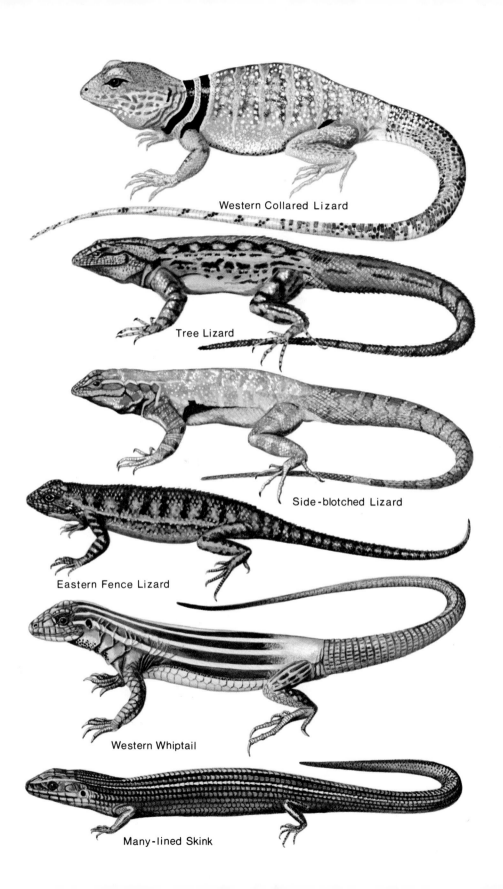

Western Collared Lizard

Tree Lizard

Side-blotched Lizard

Eastern Fence Lizard

Western Whiptail

Many-lined Skink

Plate 83. Snakes.

Striped Whipsnake, Masticophis taeniatus. *Racer Family. 40–72". Com., along streambeds. Hunts among rocks, trees and shrubs.*

Gopher Snake, Pituophis melanoleucus. *Racer Family. 48–100". Com., U Son. through Bor. zones, most habitats. When molested, mimics a rattlesnake, but is not poisonous. Told from rattlesnakes by narrow, tapering (not triangular) head and lack of rattles.*

Long-nosed Snake, Rhinocheilus lecontei. *Racer Family. 22–41". Com., U Son. zone, Ripar., Scrub, Wood. Most active dawn and dusk. Note pointed, protruding snout and partial banding. Sonoran Mountain Kingsnake* (Lampropeltis pyromelana) *has white bands encircling body. Note: the venomous and somewhat similar Arizona Coral Snake does not occur at the Grand Canyon.*

Common Kingsnake, Lampropeltis getulus. *Racer Family. 36–82". Com., L and U Son. zones, Ripar., Scrub, Wood., often among rocks and brush.*

Western Terrestrial Garter Snake, Thamnophis elegans. *Racer Family. 18–42". Com. CAN and SN Rims, Ripar., Wood. and Forest. Color variable; may appear greenish from a distance.*

Western Rattlesnake, Crotalus viridis. *Pit Viper Family. 16–64". Venomous and dangerous (see Chapter 10). Note triangular, rather than slender, head; heat-sensing pit between nostril and eye; and rattles. Snakes without these features are not rattlesnakes. Three subspecies at the Grand Canyon: (1) Grand Canyon Rattlesnake (illustrated)—CAN only; (2) Hopi Rattlesnake, pinkish, greenish or greyish, but splotches well defined—CAN and S Rim; (3) Great Basin Rattlesnake, light brown or grey, with dark, well-defined, narrow splotches—CAN and N Rim. All are Uncom., most habitats below Bor. zone. Speckled Rattlesnake* (C. mitchelii), *conspicuously speckled, with muted crossbands or blotches. Black-tailed Rattlesnake* (C. molossus) *has sharply contrasting black tail. Both species are Rare.*

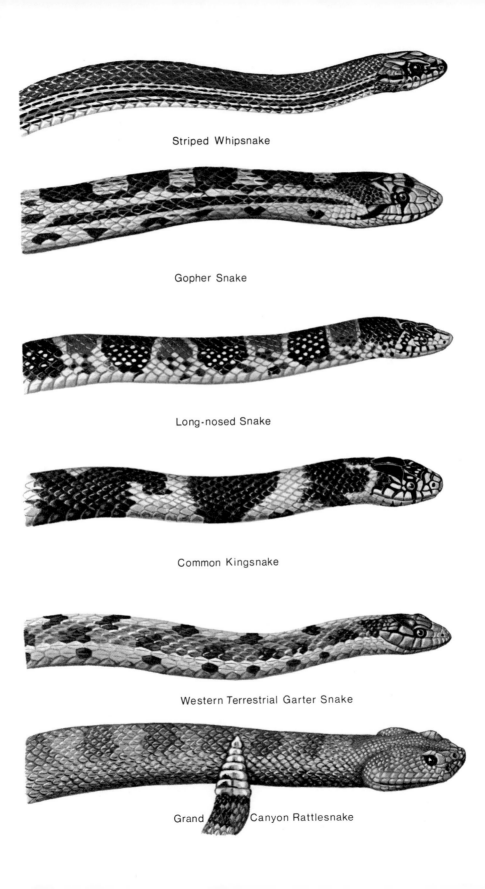

Striped Whipsnake

Gopher Snake

Long-nosed Snake

Common Kingsnake

Western Terrestrial Garter Snake

Grand Canyon Rattlesnake

Plate 84. Native Fish.

Bonytail Chub, Gila elegans. *Minnow Family. Length to 15″. Back and sides silvery-grey to metallic blue, belly silvery to white, head and lower flanks of breeding males red-orange. Note how body abruptly narrows toward tail. Once common, now endangered. Protected by law. Endemic to Colorado River system.*

Roundtail Chub, Gila robusta. *Minnow Family. Length usually to 13″. Silvery-grey with darker back. Note that mouth extends back only to front of eye (cf. Colorado Squawfish, below). Endemic to Colorado River system.*

Humpback Chub, Gila cypha. *Minnow Family. Usually under 13″ long. Silvery-grey with darker back. Note pronounced, nearly scaleless hump and protruding snout. Rare and endangered. Protected by law. Known to occur at confluence of Colorado and Little Colorado rivers. Endemic to Colorado River system.*

Colorado Squawfish, Ptychocheilus lucius. *Minnow Family. Length formerly to 6′, now 2′ or less. Olive-green back and silvery-white belly; fins of breeding males reddish. Note that mouth extends to back of eye (cf. Roundtail Chub, above). Once common, now endangered. Protected by law. Predatory fish that takes bait. Endemic to Colorado River system.*

Speckled Dace, Rhinichthys osculus. *Minnow Family. Length to 3½″. Color variable but usually dark. Breeding adults have reddish fins. Common and widespread in river systems throughout the western U.S. Native, but not endemic to the Colorado River system.*

Humpback or Razorback Sucker, Xyrauchen texanus. *Sucker Family. Length to about 3′. Back dusky to olive, belly yellow-orange (brilliantly so in breeding males). A large bottom-feeder. Once common, now endangered. Protected by law. Endemic to the Colorado River system.*

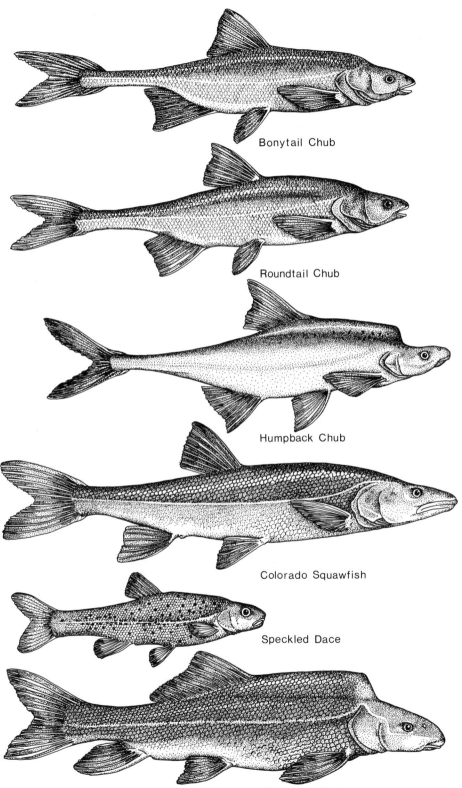

Bonytail Chub

Roundtail Chub

Humpback Chub

Colorado Squawfish

Speckled Dace

Humpback Sucker

Plate 85. Introduced Fish.

Coho or Silver Salmon, Oncorhynchus kisutch. *Trout Family. Length to 2' or more. Back metallic blue or green, sides silver, with small dark spots on back, dorsal fin and upper lobe of tail. Planted outside the canyon for anglers. Unlikely that a breeding population exists in the river. Native to Pacific Coast.*

Rainbow Trout, Salmo gairdneri. *Trout Family. Length to 2', usually under 12". Back metallic blue to brown, sides silvery with an iridescent pink or red stripe, belly silvery, white or yellowish. Native to western U.S.*

Fathead Minnow, Pimephales promelas. *Minnow Family. Length to about 3". Back brownish or olive, sides dull and dusky. Breeding males nearly black with 2 vertical stripes on each side. Bottom-feeder.*

Channel Catfish, Ictalurus punctatus. *Catfish Family. Length to 2' or more. Back and sides blue-grey, often with olive-gold tinge, belly white. Note protruding snout and long, black barbels or "feelers." Native to Missouri–Mississippi rivers.*

Green Sunfish, Chaenobryttus cyanellus. *Sunfish Family. Length to 10" or more, usually smaller. Back dark olive, sides lighter, with metallic-green flecks, underparts yellow-orange. Native to Mississippi–Missouri rivers. Closely related to Bluegill.*

Largemouth Bass, Micropterus salmoides. *Sunfish Family. Length to 2' or more, usually smaller. Back olive-grey, belly whitish, with dark stripe on each side. The chief warm water game fish in the western U.S.*

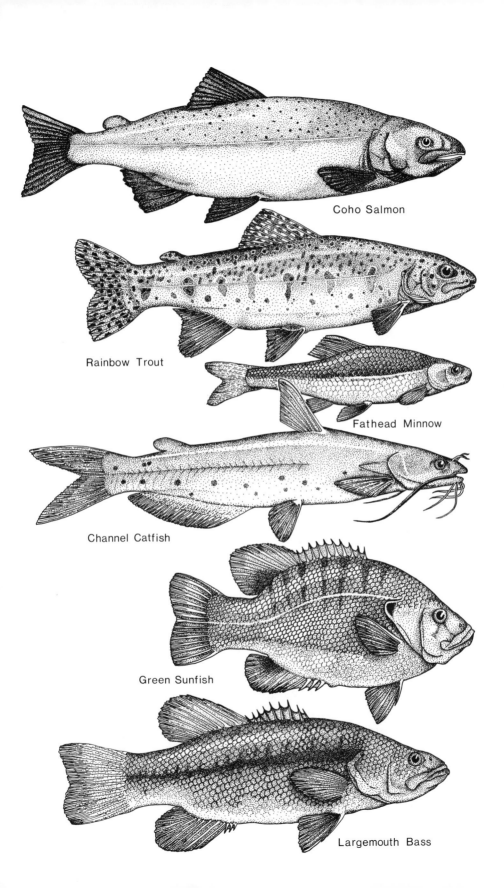

Coho Salmon

Rainbow Trout

Fathead Minnow

Channel Catfish

Green Sunfish

Largemouth Bass

Plate 86. Monarch, Brush-footed Butterflies and Others.

Monarch, Danaus plexippus. *Milkweed Butterfly Family. Abun. SN Rims, CAN, Gorge. Summer and fall. Similar to the Striated Queen (D. gilippus) but larger, lighter in color and more distinctly marked. A renowned migrant. Food: milkweeds.*

Grand Canyon Ringlet, Coenonympha ochracea furcae. *Satyr Family. Com. S Rim and CAN south of river. Late spring, early summer. Endemic to the Grand Canyon. Food: grasses.*

Arizona Sister, Adelpha bredowii. *Brush-footed Butterfly Family. Com., SN Rims, CAN, Gorge. Late spring through summer. Glides with wings held at slight angle below horizontal. Food: oaks.*

Weidemeyer's Admiral, Limenitis weidemeyerii. *Brush-footed Butterfly Family. Com., N Rim. Summer. Adults attracted to dung. Food: aspen, willows.*

The Satyr, Polygonia satyrus. *Brush-footed Butterfly Family. Com. SN Rims, streamsides. Spring and summer. Food: nettles.*

West Coast Lady, Vanessa annabella. *Brush-footed Butterfly Family. Com. N Rim. Summer. Similar to the American Painted Lady (V. virginiensis). Food: lupines, nettles, mallows.*

Mourning Cloak, Nymphalis antiopa. *Brush-footed Butterfly Family. Abun. SN Rims, CAN, Gorge, streamsides. Spring and summer. Overwinters as an adult and is often the first butterfly seen in the spring. Food: willows, cottonwood, hackberry.*

Shellbach's Fritillary, Speyeria electa shellbachi. *Brush-footed Butterfly Family. Com. N Rim, secluded draws. Adults attracted to thistle flowers. First discovered at Grand Canyon.*

Snout Butterfly, Libytheana bachmannii. *Snout Butterfly Family. Uncom., S Rim, CAN, Gorge, streamsides and side canyons. Spring through fall. Note extra-long palpi, which resemble a snout or beak. Food: netleaf hackberry.*

Monarch

Grand Canyon Ringlet

Arizona Sister

Weidemeyer's Admiral

The Satyr

Mourning Cloak

West Coast Lady

Snout Butterfly

Shellbach's Fritillary

Mormon Metalmark   Colorado Hairstreak   Nevada Copper

Alfalfa Butterfly

Ingham's Orange-tip   Western Tiger Swallowtail

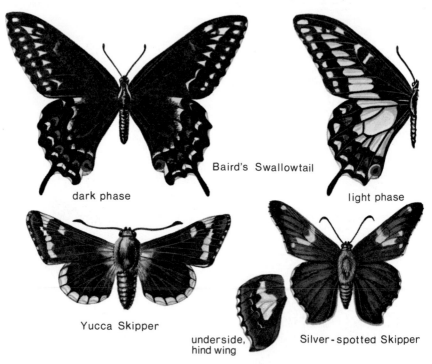

Baird's Swallowtail

dark phase   light phase

Yucca Skipper

underside,   Silver-spotted Skipper
hind wing

Plate 87. Coppers and Blues, Swallowtails, Skippers and Others.

Mormon Metalmark, Apodemia mormo. *Metalmark Family. SN Rims, CAN, Gorge. Widespread summer flier. Prefers bright sunlight. Food: wild buckwheats.*

Colorado Hairstreak, Hypaurotis crysalus. *Hairstreak, Copper and Blue Family. Uncom. SN Rims and CAN. Summer. One of the largest, showiest hairstreaks. Food: oaks.*

Nevada Copper, Lycaena arota. *Hairstreak, Copper and Blue Family. Com. U Son. through Bor. zones. Early to mid-summer. Food: gooseberries.*

Alfalfa Butterfly, Colias eurytheme. *White Family. Abun. SN Rims, CAN, Gorge. Early to mid-summer. Food: deer-vetch, clover, alfalfa and other members of the Legume or Pea Family.*

Ingham's Orange-tip, Anthocharis sara inghami. *White Family. Com. S Rim and CAN. Early fliers. Food: wild mustards.*

Western Tiger Swallowtail, Papilio rutulus. *Swallowtail Family. Com. SN Rims, CAN, Gorge, streamsides. Summer. Two-tailed Swallowtail (P. multicaudautus) is larger, with 2 tails. Also cf. light form of Baird's Swallowtail. Food: willows and aspen.*

Baird's Swallowtail, Papilio bairdii. *Swallowtail Family. Com. SN Rims, CAN and Gorge. Summer. Note light and dark forms. Female dark form difficult to distinguish from Grand Canyon Swallowtail (P. indra kaibabensis). Food: sagebrush.*

Yucca Skipper, Megathymus streckeri. *Giant Skipper Family. Uncom. S Rim, CAN, Gorge. Late spring, summer. Large, stout, swift and elusive mothlike butterfly. Food: yuccas.*

Silver-spotted Skipper, Epargyreus clarus. *Skipper Family. Uncom. SN Rims, CAN, Gorge. Summer. Largest, most conspicuous member of this well-represented family. Food: New Mexican locust.*

10. PRECAUTIONS FOR HIKERS

Few places in the lower 48 states place greater demands on a hiker's knowledge, skill and stamina than the Grand Canyon. The terrain is as steep and rugged as that of any western mountain range. In summer the heat inside the canyon is extreme. Water is scarce year-round. Winters bring subfreezing temperatures and pave many trails with hazardous coats of snow or ice.

The canyon is a harsh, demanding desert environment. One should take great care never to underestimate the difficulties of canyon travel or to overestimate one's ability or stamina. First-time Grand Canyon hikers should stay on the maintained trails. The precautions discussed below are not meant to discourage hikers, but to provide information necessary for safe, enjoyable trips.

EIGHT ESSENTIALS

The Backcountry Reservations Office recommends that all hikers carry the following eight essentials regardless of itinerary or season of travel:

1. Extra food and water
2. Pocket knife

3. First-aid kit
4. Signal mirror or reflector
5. Flashlight
6. Topographic maps, compass and the ability to use them
7. Matches
8. Reservations and permits

IN CASE OF EMERGENCY

Kaibab–Bright Angel trail corridor: Contact ranger stations at Indian Gardens, Phantom Ranch area or Cottonwood Campground (summer only). Emergency phones located along trails (see trail descriptions in Chapter 9). If unable to reach help, stay on the trail and wait for a passing hiker, a common animal on these trails.

Wilderness trails: Get as close to the trail as possible. Stay where you are. Don't wander aimlessly. Choose a place visible from the air. Signal your distress by using clothing and gear to form a cross on the ground. Keep calm and watch the skies. Use a signal mirror to alert passing aircraft. Only as a last resort, build a smoky fire from green brush.

When obtaining a backcountry permit, hikers must file their itinerary with the Backcountry Reservations Office. They are encouraged to report back to the office at the end of their trip. Single hikers are required to do so.

Many canyon trails are obscure in places. If you lose your way, backtrack immediately to the last place where the trail was clear. Do not attempt to hike cross-country unless you are an experienced canyon traveler who has notified backcountry rangers of your intended route. All hikers should carry a signal mirror, the appropriate topographic maps and a good orienteering compass.

WATER

Water is scarce in the Grand Canyon. In years of little rain even normally reliable sources may be dry. Before entering the canyon, always ask a backcountry ranger where reliable water sources are located along your route. *Do not rely on topographic maps or trail descriptions, including those in the preceding chapter, for this information.*

Water from all natural sources in the Grand Canyon should be purified before using. Halazone or commerical iodine tablets are effective for bacteria, but may not kill certain other harmful microorganisms possibly present in the water. Boiling water for five minutes will eliminate all potentially harmful organisms, but the weight of fuel consumed may make chemical treatment preferable.

Always carry water when hiking in the canyon. Allow at least two quarts per day per person for drinking purposes alone. During hot weather or on trails where water is scarce, a gallon of water per person per day is needed. Always carry more water than you need.

DEHYDRATION

Dehydration accounts for more fatalities in the Grand Canyon than any other single cause. Some victims have died with water in their canteens. It's not enough just to carry water, you must drink it. Small amounts at short intervals are better than large gulps at longer intervals.

Even mild dehydration is uncomfrotable, and as the following symptoms indicate, dehydration is a terrible way to die:

Initial symptoms: thirst, malaise, irritability, loss of appetite, flushed skin, fatigue, apathy, nausea, increased pulse.

Advanced symptoms: dizziness, headache, labored breathing, tingling, lack of saliva, bluish tongue, cottony mouth, indistinct speech, inability to walk.

Final symptoms: delirium, muscle spasms, swollen tongue, inability to swallow, dim vision, urination painful then abnormal or absent; skin progresses from shriveled to numb to cracked and bloody. Death soon follows.

Treatment for mild cases of dehydration consists of drinking as much water as possible. The patient should also rest in a cool place. In most cases full recovery will occur within 24 hours. Treatment is the same for more advanced cases, but medical help should be sought at once. This is urgent if the patient is unable to drink water because of a swollen tongue and the resulting inability to swallow.

HEAT STRESS

Heat stress poses a severe hazard to Inner Canyon hikers during the summer. It occurs hand-in-hand with dehydration and also involves a loss of essential salts. To avoid heat stress, hike only in cool weather or during the coolest times of the day—early morning and late afternoon or evening; carry plenty of water and drink it often; eat salty foods and supplement your diet with salt tablets; rest in shady places during hot weather; wear loose, lightweight clothing and a hat; and carry as little as possible.

There are three forms of heat stress:

Heat cramps result mainly from overexertion in hot weather. Symptoms: tightness and pain in leg muscles and abdomen, along with faintness and profuse sweating. Treatment: Have patient rest in a cool, shaded place. Administer salted drinking water (1 teaspoon salt per quart) and massage muscles. Heat cramps are a precursor of heat exhaustion.

Heat exhaustion results from the same causes as heat cramps, but is more serious. Symptoms: weak, rapid pulse; rapid, shallow breathing; weakness; pale and clammy skin; profuse sweating, dizziness and perhaps loss of consciousness. Treatment: same as above, but in addition, apply wet compresses or fan the patient (but do not chill). Seek medical attention at once if the patient fails to improve.

Heat stroke is a grave medical emergency. Without prompt, professional medical attention the victim will die. Heat stroke is caused by the failure of the body's sweating mechanism. Symptoms: hot, *dry* (not moist as in other forms of heat stress), flushed skin; abnormally high temperature; dilated pupils; fast pulse; abnormal breathing and possible convulsions. Treatment: same as above, but it is urgent to *seek medical attention at once*.

HYPOTHERMIA

Hypothermia is the critical loss of body heat from exposure to cold, wet, windy weather. It most often occurs at air temperatures from 30°F to 50°F, largely because people normally take adequate precautions at lower temperatures. At the Grand Canyon the danger of hypothermia is greatest from fall through spring. To prevent hypothermia, stay dry and out of the wind, wear a hat in cool weather, don warm clothes at the first signs of chill, and dress in layers to insure maximum insulation and to make it easy to adjust to changing weather. Choose wool clothing whenever possible. Wool is best because it provides insulation even when wet.

Symptoms: persistent or violent shivering, loss of memory, incoherence, slurred speech, frequent stumbling, fatigue. If someone shows these symptoms, begin treatment at once. Victims of hypothermia are often unaware that there is a problem and may deny the need for treatment. Don't take their word for it.

Treatment: get patient out of the weather. Remove wet clothes. Administer warm drinks, but not alcohol or stimulants. Build a fire if necessary. If symptoms do not subside, place the patient in a warm sleeping bag with another person. Both should be without clothes because skin-to-skin contact is the quickest way to restore body heat.

VENOMOUS ANIMALS

Venomous animals at the Grand Canyon include rattlesnakes, Gila monster, scorpions, centipedes and spiders. Hikers exercising due caution have little to fear from these creatures. Hardly anyone is troubled by them, and their presence should discourage no one from visiting the inner canyon. The following discussions are intended to provide basic information about how to avoid these animals, the nature and seriousness of their bite or sting, and first aid. Since there is some disagreement about proper first aid for some types of bites or stings, readers should consult their physicians for advice. The methods most commonly used are described here only for informational purposes and should not be taken as recommendations for treatment.

The potential hazard posed by a sting or bite depends in large measure on the amount of venom injected and the physical condition of the victim. The sick, the elderly, and alcoholics are more vulnerable to the effects of venom and in the event of a bite are likely to exhibit more severe symptoms. Children are also in greater danger because the amount of venom they receive is proportionally higher by body weight than for an adult.

Rattlesnakes

Three species of rattlesnake are found at the Grand Canyon (see Chapter 20). None are common, and the chances of meeting a rattlesnake in the canyon are slight. Even so, one should be duly cautious. In rattlesnake country hikers should do the following: (1) Wear protective clothing such as boots and long pants; 90 percent of all snakebites occur on the lower legs and arms; (2) Place hands and feet only on places in plain view; snakes often rest beneath shrubs, on shady rock ledges, in the shade of rocks or other objects and among leaves and other debris; (3) Use a flashlight when wandering about at night, even in camp. Remember, rattlesnakes do not always rattle before striking. If you do hear a rattle, freeze, locate the snake, then move away *slowly* in the opposite direction. Do not kill the snake! Given the opportunity, it will quickly retreat. Remember, too, that baby rattlesnakes are also venomous, although they cannot inject as much venom as adult snakes.

Rattlesnakes are normally retiring, striking humans only in self-defense. Their rattle is to frighten predators, their venom to immobilize and partially digest small rodents and other prey. Of the 6000 to 7000 people bitten by rattlesnakes each year in the United States, fewer than 10 victims die as a result. The great majority will recover even without first aid or other medical attention. Bites incurred on the head, neck, torso or groin are potentially more serious, even fatal, but they account for only about two percent of the total. All rattlesnake bites should be treated as medical emergencies.

There is currently a good deal of controversy concerning the proper treatment of rattlesnake bites. The traditional first-aid procedure is to apply a loose, constricting band (not a tourniquet) between the wound and the heart, cut a small incision over each fang mark and suck out the venom using either the mouth or, preferably, a special suction device of the type found in snakebite kits. Some hikers may wish to carry these kits with them into the canyon. If so, they should first become thoroughly familiar with their proper use. Instructions are included with each kit. A number of authorities, however, argue that this treatment usually causes more harm than good, usually in the form of tissue damage and infection caused by inept practitioners. Some physicians now recommend not using the procedure under any conditions. Others disagree, especially when the victim is far removed from medical help. In any case, medical attention should be obtained as soon as possible. In the meantime the victim should be kept quiet, and the afflicted part should be placed lower than the heart and kept as still as possible. The victim should also be reassured that the chances of dying from the bite are remote.

Rear-fanged Snakes

There are three species of mildly venomous, rear-fanged snakes at the Grand Canyon: the Sonora lyre snake, spotted night snake and black-headed snake. All have small mouths equipped with grooved rear fangs. Venom flows down the grooves and is worked into prey by chewing. These snakes are too small and release too little venom to pose a hazard to humans. They should be regarded as essentially harmless. All three species are uncommon in the area, and their bite has been compared in seriousness to a bee sting.

Gila Monster

The Gila monster is one of only two poisonous lizards in the world. Fortunately, it is rare here—with only three recorded observations, all from the western part of the canyon. The Gila monster is normally slow and unaggressive, but if disturbed will hiss savagely and quickly lunge at the intruder. Once it grabs hold, it hangs on tenaciously, working the venom into the victim by a continued chewing action. The venom is neurotoxic, eventually producing paralysis of the heart and respiratory muscles. Death is possible, but unlikely for a healthy adult. To minimize the amount of venom received, it is essential to pry the lizard's jaws loose as soon as possible.

Spiders and Scorpions

Spiders and scorpions, along with mites, ticks, daddy longlegs and related groups, all belong to the animal class Arachnida. Most adult arachnids have four pairs of legs, plus two pairs of mouth parts. The chelicerae, are jawlike or fanglike and are the organs used by spiders to inject their venom. The second pair of mouth parts, called pedipalpi, are feelerlike in spiders, but are enlarged in scorpions to form a pair of crablike pincers. These are used to grasp prey, while the coup de grâce is delivered by the hypodermic needlelike stinger at the end of the abdomen. All scorpions and spiders are poisonous, but only a relatively small number are potentially dangerous to humans. These harmful arachnids include the black widow and slender scorpion, both of which are present in the Grand Canyon.

Black Widow.   The name "black widow" is applied to several species of the genus *Latrodectus*. It best describes the large, glossy-black female, which often kills and eats the small, grey male upon completion of mating. Only the female poses a threat to humans. It is easily recognized by its large, globular abdomen, the underside of which bears a small red hourglass—a marking that is unique to the black widow.

Black widows prefer dark, cool, undisturbed places, including attics, basements, garages, woodpiles, rock crevices, abandoned rodent holes and the undersides of rocks, logs or other debris. The spiders are quite reticent, biting humans only when disturbed. To avoid being bitten, simply watch where you place your hands.

The poison of the black widow attacks the nervous system. Following a bite the victim experiences severe local pain, which intensifies and spreads throughout much of the body, often concentrating in the abdomen and legs. Two tiny, red fang marks will be apparent on the skin. Subsequent symptoms include nausea, vomiting, difficulty breathing, muscle spasms, excessive drooling and possible coma. Though potentially lethal, death from a black widow bite is extremely rare among adults. Small children, the sick and elderly are more prone to severe reactions to the bites. Though most victims will recover without any medical treatment, they should be taken to a physician as soon as possible. Aside from keeping the victim quiet and perhaps applying ice to the bite, there is no other useful first-aid measure.

Tarantula (genus Aphonopelma).   The imposing appearance of this large, hairy, black or brown spider has led many people to wrongly consider it to be deadly. In fact, the bite of a tarantula, though painful, is no more dangerous than that of a wasp or bee. Subsequent discomfort is more likely caused by bacterial infection than the spider's mild poison. Under no circumstances should a tarantula be molested or killed.

Though tarantulas pounce on their prey, which mostly consists of insects, they are otherwise unaggressive. Each spider lives in its own web-lined burrow, venturing forth on short hunting expeditions. It is most active on summer nights or overcast summer days. Female tarantulas may live for twenty years while males live only several years.

Scorpions.   Of the more than six species of scorpion found in the Grand Canyon, only the slender scorpion, *Centruroides sculptuatus*, is potentially lethal to humans. Between 1929 and 1948, 65 deaths in Arizona resulted from the sting of this species. During this same period, only 15 people in the state died from rattlesnake bites.

Nonlethal species, such as the giant hairy scorpion, *Hadrurus spadix*, inject a local poison that causes pain and discoloration at the site of the sting, but no other discomfort. The venom of the slender scorpion, however, is a systemic neurotoxin that can produce convulsions leading to death. The sting of the slender scorpion is painful, but this soon subsides and no swelling or discoloration occurs at the site of the sting. Instead, the area quickly becomes numb, tingly and highly sensitive to touch. This sensation soon spreads up the stung arm or leg and in extreme cases may be accompanied by tightness of the throat, difficulty in breathing and talking, excessive drooling, gastric swelling, hypertension, restlessness, convulsions and possible blindness.

First aid consists of keeping the victim quiet, applying ice to the wound and seeking medical attention as soon as possible. If possible, the scorpion should be captured for later identification. The sting of the slender scorpion can become a medical emergency.

Although the slender scorpion is difficult to distinguish from other species present in the Grand Canyon, the following characteristics may be helpful:

1. Uniform coloration is yellowish, usually straw-colored.
2. The species is short and slender, ½ to 3 inches long and no more than ⅜-inch wide in the body.
3. The tail and pincers are also noticeably slender. No more than ⅛-inch diameter, the tail has oblong rather than square-shaped segments.
4. A small barb or tooth is located at the base of the stinger. This feature may be apparent only in good light.

Scorpions habitually cling to the underside of rocks, bark, boards and the like. Most people are stung when they pick up an object without first checking the underside and thus accidentally brush or touch the scorpion. To avoid being stung by the slender scorpion—or for that matter, by nonlethal species—hikers in the inner canyon should watch where they place their hands or bare feet. It's also a good idea to shake out shoes, socks and clothing before dressing in the morning. Bedding should receive the same treatment at night and should not be left on the ground when not in use.

Miscellaneous Pests

Bees, wasps, velvet ants (actually a type of wingless wasp), true ants and kissing (or assassin) bugs can all inflict more or less painful stings or bites. Unless the victim is allergic to the venom, the result is merely a degree of local pain and swelling. The bite of the blood-sucking kissing bug (genus *Triatoma*) produces a hard, painful welt, and in some people may cause severe allergic reactions. In some parts of the Southwest, kissing bugs are known to transfer a disease-causing parasite, but it is highly unlikely that the Grand Canyon population is thus infected. Inner Canyon hikers may find the innocent-looking harvester ants (genus *Pogonomyvirex*) to be more of a threat than expected. These medium-sized Inner Gorge occupants are abundant and sting with a vengeance all out of proportion to their size. Fortunately for campers, they are strictly diurnal and return to their hives at night.

CACTUS SPINES

Cactus spines are not poisonous, but can cause severe local pain. Some are equipped with barbs or hooks and must be extracted with pliers, a distressing process; but unless a person accidentally falls into a cactus patch and receives numerous, widespread wounds, cactus spines pose no immediate danger. Should a spine break off below the skin, however, one should see a physician to have it removed surgically. Otherwise, severe pain and serious infection can result.

Prickly-pears also have tiny hairs or spines called *glochids* (see Chapter 16), which are extremely irritating when embedded in the skin. Because of their small size, they are often difficult or impossible to remove, even with the aid of tweezers. Eventually, they are dissolved by the body, but until then the afflicted area is painful when touched.

To avoid problems with cactus do not touch them and take care not to inadvertently brush up against them. If walking through brushy areas where cacti are common, long pants are recommended.

SELECTED REFERENCES

Adolf, E. F. and Associates. *Physiology of Man in the Desert*. New York: Hafner, 1969.

Arnold, Robert E. *What to Do about Bites and Stings of Venomous Animals*. New York: Macmillan, 1973; Collier (paperback), 1973.

Dodge, Natt N. *Poisonous Dwellers of the Desert*. Globe, AZ: Southwest Parks and Monuments Association, 1976.

Klauber, Laurence M. *Rattlesnakes: Their Habits, Life Histories, and Influence on Mankind*, 2 vols. Berkeley: University of California Press, 1973.

Larson, Peggy. A *Sierra Club Naturalist's Guide, The Deserts of the Southwest*. San Francisco: Sierra Club Books, 1977.

Nesbitt, Paul H., et al. *The Survival Book*. New York: Funk and Wagnalls, 1969.

Stahnke, Herbert L. *Scorpions*. Tempe: Arizona State University Bookstore, 1949.

PART II

Time, Rocks and the River

11. ROCKS AND FOSSILS

The rock formations exposed in the walls of the Grand Canyon comprise the most remarkable geological record found on earth. Nowhere else does such an ancient, extensive, relatively complete and largely undisturbed sequence of rocks outcrop over such a vast area. The oldest rocks in the canyon are the schist and gneiss that form the dark cliffs of the Inner Gorge. Extending to unknown depths, these metamorphic rocks are about two billion years old, among the more ancient exposed rocks on the planet. Above them lie sequences of younger, sedimentary rocks, ranging in age from 1.2 billion to 225 million years old. Of these the most prominent and widely outcropping are the limestones, sandstones and shales that make up the striking horizontal bands visible on the upper canyon walls. These formations accumulated layer upon layer during successive advances and retreats of the sea that occurred between 570 million and 225 million years ago. Since one layer had to be in place before the next could form on top of it, the rocks decrease in age from river to rims.

THE FOSSIL RECORD

Accumulating sediments may include the remains of plants and animals. These remains are incorporated in the resulting rocks as fossils. Most fossils consist of skeletal remains, though softer tissues, such as leaves, may leave their imprint before decaying. A sample of fossils found in the rocks of the Grand Canyon are shown on Plates 6 and 7.

Fossil-bearing strata are of particular interest to geologists. First, they provide a sample of the types of plants and animals that existed when a particular body of rock was formed. They also provide clues to the origin of the host rocks. For example, if a formation contains the remains of marine organisms, it must have formed on the sea floor. Fossils therefore indicate to some degree the types of environments that existed in a particular region in times past. And since sedimentary strata originate as a succession of deposits laid down over a certain span of time, the fossil record helps geologists to develop a picture of how the landscape of a particular region evolved during that interval.

Moreover, since each type of organism exists on the earth only for a finite period of time, its fossil remains will be found—if at all—only in rocks of that period. A fossil-bearing rock may contain a variety of organisms whose geologic ranges overlap, but those yet to appear or already extinct will not be present. By comparing the associations of plants and animals present in various rock strata, geologists are able to correlate the age of one formation with that of another.

GEOLOGIC TIME

The geologic time scale shown in Table 3 is based both on recognized rock and fossil sequences throughout the world and on absolute dates obtained by measuring the decay products of radioactive elements contained in various minerals and then calculating the age of the minerals from known rates of decay. This technique, known as radiometric dating, is applicable to granites and volcanic rocks, which form from magma through the cooling and solidification of minerals. Radiometric dating cannot be used on sedimentary rocks, which are most often made up of the weathered fragments of older rocks. Of course, sedimentary rocks that contain interbedded layers of lava or volcanic ash can be dated by this method. And if such sedimentary strata also contain fossils, otherwise undatable strata elsewhere can be dated through correlation. Most of the sedimentary rocks of the Grand Canyon have been assigned approximate dates by this method.

The geological time scale divides the history of the earth into four eras. The Precambrian Era covers the awesome gulf of time from the consolidation of the earth's crust, about 4.5 billion years ago, to the appearance of the first well-developed suites of fossils, about 570 million years ago. In the Grand Canyon the Precambrian is represented by the

Table 3. Geologic Time Scale for the Grand Canyon

Rock Formations	Years Before Present	Epoch	Period	Era
Volcanic rocks,	10,000–present	Recent	Quaternary	Cenozoic
	2.5 million–10,000	Pleistocene		
	9–2.5 million	Pliocene	Tertiary	
	25–9 million	Miocene		
	40–25 million	Oligocene		
	60–40 million	Eocene		
	70–60 million	Paleocene		
No formations	135–70 million		Cretaceous	Mesozoic
No formations	180–135 million		Jurassic	
Rocks of Cedar Mtn. and Red Butte	225–180 million		Triassic	

Rock Formations	Age of Formation in years	Period	Era
Kaibab Formation	250 million	Permian	Paleozoic
Toroweap Formation	255 million		
Coconino Sandstone	260 million		
Hermit Shale	265 million		
Supai Group	285 million	Pennsylvanian	
Redwall Limestone	335 million	Mississippian	
Temple Butte Limestone	350 million	Devonian	
No formations	500–400 million	Silurian & Ordovician	
Muav Limestone	515 million	Cambrian	
Bright Angel Shale	530 million		
Tapeats Sandstone	545 million		
Grand Canyon Supergroup	1200 million		Precambrian
Vishnu Schist	2000 million		

metamorphic rocks of the Inner Gorge and by the tilted strata comprising the Grand Canyon Supergroup, which outcrops intermittently in the eastern section of the canyon.

The Paleozoic ("ancient life") Era extends from 570 million to 225 million years before the present. It was during this era, when life began to proliferate in the sea and later move onto the land, that the prominent horizontal strata of the upper canyon walls were formed. The Paleozoic is divided into seven periods, most of which are represented by one or more rock formations in the Grand Canyon. Characteristic fossils of this era include various marine organisms and, in later periods, insects, amphibians, reptiles, ferns and seed-bearing plants.

The Mesozoic ("middle life") Era extends from 225 million to 65 million years ago. During this time, additional strata were deposited in the Grand Canyon region, but later were almost completely removed by erosion. Mesozoic rocks outcrop in the Vermilion Cliffs and Echo Cliffs to the north and east of the Grand Canyon and are the major strata exposed over the greater part of the Colorado Plateau. Near the Grand Canyon, however, these rocks outcrop only on Cedar Mountain, east of Desert View, and Red Butte, south of Grand Canyon Village. Geologists estimate that 4000 to 8000 feet of sandstone and shale have been stripped away to expose the Paleozoic rocks beneath. When these now-departed Mesozoic rocks were deposited, the Grand Canyon region was covered by tropical forest and coastal swamps, and dinosaurs ruled the earth.

The Cenozoic ("recent life") Era began 65 million years ago and continues today. It is represented in the Grand Canyon mainly by lava flows and cinder cones found near Toroweap Valley and from there west to Lake Mead. There are no Cenozoic volcanic rocks in the eastern Grand Canyon. Deposits of travertine are the only sedimentary rocks of this era to occur in the region. It was during the Cenozoic, however, that the Mesozoic rocks were stripped away, and the Paleozoic rocks were uplifted to their present position and cut through by the Colorado River to form the Grand Canyon.

The canyon itself may be anywhere from 2.6 million to ten million years old. No one knows exactly. Whatever its age, it is the merest infant compared even to the youngest rocks exposed in its walls. If the two billion years that have elapsed since the creation of the schists of the Inner Gorge were telescoped into a single day, each minute would represent about 1.4 million years. If the schist formed at 12:01 A.M. of that day, the Paleozoic Era began about 6:00 P.M. and ended three hours later. Shortly after 11:00 P.M. the Mesozoic rocks were eroded away and the Paleozoic strata were uplifted. The Colorado River began to carve the Grand Canyon sometime between 11:45 and 11:58 P.M. The entire span of human existence has occurred in the last minute before midnight.

RECOGNIZING THE ROCKS

Table 3 (page 241) lists the Grand Canyon rock formations that correspond to each period and era. Geologists define a rock formation as any body of rock sufficiently distinct from others around it that its geographic location can be shown on a map. A formation is named, if possible, for its principal rock type—limestone, granite, schist, basalt, whatever—and for the place where it was first formally recognized and described. Thus, *Redwall Limestone* refers to the nearly pure limestone formation exposed in the Grand Canyon's Redwall Cliff. A formation containing prominent exposures of two or more types of rock is simply given a geographic name. The Grand Canyon's Kaibab Formation, for example, consists mostly of limestone, but also contains beds of sandstone and lesser units of shale.

Several related formations are sometimes lumped together in groups. The Grand Canyon's Unkar Group, for example, includes formations of shales, sandstone, limestone and volcanic rocks, all of late Precambrian age. The Unkar Group, Chuar Group and Nankoweap Formation together constitute the Grand Canyon Supergroup (formerly the Grand Canyon Series), which designates all formations of late Precambrian age found in the canyon.

With a little practice, just about anyone can learn to recognize the principal rock formations of the Grand Canyon. They exhibit a number of features that can be discerned readily by an untrained observer who takes the time to examine the rocks closely. Some formations are so distinctive that they can be recognized at a glance, even from the canyon rims. The most important features to look out for are as follows:

1. Stratigraphic position. Where does the formation occur in the sequence of rocks? What formations lie above and below it? See plate 8, plus the descriptions of individual formations below.
2. Geographical location. Since formations of the Grand Canyon Supergroup, as well as certain others, are found only in certain parts of the canyon, it is necessary to know where each formation occurs. General locations are mentioned in the formation descriptions to follow. The best source of information for the eastern Grand Canyon is the *Geologic Map of the Grand Canyon National Park, Arizona,* copublished by the Grand Canyon Natural History Association and the Museum of Northern Arizona.
3. Rock type. Is the rock limestone, schist, basalt, sandstone or what? The major rock types in the Grand Canyon are described below. The

types of rock in each formation are mentioned in the formation descriptions.

4. Texture and structure. Is the rock fine-grained, coarse-grained or somewhere in between? Is it foliated or bedded? Are the beds sequential or overlapping? See the discussion of rock types and the formation descriptions.

5. Erosional features. Does the formation erode to form a cliff, slope, ledge or some combination thereof? See the formation descriptions.

6. Thickness. The formations vary greatly in thickness both among themselves and from one place to another. The thickness of each formation is given in the formation descriptions and shown in relative terms on Plate 8.

7. Color. The color of the rock can often be an important aid to identification. See the formation descriptions for this information. See also Plate 8.

8. Fossil remains. Each formation is characterized either by the presence of particular fossils or the complete absence of fossils. For illustrations of some of the more common fossils see Plates 6 and 7. In addition, the formation descriptions include partial lists of fossils.

Metamorphic Rocks

Metamorphic rocks, such as the schist and gneiss of the Inner Gorge, form through the alteration, or *metamorphosis*, of other rocks. The process is associated with mountain building, when the earth's crust is brutally buckled and folded. During such episodes, deeply buried rocks are subjected to enormous compression and extraordinarily high temperatures. In the process the minerals forming the rocks undergo dramatic changes in chemical composition and structure, producing entirely new minerals, even though the rocks themselves remain solid. In response to compression the new minerals usually assume the form of thin flakes aligned in bands perpendicular to the direction of force. Metamorphic rocks are commonly said to be *foliated* because they break apart in thin leaves along these planes.

The various types of metamorphic rock—schist, gneiss, slate, marble, quartzite and others—depend on the nature of the original rocks and the degree of metamorphosis to which they were subjected. Schist, the most common type in the Grand Canyon, is distinguished by its narrow, wavy bands of mica flakes. Dark and fine-grained, it is derived from such materials as shale, fine sandstone and volcanic rocks. Gneiss, the second most common type, forms great wandering intrusions within the schist. Usually derived from granite and related rocks, gneiss is distinguished by

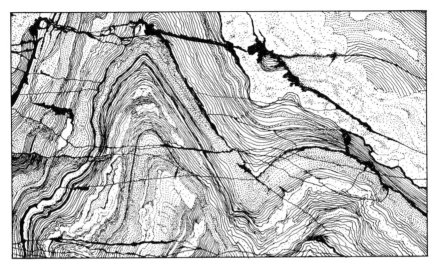

Figure 9.
   Foliated Vishnu Schist with light-colored, discontinuous bands of felsic gneiss of probable granitic origin. Such mixtures of schist and gneiss—known as migmatites—are conspicuous at the mouths of Pipe and Bright Angel creeks.

its lighter color, coarser texture and broad, highly contorted bands of quartz and feldspars, which alternate with thinner, darker bands of mica.

Sedimentary Rocks

The great majority of rocks exposed in the Grand Canyon are limestone, sandstone or shale. Such rocks originate as accumulations of sediments, which include weathered rock particles, organic remains and chemical precipitates. Sediments are most commonly transported and deposited by streams, but they may also be worked by winds. Limestones, as a rule, originate on the sea floor from debris drifting downward from above. Whatever the mode of deposition, sedimentary deposits accumulate in essentially horizontal beds. Sediments become compacted as additional materials pile on top of them. At the same time, water seeping through the particles deposits mineral cements that bind the particles together. When sediments become so compacted and cemented that they will break rather than crumble, they are sedimentary rocks.

Many sandstones and shales in the Grand Canyon exhibit cross-beds of the sort produced when shifting stream or tidal currents deposit sediments in overlapping layers. The enormous wedge-shape cross-beds in the Coconino Sandstone, however, are the preserved remains of ancient sand dunes. Ripple marks produced by winds or currents are also evident on the surface of many strata. Some of the sediments must have lain above water for a time because the rock surfaces are now pocked with shallow raindrop impressions or fractured into networks of mud cracks. For such features as ripple marks, raindrop impressions and mud cracks to have been preserved, the sediments must have been little disturbed and later gently covered by other materials.

Limestone mainly consists of calcium carbonate, a mineral abundant in seawater and present in the shells of marine animals. Most limestones originate in deep ocean waters, but a common type known as dolomite forms in shallow tidal flats through the chemical alteration of normal limestone. In this process, magnesium replaces some of the calcium in calcium carbonate to produce calcium–magnesium carbonate, the mineral dolomite. Dolomitic limestones are rather common in the Grand Canyon.

Though the vast majority of limestones are of marine origin, freshwater forms are not uncommon. Since calcium carbonate and dolomite are soluble in fresh water, limestone formations are typically riddled with caverns hollowed out by underground streams. The many springs in the Grand Canyon occur where such streams finally emerge at the base of limestone formations. Their waters are typically saturated with carbonate minerals, which form deposits of travertine, the type of limestone that composes stalactites and stalagmites. Travertine deposits are widely scattered through the Canyon, but are most spectacular along Havasu Creek. Precipitation of carbonate minerals from the water, which originates in the Kaibab Limestone of the Coconino Plateau, has produced terraced pools dammed by semicircular dikes of travertine. The cliffs adjacent to the waterfalls along the stream are hung with bizarre travertine curtains where windblown spray has evaporated from the rock surface.

Limestones are usually fine-textured and light-colored, whites and greys predominating. The limestone of the Redwall Cliff is actually grey, but has been stained by iron oxides washed down from the overlying Supai Group. Limestones are commonly rich in marine fossils.

Sandstone, as one might guess, is derived from sand, the smallest type of rock particle visible to the naked eye. Sands may consist of almost any mineral, but quartz and feldspars are most common. Sandstones are fine- to coarse-grained and come in a wide range of colors, depending on their constituent minerals. They usually originate as stream deposits in shallow coastal waters or floodplains. They also accumulate in desert basins fed by landlocked streams. The Coconino Sandstone of the Grand Canyon consists of petrified sand dunes that were piled up by the wind.

Shale originates as deposits of clay, silt or mud, the latter being a blend

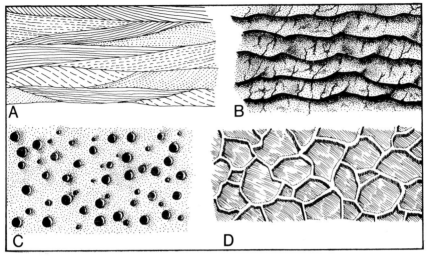

Figure 10.
  Features preserved on the surfaces of sedimentary beds provide clues to the environment in which the rocks were formed. Cross-beds (A) are produced as water currents or wind deposit overlapping layers of sediment. Ripple marks (B) are typically produced by gentle, shallow-water currents of the type found in estuaries, lagoons and tidal flats. Ripple marks in the Coconino Sandstone, however, were produced by wind blowing over the surface of ancient dunes. Raindrop impressions (C) indicate deposition in a terrestrial environment, as do mud-crack casts (D), which also suggest desertlike conditions.

of silt and clay. Geologists distinguish between mudstone, siltstone and other types, but here all are simply called shale. Shale particles are so minute as to be invisible even under a hand lens. Because its constituent particles are microscopic, shale is extremely fine-grained. When weathered, it breaks into small, thin chips or flakes. Most shales originate as stream deposits in deeper coastal waters, floodplains and river deltas, and large, deep lakes. Like sandstone, shale comes in various colors, but in the Grand Canyon it is mostly bright red from abundant iron oxides present in the rocks. Because of its soft texture, shale erodes to form slopes rather than cliffs or ledges.

  Conglomerate and *breccia* consist of gravels (rock fragments larger than sand) embedded in a matrix of finer particles, either sands or muds, sometimes limestone. Conglomerate gravels are rounded, indicating stream action. Breccia gravels, however, retain their angularity. Some breccias are of volcanic origin, while others form from rocks crushed along geological faults or where slide debris is buried by finer sediments. Conglomerates and breccias are fairly common in the Grand Canyon and in places form extensive outcrops.

Igneous Rocks

Igneous rocks originate from the cooling and solidification of molten rock, or magma, which forms deep within the earth. If the magma erupts on the surface of the earth as lava or *pyroclastic* ("fire broken") materials, such as volcanic ash, it forms volcanic rocks such as basalt, andesite and rhyolite. If the magma remains deep within the earth where it cools more slowly, it solidifies to form granite and similar coarse-grained igneous rocks, which may later be exposed by erosion of overlying rocks.

John Wesley Powell, on his first expedition through the Grand Canyon, named the river corridor Granite Gorge for its extensive outcrops of crystalline rocks. The name has stuck, but remains a misnomer, for these rocks are mostly schist and gneiss. The gneiss, however, originated as granite intruded into the surrounding schist. Later, it too was metamorphosed to produce the light-colored foliated rocks exposed in the cliffs. Here and there among the metamorphic rocks are dikes and sills of unaltered granitic rocks called aplite if fine-grained, and pegmatite if coarse-grained.

Volcanic rocks are scarce in the eastern Grand Canyon but common from near Toroweap Valley west to Lake Mead. Most are basalts, a dark, extremely fine-grained volcanic rock that originates as highly fluid lava. Lava flows have occurred on the Uinkaret and Shivwits plateaus and have filled Toroweap Valley, Prospect Canyon and Whitmore Wash. Cinder cones composed of pyroclastic materials are scattered over both plateaus; Vulcan's Throne, at the foot of the Toroweap Valley, is one of these.

GRAND CANYON ROCK FORMATIONS

The principal features of the rock formations exposed in the Grand Canyon are given below. The formations are listed in the order one might encounter them if hiking from the canyon rims to the river. Nowhere, however, will one encounter every formation. The descriptions apply to the formations as they appear in the eastern Grand Canyon, from Nankoweap south to below Desert View and west to Havasu and Kanab canyons. Most of the formations continue westward, but change somewhat in their composition and appearance.

Paleozoic Strata

KAIBAB FORMATION (Kaibab Limestone). Mostly fine-grained, thick-bedded, sandy limestone, with a bed of sandstone beneath and minor units of sandstone and shale above. Forms the surface of the Kaibab and Coconino plateaus. Color: cream to greyish-white. Thickness: 300'. Fossils: brachiopods, corals, mollusks, sea lilies, worms and fish teeth. Erodes to form a cliff.

TOROWEAP FORMATION. Similar in composition and structure to the Kaibab Formation. Color: pale yellow and grey. Thickness: 250'. Fossils: marine fossils like those of the Kaibab Formation. Erodes to form a sequence of ledgy cliffs and slopes.

COCONINO SANDSTONE. Fine-grained quartz sandstone with large, prominent, wedge-shape cross-beds. Color: white or cream. Thickness: 300–350'. Fossils: tracks of scorpions, insects and lizards. Erodes to form a massive cliff.

HERMIT SHALE. Extremely fine-grained shale, with mud cracks and raindrop impressions. Color: deep red. Thickness: 300'. Fossils: conifers, ferns and other plants; tracks of amphibians and reptiles. Erodes to form a slope. In the western Grand Canyon, the soft Hermit Shale has been stripped off the underlying Supai Formation to form the Esplanade.

SUPAI GROUP. Mostly shale, interbedded with minor limestone units and capped by three sandstone beds. Limestone becomes increasingly prominent westward. Color: deep red with tan sandstone beds. Thickness: 600'. Fossils: terrestrial plants and tracks of amphibians and reptiles; marine fossils in western limestones. Cross-beds, raindrop impressions and mud cracks. Erodes to form a slope topped by three small cliffs (sandstone beds).

REDWALL LIMESTONE. Nearly pure marine limestones and dolomites. Upper surface shows depressions caused by erosion prior to the deposition of the Supai Group. Color: light grey, stained bright red by iron oxides washed down from above. Thickness: 500'. Fossils: abundant marine fossils, including sea lilies, corals, brachiopods, trilobites, clams, snails, fish and algae. Erodes to form the massive red cliff just above the Tonto Plateau. Riddled with caves and often featuring deep alcoves.

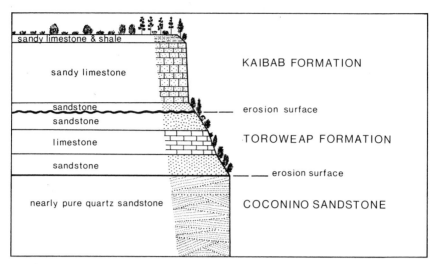

Figure 11.

The cream-colored Kaibab Formation forms the surface of the Kaibab and Coconino plateaus. The similar, but less resistant Toroweap Formation forms the wooded slope just beneath the Kaibab cliff. The massive white cliff of the Coconino Sandstone drops abruptly from the Toroweap slope and rests on the deep red Hermit Shale. Together, the Kaibab Formation, Toroweap Formation and Coconino Sandstone make up the conspicuous, creamy white bands on the uppermost walls of the Grand Canyon.

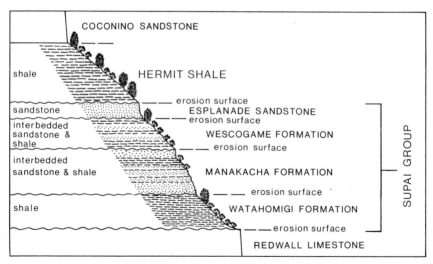

Figure 12.

The thick, deep-red slope lying between the Coconino and Redwall cliffs is formed by the Hermit Shale and Supai Group. In the western Grand Canyon, the easily eroded Hermit Shale has been stripped away from the Supai Group to form the Esplanade. The Supai Group, until recently considered a single formation, consists of four separate formations that together form a series of small cliffs and ledgy slopes.

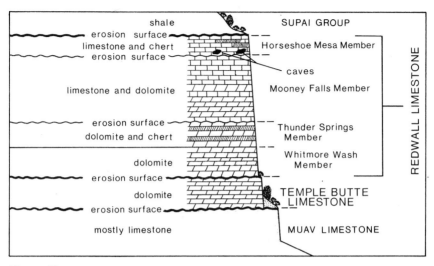

Figure 13.

Beneath the Supai Group lies the resistant Redwall Limestone, which represents nearly 50 million years of more or less continual deposition in a marine environment. It consists of remarkably even beds of various types of limestone and dolomite and contains beds and lenses of chert, a hard, flinty, microscopically grained variety of quartz derived from seawater. Redwall Limestone forms the massive red cliff located about midpoint on the canyon walls between the rims and the river. Although the rocks are mostly grey, the cliff has been stained red by iron oxides washed down from the overlying Supai shales. In the eastern Grand Canyon Temple Butte Limestone exists as intermittent deposits filling channels eroded in the underlying Muav Limestone. In the western canyon, however, Temple Butte Limestone forms continuous, massive cliffs.

TEMPLE BUTTE LIMESTONE. In eastern Grand Canyon, gnarly, sugary-textured freshwater limestone of intermittent occurrence. Color: purplish. Thickness: less than 100'. Fossils: armored plates of a primitive freshwater fish. Erodes to form a cliff. Deposited in stream channels cut into the underlying Muav Limestone. In the western Grand Canyon, the formation consists of continuous beds of grey or creamy dolomite forming massive cliffs hundreds of feet high.

MUAV LIMESTONE. Fine- to medium-grained marine limestone, with cavities, passages and some springs. Interbedded with minor units of sandstone, shale and conglomerate. Color: mottled grey. Thickness: 400'. Fossils: sparse, but include numerous species of trilobites and some brachiopods. Erodes to form a cliff with sandstone ledges and shale recesses.

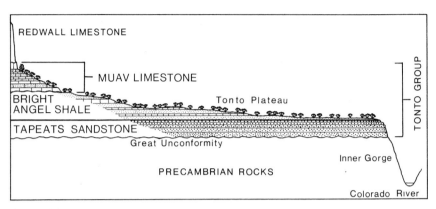

Figure 14.

The Tonto Plateau is the broad bench perched above the Grand Canyon's Inner Gorge. It occurs where the easily eroded Bright Angel Shale has been nearly stripped away from the surface of the resistant Tapeats Sandstone below. Muav Limestone forms a ledgy slope transitional between the Tonto Plateau and the Redwall above. Together, the Muav Limestone, Bright Angel Shale and Tapeats Sandstone are sometimes called the Tonto Group.

BRIGHT ANGEL SHALE. Extremely fine-grained mudstone shale, interbedded with thin units of siltstone, sandstone and sandy limestone. Color: greenish. Thickness: 350–400′. Fossils: trilobites, brachiopods, *hyolithes* and the trails of various marine animals. Erodes to form a gentle slope. Bright Angel Shale has been nearly stripped away from the underlying Tapeats Sandstone to form the broad terrace of the Tonto Plateau.

TAPEATS SANDSTONE. Medium- to coarse-grained sandstone, with extensive cross-bedding. Color: dark brown. Thickness: 100′. Fossils: trilobite trails. Ripple marks are widespread. Erodes to form the cliff at the brink of the Tonto Plateau. Sits atop either early or late Precambrian rocks.

Late Precambrian Rocks—The Grand Canyon Supergroup

The Grand Canyon Supergroup consists of tilted sedimentary strata of late Precambrian age. The strata outcrop over a wide area in the eastern Grand Canyon from Nankoweap to Hance Rapids at the mouth of Red Canyon. From there westward they occur intermittently, often in side canyons. The Grand Canyon Supergroup includes the Chuar Group, Nankoweap Formation and Unkar Group.

Chuar Group

SIXTYMILE FORMATION. Medium-grained sandstone with breccia and minor units of shale. Outcrops only in Awatubi and Sixtymile canyons and as cap rock on Nankoweap Butte. Color: tan to buff. Thickness: 120'. Erodes to form a ledgy cliff.

KWAGUNT FORMATION. Shale and limestone, with a thick sandstone bed at the base of Carbon Butte. Color: red to purplish. Thickness: up to 2218'. Fossils: stromatolites (the oldest fossils found in the Grand Canyon) and Chuaria. Features mud cracks, ripple marks and raindrop impressions. Erodes to form a ledgy slope. Outcrops from Nankoweap Canyon south to Chuar Canyon on the west side of the river.

GALEROS FORMATION. Interbedded limestone, shale and sandstone. Color: ocher to yellow-green. Thickness: 570–4272'. Fossils: stromatolites. Features ripple marks and raindrop impressions. Outcrops from Nankoweap Canyon south to Basalt Canyon, on the west side of the river.

NANKOWEAP FORMATION. Coarse-grained, thick-bedded sandstone, with some cross-bedding and mud cracks. Color: white, brown and purple. Thickness: 330'. Erodes to form a cliff. Outcrops in Nankoweap Canyon and below Desert View.

Unkar Group

CARDENAS LAVAS AND INTRUSIVES. Basaltic lava flows and diabase sills (diabase is an intrusive form of basalt). Extremely fine-grained. Color: dark brown to black. Thickness: up to 980'. Erodes to form cliffs. The lava flows occur just above the Dox Formation. The diabase sills are scattered among the Unkar rocks.

DOX FORMATION (Dox Sandstone). Sandstone interbedded with shale. Features ripple marks and mud cracks. Color: reddish. Thickness: up to

3122'. Erodes to form gentle hills and valleys. Outcrops widely below Desert View; scattered outcrops westward, mostly in side canyons.

SHINUMO QUARTZITE. Medium- to coarse-grained sandstone with a thick bed of quartzite (a hard sandstone cemented with silica rather than calcite). Color: purple, red, white and brown. Features some cross-beds. Erodes to form a massive cliff. Scattered outcrops in side canyons west of Escalante Creek, below Papago Point.

HAKATAI SHALE. Shale with minor beds of sandstone. Often cross-bedded, with ripple marks, raindrop impressions and mud cracks. Color: vivid red-orange. Thickness: 600–800'. Erodes to form slopes and benches. Scattered outcrops from Red Canyon west.

BASS FORMATION (Bass Limestone). Mostly fine-grained limestone interbedded with shale. Color: grey. Thickness: up to 327'. Fossils: stromatolites. Features ripple marks. Erodes to form a ledgy cliff. Scattered outcrops from Mineral Canyon west. Includes the Hotauta Conglomerate, which lies in channels eroded in the underlying Vishnu Schist.

Early Precambrian Rocks

VISHNU SCHIST. Mostly foliated mica schist. Also includes Zoroaster Gneiss, Elves Canyon and Trinity gneisses, quartzite units, dikes and sills of aplite and pegmatite, and other materials. Color: schist is dark grey to nearly black, with numerous wavy bands; gneiss has broader, wavy bands and is pink or light grey. Thickness: about 800–1500'. Outcrops in the cliffs of Lower, Middle and Upper Granite Gorge, but the rocks extend to unknown depths. Erodes to form steep cliffs.

THE STORY OF THE ROCKS

Early Precambrian Rocks

About two billion years ago, the Grand Canyon region lay beneath an ancient sea. Rivers draining a nearby landmass dumped tons of silt and clay in the area. Smaller amounts of sand were also deposited, and layers of limey mud accumulated on the sea floor. From time to time, offshore volcanos covered the sediments with layers of lava and volcanic ash. For tens of millions of years these materials accumulated to a depth of five miles and consolidated to form shale interbedded with minor layers of limestone and sandstone. With the addition of further sediments, these rocks were buried perhaps ten miles below the earth's surface. Then, about 1.7 billion years ago, the buried strata were buckled and folded as the land rose to form a mountain range comparable to today's Rockies. In the process, intense heat and pressure altered the rocks to form the Vishnu Schist of the Inner Gorge. At the same time, great plumes of molten rock intruded into the surrounding schist, cooling at depth to form granite. This rock was then metamorphosed along with the shale to form gneiss, the other major type of rock today exposed in the Inner Gorge.

Precambrian Unconformity

Over the next half-billion years or so, the mountains eroded gradually to form a low plain. Streams carved channels across the plain and filled these channels with the gravels and other sediments that today form the Hotauta Conglomerate. Periods when regions are being eroded rather than receiving sediments form gaps in the geological record. The Vishnu Schist erosion surface represents a gap of about 500 million years, the time that elapsed between the formation of that surface and its burial beneath the Bass Limestone. Such breaks in the orderly sequence of rocks are called unconformities. Since this one separates formations of Precambrian age, it is known as the Precambrian Unconformity.

Late Precambrian Rocks

About 1.2 billion years ago, the land subsided and was invaded by the sea. Marine algae, the earliest forms of life known to have existed in the Grand Canyon region, secreted calcium carbonate, which combined with silts and clays washed in from nearby lands to form limey muds. These later became the Bass Limestone. At times the sediments must have lain in a shallow, tidal-flat environment, for the limestone includes dolomite and is interbedded with thin units of shale on which ripple marks are apparent. Fossils from this time include small discs of crushed and carbonized organic matter (*Chuaria*) and thinly laminated mounds (stromatolites) thought to consist of limey secretions of mat-forming marine algae. These fossils are the oldest in the Grand Canyon.

During late Precambrian time, the sea must have advanced and retreated over the region many times. The sandstones and shales that form the remainder of the Grand Canyon Supergroup are often cross-bedded and bear ripple marks, features that suggest a coastal floodplain or river-delta environment. Some of the rocks also have raindrop impressions and mud cracks, indicating that they were not continuously submerged. The mud cracks also suggest a hot, arid climate for at least part of the time.

Midway through the late Precambrian, lavas erupted on the sea floor and basaltic magma intruded into the upper rock strata. Subsequent eruptions poured lava and ash onto the land. Evidence of this activity is preserved in the form of the basaltic cliffs and diabase intrusions of the Cardenas Lavas.

Following this volcanic activity, the Grand Canyon region continued to alternate between marine and coastal environments. Evidence is provided by the beds of shale, sandstone and limestone that comprise the Chuar Group. Many of these rocks exhibit raindrop impressions, ripple marks, cross-bedding and mud cracks.

Toward the end of the late Precambrian, the strata of the Grand Canyon Supergroup were tilted and uplifted along geologic faults to form another mountain range. This range, like the one before it, eroded away. As much as 15,000 feet of rock was removed, leaving a low plain covered with scattered hills. The Vishnu Schist formed the surface of the plain, and the scattered outcrops of late Precambrian rocks found in the Grand Canyon today were the hills.

The Great Unconformity

At the onset of the Paleozoic Era, about 600 million years ago, this landscape was gradually submerged beneath a sea advancing from the west. Sands were deposited over the region, burying both the plain and the hills. These sands are preserved today in the Tapeats Sandstone, and the boundary between it and the Precambrian rocks beneath is called the Great Unconformity (see Plate 9). It represents a break in the record of between 600 million and 1.4 billion years. The Great Unconformity occurs throughout the Grand Canyon, but is especially striking near

Desert View where the Tapeats Sandstone sits directly on top of the tilted strata of the Unkar Group.

Paleozoic Rocks

The Tapeats Sandstone is probably the remains of beaches that lined the margins of the Cambrian sea. The sands are commonly cross-bedded and exhibit ripple marks and trails made by trilobites, all of which suggest a shallow, clear-water environment.

As the sea continued to advance eastward over the region, layers of mud, silt and fine-grained sand were deposited in deeper waters atop the Tapeats Sandstone. These sediments today comprise the Bright Angel Shale. They were covered in turn by deep-water limestones of the Muav Formation. Conglomerates interbedded in the limestone suggest periodic retreats of the sea.

In mid-Cambrian time the sea retreated westward and remained there for perhaps 150 million years. During this time, much of the accumulated rock was removed, exposing the Muav Limestone. In Devonian time, the sea returned. Stream channels cut in the surface of the Muav Limestone were filled with Temple Butte Limestone. To the west, thick beds of dolomite formed in shallow tidal flats. The presence of fossilized plates of a primitive freshwater fish in the Temple Butte Limestone, suggest that the channels represent ancient stream meanders in an estuarine or river-delta environment.

During the following tens of millions of years, the Devonian sea retreated, and the exposed land was eroded to a level plain. Then, in Mississippian time, the sea advanced and retreated three times over the region. The nearly pure limestones deposited during these advances today form the massive Redwall Cliff. The Mississippian seas were rich in life, leaving an abundance of marine fossils in the Redwall.

The retreat of the third and final Mississippian sea exposed the surface of the Redwall Limestone to profound weathering in a warm, humid, tropical environment. Abundant rains fed underground streams, which carved caverns through the Redwall. The land was weathered to low relief and here and there marked by sinkholes, where cavern roofs collapsed. Such terrain is typical of what geologists call Karst topography, after a region in Yugoslavia. Today, Karst topography similar to that developed in the Redwall Limestone can be seen on the Kaibab Plateau and, less dramatically, the Coconino Plateau.

During Pennsylvanian time, the sea once again advanced over the region, but not so far as before. The vicinity of Grand Canyon Village was then covered by low-lying coastal swamp not unlike that found today along the Gulf Coast. Sluggish rivers deposited the silts, clays and sands of the Supai Formation. To the west, in deeper waters, limestone accumulated on the sea floor.

The sandstone cap of the Supai Formation suggests that the sea was retreating by Permian time. After a period of erosion, the Grand Canyon region once again formed a vast floodplain. Rivers draining lands to the north and east deposited thick layers of mud over the region. This mud today forms the Hermit Shale. Preserved in the shale are mud cracks, raindrop impressions and the tracks of amphibians and reptiles. Fossil seed ferns and other land plants suggest a semiarid environment.

As the Permian period progressed, the climate became increasingly arid until desert conditions prevailed over the region. Winds piled up vast fields of sand dunes much like those found in the Sahara Desert. These dunes, along with the tracks of reptiles that scurried over their surface, are preserved in the Coconino Sandstone. The shape of the ancient dunes can be seen today in the enormous wedge-shape cross-beds of this formation. The sands are nearly pure quartz. Viewed under a hand lens, the grains are seen to be rounded and minutely pitted, giving them a frosty appearance. The pits were probably produced by collisions with other particles during desert windstorms.

In mid-Permian time the desert was twice inundated by advancing seas. The limestones of the Toroweap and Kaibab formations originated during these advances. The sandstone beds on either side of the limestone record times during each advance and retreat when the region lay along the coast. Both formations contain numerous marine fossils.

Mesozoic Rocks

At the opening of the Mesozoic Era, following the retreat of the last Permian sea, the Kaibab Limestone was eroded to form a low, coastal plain. At that time, dinosaurs roamed the Grand Canyon region in a swampy, tropical environment. Over the next 150 million years, the Kaibab Limestone slowly subsided as rivers deposited mud, silt and sand over the region. At the end of that time, the region still lay near sea level, but the Kaibab Limestone was buried beneath 4000 to 8000 feet of sediments.

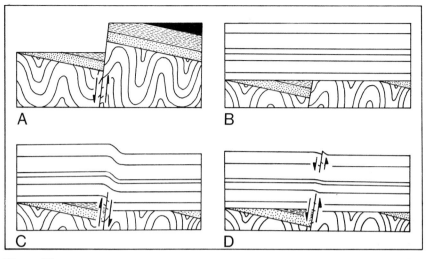

Figure 15.
Development of faults and monoclines at the Grand Canyon. (A) Faults developed as Precambrian rocks were uplifted to form a mountain range. (B) Eventually the range was eroded to a gentle plain and then covered by Paleozoic strata. (C) When regional uplift commenced again in late Mesozoic time, faulting and monoclinal folding of the Paleozoic strata occurred along the lines of the older faults, but in a reverse direction. (D) In some places a second reversal of fault movement also occurred.

Toward the end of the Mesozoic Era and continuing well into the Cenozoic, mountain-building forces began to uplift the entire Colorado Plateau Province. In the Grand Canyon region, the rocks were bowed upward to form a broad dome called the Kaibab Upwarp. In the process, numerous geological faults developed where the strata broke under the strain. In other places the rocks simply bent without breaking, producing the great monoclinal folds seen today along both sides of the Kaibab Plateau and on the eastern portion of the Coconino Plateau. Later faults then developed along the monoclines as uplift continued. The staircase of plateaus along the north side of the Grand Canyon was produced by these episodes of faulting.

Another result of the uplift and deformation of the rocks was that the Mesozoic strata were almost completely removed from the Grand Canyon region. All that remain today are the outcrops on Cedar Mountain and Red Butte, both near the South Rim. The contact between the Kaibab Limestone and Mesozoic strata is best seen, however, northeast of the Grand Canyon, where the Echo Cliffs and Vermilion Cliffs rest on the surface of the Marble Platform.

Cenozoic Rocks

Rock formation in the last 70 million years has been limited to the deposition of travertine (see *Sedimentary Rocks*, page 245) and volcanic eruptions in the western Grand Canyon. About six million years ago, when the main stem of the Colorado River had begun to carve its way down through the Kaibab Upwarp, volcanos on the Shivwits, Uinkaret and western Coconino plateaus began to belch lava and ash. Over the next few million years, repeated eruptions from such sources as Mt. Trumbull created the spectacular volcanic landforms of the western Grand Canyon. These include extensive basalt flows on the Uinkaret Plateau, lava-filled side canyons, petrified lava falls on the cliffs of the Inner Gorge, basalt columns, the volcanic neck of Vulcan's Forge, and numerous cinder cones, including Vulcan's Throne, at the foot of Toroweap Valley.

By piecing together scraps of information gleaned from fossils, rock types, erosion surfaces, the structure and position of the strata, superficial features such as ripple marks and other sources, geologists have been able to reconstruct in broad outline the sequence of events and landscapes that preceded the formation of the Grand Canyon. Ironically, the age and origin of the Grand Canyon itself remain uncertain. Authorities agree that the canyon is a river-cut gorge. But whether the Colorado River was the principal agent or a late arrival after the work had been initiated by another stream or streams is a subject of spirited debate.

SELECTED REFERENCES: See page 267.

12. FORMATION OF THE GRAND CANYON

Many people fine it almost incredible that the Colorado River could have carved the Grand Canyon. The canyon's extravagant scale and elaborate rock sculpture are so unlike those of any landscape encountered before that they seem to require extraordinary causes. A monumental earthquake, perhaps, a catastrophic collapse of the earth's crust. Anything but the operation of normal erosional processes over the vast stretches of time. Yet the identical sequences of strata on both sides of the canyon leave no doubt that the Kaibab and Coconino plateaus once formed a continuous surface down through which the Colorado River carved its gorge.

PROCESSES OF CANYON FORMATION

A river deepens its channel principally by scraping and gouging its bed. Its tools are the cobbles and boulders swept along by the current. As a river cuts downward, it exposes canyon walls to the forces of weathering and erosion, which waste them back from the water's edge to form a V-shape gorge.

The profile of the Grand Canyon, however, is not a simple V, but consists of a giant staircase of cliffs, slopes and terraces. This sequence of

261

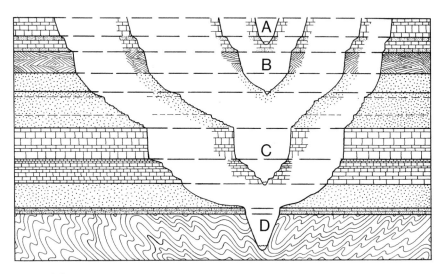

Figure 16.

The Grand Canyon began as a narrow V-shape gorge (A). Chemical and mechanical weathering wore back the walls at varying rates depending on the hardness of the rock strata, producing a series of cliffs, slopes and terraces. At the same time, the river continued to cut more deeply (B and C). Together, river cutting and weathering of the canyon walls produced the Grand Canyon as it exists today (D). Millions of years hence continued erosion will have reduced the Grand Canyon to a broad river valley.

landforms reflects the different rates at which the various strata are eroded. Sandstone, limestone and schist are hard, resistant rocks and therefore weather slowly to form cliffs. Softer shales wear away to slopes. Broad terraces such as the Esplanade and Tonto Platform occur where shales have been almost entirely stripped away from more resistant rocks below.

Weathering is the process whereby the elements—heat, cold, running water, frost and ice—break down rocks into sediments. Weathering may be either chemical or mechanical. Chemical weathering occurs when moisture seeping into rocks chemically alters their minerals, dissolving some, breaking down others to form clay.

Since carbonate minerals are soluble in water, rainwater seeping into limestone slowly hollows out caverns and underground channels. Numerous caves formed in this way are evident in the Redwall Cliff. Runoff seeping into fractures in the Redwall eventually weathers the rocks to a point where large sections may no longer adhere to the rest of the cliff. Resulting rock falls leave niches or panels in the cliff. The deep

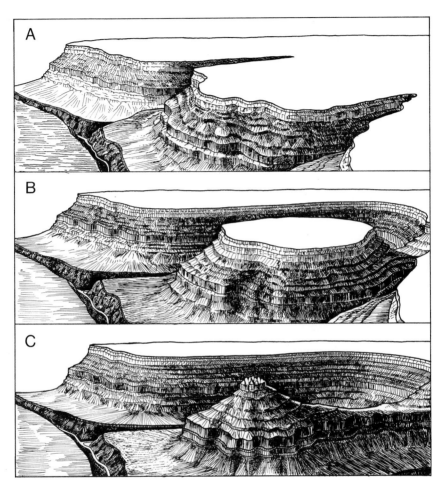

Figure 17.

Evolution of temples and amphitheaters. (A) A hypothetical section of the North Rim into which tributary streams have cut a pair of side canyons. The portion of the rim between the canyons forms a promontory. (B) Continued headward erosion by tributary streams, coupled with weathering of the canyon walls, cuts off the promontory from the rim, producing an isolated plateau. (C) Erosion of the plateau produces a temple, which is connected to the rim by a low saddle. The heads of the side canyons now form broad amphitheaters.

alcoves, or embayments, that scallop the Redwall are produced over long periods by successive rockfalls.

Chemical weathering rapidly weakens the bonds uniting the microscopic particles of silt and clay that make up shale. At some point a shale formation becomes so unstable that it is no longer able to support overlying strata of more resistant rocks. As a result the undermined cliffs slump downward along with the shale, producing a landslide. Massive landslides are historically rare in the Grand Canyon, but have nevertheless occurred with regularity throughout its geologic history. The most spectacular example can be seen in Surprise Canyon, where two cliff blocks with a total volume of about one cubic mile slid 1500 feet. Small slides are fairly common, though there is little chance of actually witnessing one. Landslides are the chief mechanism by which the Grand Canyon cliffs have worn back to their present positions. The canyon's spectacular width, then, is due primarily to the occurrence of soft shale strata between harder layers of rock. If the shales were not present, the canyon would probably be a much narrower, V-shape gorge like that carved by most rivers.

The chief form of mechanical weathering is frost riving. During the winter, when freezing temperatures are common in all but the deepest parts of the canyon, and are not unknown there, frost forms in cracks and crevices and slowly wedges the rocks apart. The wedging occurs because water expands as it freezes. When the frost melts, the crevice contracts a bit. Alternating hot days and cold nights also cause the rocks to expand and contract. If soils form in a crevice and plants become established, their roots help pry the rocks farther apart. Moist soils covering crevice surfaces also provide suitable conditions for chemical weathering. Though such processes operate slowly, they ultimately cause rock fragments to be dislodged from the cliffs. If a cliff is densely fractured, mechanical and chemical weathering in conjunction may cause an entire section to collapse all at once. Fallen debris accumulates at the base of a cliff to form a steep apron called a talus slope.

Had the Colorado River been the only stream at work, the Grand Canyon would not be so wide nor complex as it is. But as the river cut downward, tributary streams draining the rims simultaneously cut a host of side canyons. In the process they exposed new areas of cliff to weathering. The ridges separating the side canyons were eroded to produce the Grand Canyon's magnificent buttes, or "temples."

Since a side stream cannot erode its channel below that of the river, the growth of side canyons proceeds in a headward, that is, upstream, direction. In other words, the tributary streams cut back into the canyon walls, scalloping the rims into an alternation of recesses and promontories. The large amphitheaters that have formed at the heads of many side canyons were produced by slides and rockfalls.

The recesses in the North Rim are cut back more deeply than those in the South Rim partly because the former receives more precipitation. As a result, its streams are more vigorous and are thus able to excavate their canyons more rapidly. Moreover, the Kaibab Plateau tilts toward the Canyon, while the Coconino Plateau slopes away from it. Consequently, North Rim streams flow into the canyon, South Rim streams do not.

Since there are few permanent tributary streams in the Grand Canyon, the great majority of side canyons were carved by seasonal torrents, flash floods generated by rains. Flash floods constitute the single most important agent of erosion in arid regions, especially in steep, rocky terrain. The bare cliffs and sparsely vegetated slopes of the Grand Canyon shed enormous amounts of runoff following a storm. The waters rapidly funnel into side canyons and from there down to the river. In the process they transport huge amounts of rock debris from the sides to the bottom of the canyon. The river uses the rocks weathered from the cliffs to scour its channel yet more deeply, and thus the cycle of canyon formation comes full circle.

ORIGIN OF THE GRAND CANYON

Few places on earth have received closer scrutiny from geologists than the Grand Canyon. And while much of its story is known with reasonable certainty, there remains one mystery that all the time, labor and intelligence of dozens of workers have failed to unravel. Since water can't flow uphill, exactly how and when did the ancestral Colorado River manage to establish its course across the Kaibab Upwarp, which now stands 2000 to 3000 feet above the lands upstream?

John Wesley Powell suggested that the river was already flowing across the region before uplift began. Then, as the land rose, the river responded by cutting its canyon ever more deeply. Unfortunately, this straightforward explanation is contradicted by evidence uncovered since Powell's time. At Grand Wash, where the Colorado now leaves the canyon, sediments of the Muddy Creek Formation have been assigned a radiometric date of six million years. These sediments lie *beneath* river gravels, which means that the river began to flow through this area after the sediments were in place. In other words, Lower Granite Gorge, the final section of the Grand Canyon, is less than six million years old. Yet evidence suggests that the Kaibab Upwarp had reached nearly its present elevation about 65 million years ago. So when did the river cross the upwarp?

One current theory suggests that before six million years ago the ancestral Colorado River flowed south along the eastern base of the Kaibab Upwarp, much as it does today. But instead of swinging westward across the rise, it turned southeastward through the channel now occupied by the Little Colorado River. Meanwhile, the theory goes, a second river, the Hualapai, was cutting headward into the western flank of the Upwarp. Eventually, it cut backward completely through the bulge, capturing the Colorado River, which was diverted westward along roughly its present course. This act of river piracy would have occurred some time after the deposition of the Muddy Creek Formation about six million years ago. If this theory is correct, geologists should have uncovered some trace of the ancestral Colorado's southeastward course, but so far no substantiating evidence has turned up.

Alternate theories suggest that the ancestral Colorado River cut across the upwarp after the land had been uplifted, but before erosion had lowered the surface of the Marble Platform upstream. In other words, the river established its channel when the platform and upwarp together formed a continuous surface at roughly the same elevation. Later, erosion lowered the platform by removing a couple of thousand feet of Mesozoic rocks.

If this scenario is true, the ancestral Colorado River would have cut through the upwarp some time between 25 and 65 million years ago. West of the upwarp, the river would have had to leave the area by a different route than it does today, since Lower Granite Gorge was carved less than six million years ago.

According to one view, the river established its course across the Kaibab Upwarp between 25 million and 30 million years ago, exiting the region via Peach Springs Canyon, at the upper end of Lower Granite Gorge. From there, it flowed southwestward across northwestern Arizona to its present channel along the Arizona–California border, where—as it does today—it flowed southward to the Gulf of California. Then, about 18 million years ago, the river was ponded for a time at the head of Lower Granite Gorge. Drainage occurred by means of a subterranean stream that flowed through cavernous limestone northwest along the gorge's present course to Grand Wash. Eventually, the river opened up this course to carve the gorge itself. The major hitch to this scenario is that subsequent evidence has revealed that the Gulf of Mexico probably formed only four to five million years ago and therefore could not have received the waters of the ancestral Colorado before that time.

Another theory suggests that the river cut through the upwarp about 65 million years ago and from there flowed northwestward into landlocked basins in southern Utah. Then, about three million years ago, its flow was diverted to its present course by a second stream cutting headward from the "recently" opened Gulf of California. The main problem with this theory is that the river would have had to carve Lower Granite Gorge at a fantastic rate. In addition, the rough-hewn profile of the eastern Grand Canyon seems too youthful. Nevertheless, until a thorough investigation of the Utah basins confirms or denies the presence of the ancestral Colorado, the theory remains a plausible alternative.

All the above scenarios represent conscientious attempts to explain the origin of the Grand Canyon in the light of available evidence. So far, the rocks have revealed precious few clues, but more are bound to turn up as investigation continues. And while no one of the theories is entirely satisfactory in all its details, refinements of one sort or another may be expected in the future. Finally, it should be remembered that there is no disagreement whatsoever regarding the role of river cutting and erosion in the formation of the Grand Canyon.

The forces that produced the Grand Canyon operate at an exceedingly slow pace. But by any measure they have had millions of years in which to work. The rockfalls and landslides that continue to occur indicate that the canyon is growing ever wider. As the Colorado River approaches sea level, it will carve its channel ever more slowly. Yet the walls will continue to waste away. Barring renewed uplift in the region, a broad valley will probably replace the Grand Canyon in another few million years. Enjoy it while you can.

SELECTED REFERENCES FOR CHAPTERS 11 AND 12

Baars, Donald L. *Red Rock Country: the Geologic History of the Colorado Plateau.* Garden City, NY: Doubleday/Natural History Press, 1972.

Beal, M. D. *Grand Canyon: the Story behind the Scenery.* Las Vegas: K. C. Publications, 1978.

Breed, William J., and E. C. Road, eds. *Geology of the Grand Canyon.* Flagstaff, AZ: Museum of Northern Arizona/Grand Canyon Natural History Association, 1974.

Collier, Michael. *An Introduction to Grand Canyon Geology.* Grand Canyon, AZ: Grand Canyon Natural History Association, 1980.

Hamblin, W. Kenneth, and Joseph R. Murphy. *Grand Canyon Perspectives.* Provo, UT: Brigham Young University Printing Services, 1969.

McKee, Edwin D. *Ancient Landscapes of the Grand Canyon Region*, 28th ed. Flagstaff, AZ: Northland Press, 1978.

McKee, Edwin D., et al. *Evolution of the Colorado River*. Flagstaff, AZ: Museum of Northern Arizona, 1964.

Rahm, David A. *Reading the Rocks: a Guide to the Geologic Secrets of the Canyons, Mesas and Buttes of the American Southwest*. San Francisco: Sierra Club Books, 1974.

Rigby, J. Keith. *Southern Colorado Plateau*. Dubuque, IA: Kendall/Hunt Publishing Co., 1977.

Shelton, John S. *Geology Illustrated*. San Francisco: W. H. Freeman, 1966.

Simmons, George C., and David L. Gaskill. *River Runner's Guide to the Canyons of the Green and Colorado Rivers, with Emphasis on Geologic Features*, vol. 3, *Marble Gorge and Grand Canyon*. Flagstaff, AZ: Northland Press, 1969.

Stokes, William Lee. *Scenes of the Plateau Lands and How They Came to Be*. Salt Lake City, UT: Publishers Press, 1973.

United States Geological Survey. *The Colorado River Region and John Wesley Powell*. Professional Paper 669-C, Washington, D.C.: Government Printing Office, 1969.

PART III

Plants

13. FERNS AND FERN ALLIES

Ferns and fern allies (horsetails, club mosses, spike mosses and others) have vascular tissue for support and for circulating water and nutrients, but unlike flowering plants, reproduce from spores rather than seeds. Seed-bearing plants, no matter how fernlike they may seem at first glance, are not ferns. *Fern allies* is an umbrella term covering a variety of spore-bearing vascular plants that differ from true ferns in one way or another.

Though not closely related, ferns and fern allies probably evolved from a common ancestor. They are the oldest vascular land plants in the fossil record, first appearing about 400 million years ago. In the Grand Canyon, fossil ferns have been found in the Hermit Shale. Today there are about 10,000 types of ferns and fern allies, of which about 80 species occur in Arizona and nearly 20 in the Grand Canyon.

This chapter depicts 11 species of ferns found in and near the canyon, including all the common ones and at least one representative of each genus. Many are adapted to growing in cliff crevices, where soil and moisture are more abundant than elsewhere. A few species are largely restricted to seeps, springs, stream banks or similar moist places. A few, however, thrive in rather arid habitats. Among the cliff-dwelling forms, some prefer or at least grow more abundantly on limestone, a habit that may help to distinguish them from certain other types.

LIFE CYCLE AND REPRODUCTION

The life cycle of a fern consists of two distinct stages or generations, each represented by a separate plant. The plants normally called ferns actually represent only the asexual, spore-bearing (sporophyte) generation. Spores are produced in minute cases (sporangia). Clusters of spore cases, called *sori* (or "fruit dots"), are borne on the undersides of leaves. These usually appear during the summer and at first may be covered by a membrane called the *indusium*. Some ferns lack indusia, however, and instead bear the sori beneath rolled-over leaf margins. Sori may be missing if a plant is too young, the season is wrong or the leaf is sterile.

Upon maturity, spore cases open slowly, then snap shut, slinging out spores in the process. Borne by the wind, spores that land in suitable places germinate and develop into simple, heart-shaped plants called prothalli (singular *prothallus*). Smaller than a thumbnail, each prothallus is a self-supporting green plant bearing the male and female reproductive cells. These reproductive cells unite and grow into the plants we know as ferns, thus completing the cycle. Normally, only one fern plant develops from each prothallus. It remains attached to the prothallus, which continues to provide water and nutrients until the young fern is established. Then the prothallus withers away.

Reproduction is essentially the same for fern allies. They do not, however, bear spores on the undersides of their leaves. Scouring rushes bear spores in conelike spikes atop the stems; spikemosses, in special chambers between the leaves; and pepperworts, in individual cases (sporocarps) attached to stalks rising from the base of the plant. Despite these and other differences, ferns and fern allies share the two-stage life cycle consisting of an asexual and a sexual generation.

IDENTIFYING FERNS

When identifying ferns, pay special attention to the structure of the leaves, the location of the sori, and whether the fruitdots are covered by an indusium or rolled-over leaf margin. If sori are not present, some ferns may be difficult to distinguish. The parts and leaf structure of ferns and fern allies are shown in Plate 10. Species descriptions are limited to features that may be perceived without special training or equipment *and without disturbing the specimen plant.* These features may not always be sufficient for distinguishing a particular specimen, but they will serve in most cases.

SELECTED REFERENCES

Cobb, Broughton. A *Field Guide to the Ferns and Their Related Families.* Boston: Houghton Mifflin, 1963.

Cronquist, Arthur, et al. *Intermountain Flora: Vascular Plants of the Intermountain West, U.S.A.*, vol. I. New York: Hafner, 1972.

Dittmer, Howard J., et al. *The Ferns and Fern Allies of New Mexico.* Albuquerque: University of New Mexico Press, 1954.

Grillos, Steve J. *Ferns and Fern Allies of California.* Berkeley: University of California Press, 1971.

Kearney, Thomas H., and Robert H. Peebles. *Arizona Flora*, 2nd ed. with supplement. Berkeley: University of California Press, 1960.

McDougall, W. B. *Checklist of Plants of Grand Canyon National Park.* Natural History Bulletin no. 10. Grand Canyon, AZ: Grand Canyon Natural History Association, 1947.

Mickel, John T. *How to Know the Ferns and Fern Allies.* Dubuque, IA: William C. Brown Co., 1979.

Patraw, Pauline. *Checklist of Plants of Grand Canyon National Park.* Natural History Bulletin no. 6. Grand Canyon, AZ: Grand Canyon Natural History Association, 1936.

Phillips, W. S. "A Checklist of the Ferns of Arizona," in *American Fern Journal* 36(1946): 97–108 and 37(1947): 13–20, 39–51.

14. FLOWERING PLANTS

The Grand Canyon, with its varied topography and climate, supports a large flora, which includes more than 1500 species of flowering plants. This guide depicts more than 230 of the more common types. They have been separated into groups: wildflowers (Chapter 15), cacti (Chapter 16) and trees and shrubs (Chapter 17).

The term *wildflower* has no precise botanical meaning, referring to all flowering plants growing outside of cultivation. In common usage, however, it refers to nonwoody (herbaceous) plants with stems that form anew each year and die back after seed production. Annuals sprout each year and complete their life cycle in a single growing season. Perennial herbs live for several seasons, but are reduced during months of dormancy to persistent underground parts such as bulbs, corms, tubers, rhizomes or root crowns. Some perennial herbs die back to woody bases, but each year's new growth is herbaceous. In addition to reproducing from seed, some perennials may form new plants through such means as the division of bulbs and corms, the sprouting of tubers, and sprouting along rhizomes (underground stems) or runners (aboveground stems).

Trees and shrubs have woody stems that persist, with or without leaves, from one year to the next. A tree is often defined as a woody plant with a single main stem (trunk) at least three inches in diameter and with a crown of branches reaching to heights of 15 feet or more. A shrub, therefore, is a woody plant less than 15-feet tall, with several main stems, most less than three inches in diameter. The distinction is neat in theory but often difficult to apply with certainty in the field. Numerous species of woody plants may grow as either trees or shrubs depending on environmental conditions. In arid regions such as the Inner Canyon, plants that elsewhere typically form trees may be stunted by insufficient moisture. For this reason, trees and shrubs are treated together in this guide.

Cacti, too, can be considered either trees or shrubs, depending on size, but have fleshy rather than woody stems. The types found in the Grand Canyon are shrubby and leafless. Cacti are so distinct that they are treated in a separate chapter. For a more detailed description of this fascinating group of plants, see the introduction to Chapter 16.

PLANT ADAPTATIONS

The desert conditions of the Inner Canyon and the cold, snowy winters of the Kaibab Plateau represent the extremes of climate at the Grand Canyon. Both regimes pose severe challenges to plants, challenges that limit the kinds and numbers of plants able to grow in either place. Those that inhabit such extreme environments have evolved a variety of ingenious strategies for survival.

Plants in the Inner Canyon must contend with high air temperatures, low humidity and scant rainfall. If air temperatures are too high, basic metabolic processes slow down or stop. Extreme heat may even cook plant tissues. The usual consequence of hot weather, however, is moisture loss by means of evaporation from leaves and stems. In desert conditions plants are in danger of losing moisture faster than they can replace it from the soil. In effect, the hot, dry air acts as a sponge. Heat and drought, then, are intimately connected in the sense that adaptations to one also usually apply to the other.

Some plants found in desert regions solve the twin problems of heat and drought by growing only in places where these conditions are alleviated to some degree. At seeps, springs and streamsides, for example, water loss is not a problem. A shady crevice dampened by seepage is also a desirable site. In the Inner Canyon all such places tend to support distinctive plant associations made up of species rare or absent in other situations.

The very sparseness of desert vegetation is itself an accommodation to drought. Plants in the Inner Canyon tend to be widely spaced in order that each may obtain adequate moisture. Young plants that attempt to invade territories already occupied by older, established plants will probably not succeed since the latter will suck up most available moisture.

Most desert wildflowers are short-lived herbaceous annuals that avoid moisture stress by growing only when soils are moist and temperatures mild. As a rule they germinate in early spring following a wet winter. If rains are below normal, however, the seeds may remain dormant for several years. Following germination, the development of roots and shoots is rapid. Flowers and seed are normally produced within a few weeks, after which the plants die. Such short-lived, opportunistic plants are appropriately called ephemerals.

The majority of Inner Canyon plants have adapted to heat and drought by means of special modifications to leaves and stems. These modifications include:

1. Reduced leaf surfaces from which moisture loss can occur. Cacti have abandoned leaves altogether. Many plants sprout tiny leaves shortly after a rain, quickly shedding them as drought returns.
2. Self-pruning. Some desert plants shed twigs and branches during times of drought. This reduces the number of shoots that must be supplied with water.
3. Green stems. Green stems allow plants to carry out photosynthesis in the absence of leaves.
4. Coated leaves. Some desert plants have waxy or leathery leaves which reduce evaporative moisture loss.
5. Succulence. Cacti and certain other plants avoid drought by storing moisture in their leaves or stems.
6. Dormancy. Many desert plants reduce or shut down metabolic processes during times of heat and drought. Dormancy is usually attended by leaf loss and self-pruning.
7. Special root systems. Some desert plants have long taproots for securing moisture well below the ground surface. Others have extensive surface roots that allow them to take advantage of even light rains.
8. Hairs and thorns. Most desert plants are densely covered with hairs or thorns, which filter sunlight and thereby reduce heating and moisture loss.
9. Heat and drought tolerance. Most desert plants can carry out basic metabolic processes at temperatures well above and moisture levels well below those tolerable to other plants.

During the winter, plants at higher elevations on the Kaibab Plateau (and to a lesser degree on the Coconino Plateau) are subject to freezing temperatures, cold winds and snow. The summer growing season is relatively brief and may bring freezing nighttime temperatures. Most plants growing on the plateau are perennials, which become dormant during the winter, but are able to put out new shoots rapidly at the onset of summer. The period of dormancy for most species begins with the cold nights and first snows of autumn. It ends shortly after the snowpack melts, if not earlier.

Perennial herbs die back during the winter to root crowns, bulbs and other underground parts, in which nutrients are stored to quickly fuel new growth the following year. Trees and shrubs are protected from cold by thick bark and woody tissue. At the onset of cold weather they begin to reduce the water content of their sap. Like antifreeze, the resins that remain freeze at lower temperatures than water, thus making the plants more resistant to frost damage. Deciduous plants drop their leaves, which would be killed by cold in any case. Conifers and evergreen broadleaf plants have leaves thickly coated with cutin, a waxy varnish that protects them from cold and moisture loss.

Trees and shrubs growing in cold-winter climates typically have flexible limbs that bend rather than break under the weight of snow. The conical form of many conifers permits them to shed snow easily. On steep slopes, young trees are often bent just above the base by the downward creep of the snowpack. The resulting deformation, known as a snow knee, persists in the mature plant.

Seedlings and small shrubs are actually protected by the snow, which covers them with an insulating blanket. If exposed to icy winds, evergreen plants can lose shoots to frost damage, moisture stress or abrasion by wind-blown snow. Moisture stress occurs because the wind causes evaporation at the leaf surfaces at a time when the ground is frozen and replacement water is therefore unavailable.

IDENTIFYING FLOWERING PLANTS

As used here, the term *flowering plants* includes cone-bearing plants (gymnosperms) as well as true flowering plants (angiosperms). The latter bear seeds in protective capsules, or ovaries. Gymnosperms bear naked seeds on the undersides of cone scales, or bracts.

In order to identify flowering plants, one must often be able to recognize and distinguish various types of flowers, flower clusters, flower parts and leaves. Closely related species are often distinguishable only by small differences among these features. Botanists have developed a large special vocabulary to describe all of the various parts and characteristics of flowering plants. Wherever possible, common words have been substituted for technical jargon in the species descriptions in this book. In some cases, however, there are no popular equivalents and the technical terms had to be retained.

Before referring to species descriptions, readers should acquaint themselves with the flower and leaf parts and types shown on Plates 14–17. The terms used in the species descriptions are defined in words and pictures on each plate.

SELECTED REFERENCES FOR CHAPTERS 14–17.

Arnberger, Leslie P. *Flowers of the Southwest Mountains*, 5th ed. Globe, AZ: Southwest Parks and Monuments Association, 1974.

Benson, Lyman. *The Cacti of Arizona*, 3rd ed. Tucson: University of Arizona Press, 1969.

Benson, Lyman, and Robert A. Darrow. *The Trees and Shrubs of the Southwestern Deserts*. Tucson and Albuquerque: University of Arizona Press and University of New Mexico Press, 1954.

Brockman, C. Frank. *Trees of North America*. New York: Golden Press, 1968.

Craighead, J. J., et al. *A Field Guide to Rocky Mountain Wildflowers*. Boston: Houghton Mifflin, 1963.

Dodge, Natt N. *Flowers of the Southwest Deserts*. 9th ed. Globe, AZ: Southwest Parks and Monuments Association, 1976.

―――. *100 Desert Wildflowers in Natural Color*. Globe, AZ: Southwest Parks and Monuments Association, 1963.

―――. *100 Roadside Wildflowers of Southwest Uplands*. Globe, AZ: Southwest Parks and Monuments Association, 1967.

Elmore, Francis H. *Shrubs and Trees of the Southwest Uplands*. Globe, AZ: Southwest Parks and Monuments Association, 1976.

Kearney, Thomas H., and Robert H. Peebles. *Arizona Flora*. 2nd ed. with supplement. Berkeley: University of California Press, 1960.

Little, Elbert L., Jr. *The Audubon Society Field Guide to North American Trees*. New York: Knopf, 1980.

―――. *Southwestern Trees*. Agriculture Handbook no. 9, reprint. Washington, D.C.: Government Printing Office, 1968.

McDougall, W. B. *Checklist of Plants of Grand Canyon National Park*. Natural History Bulletin no. 10. Grand Canyon, AZ: Grand Canyon Natural History Association, 1947.

————. *Grand Canyon Wildflowers*. Flagstaff: Museum of Northern Arizona and Grand Canyon Natural History Association, 1964.

————. *Seed Plants of Northern Arizona*. Flagstaff: Museum of Northern Arizona, 1973.

Niehaus, Theodore F., and Charles L. Ripper. A *Field Guide to Pacific States Wildflowers*. Boston: Houghton Mifflin, 1976.

Patraw, Pauline. *Checklist of Plants of Grand Canyon National Park*. Natural History Bulletin no. 6. Grand Canyon, AZ: Grand Canyon Natural History Association, 1936.

————. *Flowers of the Southwest Mesas*. 6th ed. Globe, AZ: Southwest Parks and Monuments Association, 1977.

Peattie, Donald Culross. A *Natural History of Western Trees*. New York: Bonanza, 1975.

Phillips, Arthur M., III. *Grand Canyon Wildflowers*. Grand Canyon, AZ: Grand Canyon Natural History Association, 1979.

Rickett, Harold W. *Wildflowers of the United States*, vol. 4, pts. 1, 2 and 3, *The Southwest States*. New York: McGraw-Hill, 1970.

Spellenberg, Richard. *The Audubon Society Field Guide to North American Wildflowers, Western Region*. New York: Knopf, 1979.

Stockert, John W. and Joanne W. *Common Wildflowers of the Grand Canyon*. 5th ed. Salt Lake City: Wheelwright Press, 1979.

Venning, Frank D. *Cacti*. New York: Golden Press, 1974.

Vines, Robert A. *Trees, Shrubs and Woody Vines of the Southwest*. Austin: University of Texas Press, 1960.

15. WILDFLOWERS

The term *wildflower* may be properly applied to any naturally occurring flowering plant, but it is more often used to designate herbaceous plants with more or less showy flowers. There are roughly 650 species of herbaceous plants at the Grand Canyon. Of these, 130 of the more common and showy types are depicted in this guide. Those selected represent most of the important taxonomic groups and include species common to each of the principal life zones and plant communities.

For easy reference, the flowers are grouped by color. As an aid to locating each section quickly, the upper outside corner of each plate bears an index tab of the appropriate color. Within each color section the plants are grouped by family.

Color alone is an unreliable field mark for many species. Some have flowers that change color with age. Others have flowers of different shades, though seldom on the same plant. Some of the plates show both principal color and variations. More often, the variation is only mentioned in the description. It is important to remember that flower and leaf characteristics may be more important than color to proper identification. The color sections are merely convenient places to begin searching. If a plant in question does not appear in one color section, look for similar plants in other sections. Compare them with the specimen plant and read the species descriptions to find out if the flowers vary in color.

Species descriptions contain the following information:

WILDFLOWERS

1. Common and scientific names and family affiliation;
2. Abundance and distribution;
3. Overall height of plant expressed in feet or inches. Unless otherwise indicated, a plant is erect or nearly so;
4. Stem characteristics. Unless otherwise indicated, a stem is smooth and entirely nonwoody;
5. Leaf characteristics, including type, shape, texture, margin type, arrangement and mode of attachment. Unless otherwise indicated, a leaf is simple, alternate, entire, smooth and attached by means of a petiole. See Plates 16 and 17.
6. Flower characteristics, including type, ovary position, size, number of petals, type of inflorescence and color variations. Unless otherwise indicated, a flower is regular, has a superior ovary, blooms singly and lacks significant color variations. See Plates 15 and 16.
7. Blooming season, expressed in months. The period indicated refers to all the plants of that species occurring in the area covered by this book. Moreover, the periods given are for normal years, and some variation may occur.

The species descriptions employ the following abbreviations:

Ht. = Height
Lvs. = Leaves
Flrs. = Flowers
Diam. = Diameter
Cf. = Refer to
Abundance: Com. = common, Uncom. = uncommon
Habitat: Aquat. = aquatic; Ripar. = riparian (streamsides); Grass. = grassland; Scrub = desert scrub; Wood. = pinyon-juniper or oak woodland; Forest = pine, fir or spruce forest.
Geographic Distribution: S Rim = South Rim, N Rim = North Rim, SN Rims = both rims, CAN = canyon, Gorge = Inner Gorge.

16. CACTI

Cacti comprise a distinctive family of flowering plants, one not closely related to any other. They are confined almost exclusively to the New World, ranging from southern Canada to Tierra del Fuego. Of some 1500 different species, 60 are found in Arizona and about two dozen in the Grand Canyon. Fifteen are shown in the following plates.

Most cacti have fleshy, leafless green stems, but in Tropical America the family also includes woody vines, shrubs and trees with well-developed leaves. Such plants are probably much like those from which typical cacti evolved. Prickly-pears and chollas (genus *Opuntia*) bear tiny relict leaves on new stems, but drop them soon after.

In the absence of leaves, typical cacti carry out photosynthesis by means of green, fleshy stems, which also function as storage places for water. The waxy coat on the stems inhibits moisture loss. At a distance, cacti may not appear green because of their dense spines. The spines are actually modified leaves that grow in clusters typically consisting of one or more central spines and numerous, usually shorter radial spines. They may be straight or curved; needlelike, barbed or hooked; smooth or rough. Most cacti bear spines over all or nearly all their stem surfaces. A few have spines only in certain places, and still others are spineless. Since the shape, arrangement and distribution of spines is more or less distinctive for each type of cactus, spines are among the more important features to note when attempting to identify a specimen.

Prickly-pears and chollas also bear tiny barbed bristles called glochids (pronounced GLOCK-ids). Unlike spines, these bristles detach readily from the plant. Embedded in the skin, glochids can be more unpleasant than spines and are removed only by means of tweezers. The process is difficult and painful.

Cacti are noted for their exquisite flowers, which are typically large and vividly colored. The blossoms of Grand Canyon cacti are mostly red or reddish purple, less often various shades of yellow. Color variations are common within a single species and even on a single plant. Flowers are regular, with numerous, nearly identical petals and sepals. The pistil consists of an inferior ovary, a single style and several stigmas. It is surrounded by numerous stamens, which along with the pistil form a conspicuous central cluster.

Spines, glochids, flowers and new stems sprout from small, well-defined places called areoles. Arranged on stems in spirals, areoles are one of the features that distinguish cacti from other flowering plants. Prickly-pears have more or less smooth stems, with areoles well distributed over the entire surface. Stems of other species may either be ribbed or covered with nipplelike bumps called tubercles. Ribbed cacti have areoles spaced along the rib crests. Tuberculate cacti have a single areole atop each tubercle.

Cacti at the Grand Canyon tend to be shrubby, typically forming low mats or clumps. Prickly-pears and chollas have branched stems consisting of a series of flattened, globular or cylindrical joints. Stems of other canyon species are unbranched, solitary or in clusters, and shaped like globes, barrels or columns. At the Grand Canyon the number and variety of cacti are greatest in the Inner Canyon, where they typically grow in hot, arid places among rocks, grasses and shrubs. Even so, a few species also occur on both rims, where the climate is somewhat more humid and significantly cooler.

Among the flowering plants, none have proved more difficult to classify than cacti. The distinctions among closely related species are often obscure and variable. Many species hybridize freely in the wild, producing intermediate forms that even professional botanists are hard put to classify. The beginning student, then, should not be dismayed to encounter forms that do not correspond in all respects with the species described hereafter. The descriptions apply only to typical adult specimens. Juvenile plants may be quite different.

The species descriptions employ the following abbreviations:

Var. = Variety

Ht. = Height

Diam. = Diameter

Habitat: Grass. = grassland; Scrub = desert scrub; Wood. = pinyon-juniper or oak woodland; Forest = pine, fir or spruce forest.

Geographic Distribution: S Rim = South Rim, N Rim = North Rim, SN Rims = both rims, CAN = canyon, Gorge = Inner Gorge.

17. TREES AND SHRUBS

Trees and shrubs are plants with persistent woody stems. About 200 species occur at the Grand Canyon of which roughly ten percent are conifers. Trees dominate the woodlands and forests of higher elevations. Shrubs dominate the desert areas of the South Rim and Inner Canyon. As noted in Chapter 14, many plants grow either as trees or shrubs, depending on local conditions. The most important trees and shrubs in each plant community are listed in Table 2, page 32. The following plates depict 84 of the more common and conspicuous trees and shrubs at the Grand Canyon.

Unlike herbaceous plants, which tend to catch our attention only when they are in bloom, trees and shrubs are conspicuous whether flowers are present or not. For this reason, woody plants are grouped here according to leaf characteristics, rather than flower color. Within each section, species are grouped by family. Terms used in species descriptions are defined and illustrated in plates 14–17, in Chapter 14. Readers should take special care to become thoroughly familiar with leaf characteristics.

The species descriptions employ the following abbreviations:

Lvs. = Leaves
Flrs. = Flowers
Diam. = Diameter
Cf. = Refer to
Abundance: Com. = common, Uncom. = uncommon

Habitat: Ripar. = riparian (streamsides); Grass. = grassland; Scrub = desert scrub; Wood. = pinyon-juniper or oak woodland; Forest = pine, fir or spruce forest.

Geographic Distribution: S Rim = South Rim, N Rim = North Rim, SN Rims = both rims, CAN = canyon, Gorge = Inner Gorge.

Life Zones: L Son. = Lower Sonoran, U Son. = Upper Sonoran, Tran. = Transition, Bor. = Boreal (Canadian and Hudsonian zones).

KEY TO TREES AND SHRUBS SHOWN IN THE PLATES

The following key, based on leaf characteristics, makes it easy to narrow down the number of plates on which a specimen plant is likely to appear. The key consists of ten pairs of statements. First read statements 1A and 1B. Only one of these should apply to the plant you want to identify. Choose the one that fits more closely and proceed as instructed by the key. Continue in this fashion until you are directed to a particular plate or plates. When using the key, don't rely on a single leaf or even the leaves on a single branch or plant, for many species have variable leaves. If the plant is woody only toward the base, see Chapter 15, *Wildflowers*. If the plant has fleshy rather than woody stems, see Chapter 16, *Cacti*.

1A. Lvs. conspicuous and more or less numerous. See 2.
1B. Lvs. inconspicuous, sparse or absent. Plate 57.
2A. Lvs. awl-shaped, needlelike or scalelike, overlapping and tightly pressed on stems. Plates 44 and 45.
2B. Lvs. unlike 2A. See 3.
3A. Lvs. simple. See 4.
3B. Lvs. compound. Plates 55 and 56.
4A. Lvs. attached to stems. See 5.
4B. Lvs. mostly or entirely basal. Plate 57.
5A. Lvs. opposite. Plates 53 and 54.
5B. Lvs. alternate. See 6.
6A. Leaf margins entire. Plates 47, 48 and 49.
6B. Leaf margins not entire. See 7.
7A. Leaf margins lobed. Plate 46.
7B. Leaf margins toothed, scalloped or wavy. Plates 50, 51 and 52.

PART IV

Animals

18. MAMMALS

Mammals are four-legged, fur-bearing animals that suckle their young. Like birds, their body temperature is regulated internally. Most mammals escape excessive daytime heat by seeking shelter in burrows, caves, rock crevices, tree cavities and similar cool retreats. Protection from cold is provided by the fur coat, or pelage, which consists of durable outer guard hairs and short, soft inner fur that provides insulation.

The young are born live and are thereafter nourished by milk secreted from the mother's mammary glands. The young of some species, notably rabbits, rodents and most carnivores, are born naked, blind and helpless. Those of jackrabbits and hoofed mammals, however, are fully active and alert shortly after birth.

Most mammals have acute senses of smell, hearing and vision. Many species also possess sensitive facial whiskers that convey information through touch. Along with excellent night vision and a sharp sense of smell, these vibrissae, as they are called, are adaptations to nocturnal activity.

Many mammals are wholly or partly nocturnal and therefore are rarely seen. Small mammals, with the notable exception of most squirrels, tend to be nocturnal because at night they are less conspicuous to predators. In response, predatory mammals are usually at least partly nocturnal as well. And since nocturnality is also an excellent way to beat the heat, mammals are preadapted, so to speak, to desert conditions.

A large desert mammal, such as the bighorn sheep, is able to range widely for water. Ground squirrels, mice and rats, however, are too small to make the long journeys that often would be necessary to obtain water in the Inner Canyon. Instead, they are able to derive sufficient moisture from their food. A few small rodents, such as kangaroo rats, are able to subsist on the small amounts of water produced as a normal byproduct of food metabolism. Most, however, require green vegetation or some surface water, such as vernal pools or even dewdrops clinging to plants. The grasshopper mouse obtains most of the water it needs from its prey, which are chiefly insects but also may include other mice.

The antelope ground squirrel is a highly specialized desert rodent. Though mostly vegetarian, it supplements its diet with insects, thereby increasing its moisture supply. Though it occupies the hottest, most arid parts of the Grand Canyon, it may be seen abroad even on the hottest days. It keeps cool by foraging in the shade of rocks and shrubs and by retreating to its burrow for short rests. Its light fur tends to reflect heat. The bottom of its tail, which it often holds over its back like a parasol, is white. When overheated, the ground squirrel slobbers onto its chest fur, where the saliva cools through evaporation.

The kangaroo rat escapes intense heat by spending the day in its burrow. Because of the insulative qualities of soil, a burrow even a few inches belowground will be substantially cooler than at the surface. By plugging the burrow opening, the kangaroo rat prevents hot air and predators from entering and cool, relatively moist air from escaping. The rodent derives metabolic water from its food, which mostly consists of seeds. Since its diet contains little protein, it urinates infrequently. Oddly enough, considering how well adapted the kangaroo rat is to desert conditions, it is found only on the rims of the Grand Canyon.

Heat and drought do not pose problems for mammals living on the Kaibab Plateau. Instead, large mammals must contend with winter food shortages brought on by cold weather and deep snow. Some small mammals such as voles and pocket gophers continue to forage under the protective insulation of the snow cover. They encounter difficulty only when extreme cold combined with a lack of snow cover (or when it rains and freezes) either prevents them from foraging or allows them to forage only by expending a great deal of energy. Cold by itself, however, is rarely a problem, for most mammals are protected by their fur from all but extreme cold.

Some mammals, such as the mule deer, cope with winter food shortages by migrating downslope into the pinyon-juniper woodland, where food is more plentiful. In spring the mule deer follow the retreating snow line upslope, feeding on newly sprouted grasses and shrubs. Their constant, though unwelcome, companion in this semiannual trek is the mountain lion, which feeds chiefly on deer and must therefore go where they go.

Most tree squirrels cope with winter food shortages by living off caches of seeds stored during the summer. The Abert and Kaibab squirrels, however, feed in winter off the cambium layer of twigs. Ground squirrels and chipmunks hibernate, living off layers of fat put on for that purpose during the late summer. When hibernating, their body temperature and overall metabolism are reduced to maintenance levels, thereby reducing the need for food and water.

The black bear, which is now very rare at the Grand Canyon, also sleeps away much of the winter, living off body fat in the manner of chipmunks. This is not true hibernation, though, since the bear's body temperature remains near normal. During warmer periods, male bears may even venture abroad for a spell. Female bears, who give birth and suckle their young in the winter, wake up frequently but remain with the cubs in their shared den.

Most carnivores are active throughout the winter, though some migrate downslope if food becomes too scarce. Even at higher elevations, however, prey species such as tree squirrels, rats and mice, as well as numerous small birds, remain active throughout the winter, holing up only during nasty weather.

MAMMAL DISTRIBUTION

More than 70 species of mammals have been observed in Grand Canyon National Park. Several others may be present at least part of the time, though their presence has not been substantiated by specimens or photographs. Mammals occupy every life zone and plant community. Large mammals tend to range freely from one zone or community to another, though each species usually has a preferred habitat for bearing and suckling young. Small mammals are more restricted, though many appear in more than one community or zone.

The canyon itself and perhaps the river in particular have posed a barrier to the movement of some species from one rim to the other. Eleven species are restricted to the north side of the river, nine to the south. Of the former, at least four are absent from the south for lack of suitable habitats. The remainder, however, are missing despite the existence of such habitats. Apparently, they were unable to bridge either the canyon or the river. Mammals restricted to particular geographic areas at the Grand Canyon are listed in Table 4.

Table 4. Mammal Distribution

Found Only North of the River	Found Only South of the River	Found Only in the Canyon
Dwarf Shrew	Spotted Ground Squirrel	California Myotis
Nuttall Cottontail	Gunnison Prairie Dog	Ringtail
Golden-mantled Ground Squirrel	Abert Squirrel	Spotted Skunk
	Silky Pocket Mouse	White-tailed Antelope Ground Squirrel
Least Chipmunk	Rock Pocket Mouse	
Uinta Chipmunk	Stephens Wood Rat	Rock Pocket Mouse
Kaibab Squirrel	White-throated Wood Rat	Long-tailed Pocket Mouse
Red Squirrel	Mexican Wood Rat	Canyon Mouse
Northern Pocket Gopher	Mexican Vole	Cactus Mouse
		Desert Wood Rat
Long-tailed Pocket Mouse		Bighorn Sheep
Bushy-tailed Wood Rat		*Found only along the river or tributaries*
Long-tailed Vole		Raccoon
		River Otter
		Beaver

(From Hoffmeister: *Mammals of Grand Canyon*, 1971)

Of the mammals restricted to one or the other of the rims, the most famous are the two tassel-eared squirrels, which are quite similar except for the coloration of their undersides and tails. The Kaibab squirrel of the North Rim pine forest occurs nowhere else in the world. The Abert squirrel, which inhabits the pine forest of the South Rim, occurs as far north as Colorado and as far south as Mexico. It seems likely that the Abert squirrel managed to cross over to the North Rim at a time when pines were more widespread. Later, as the climate became more arid and the pine forests retreated to higher elevations, the squirrels on the North Rim were isolated from their kin. Mammalogists differ as to whether the Abert and Kaibab squirrels should be treated as separate species or as races of a single species. The former classification is used here largely as a practical device for illustration and discussion.

IDENTIFYING MAMMALS

The plates in this guide depict 39 species of mammals found at the Grand Canyon. These include most of the mammals one is likely to see plus a few that are uncommon but especially interesting. Many of the smaller mammals can be distinguished with certainty only by an expert holding a specimen in hand. Of such groups, one or two species are selected for illustration. Bats, which are well represented at the Grand Canyon, are nonetheless not illustrated because their small size, mostly nocturnal habits and rapid, erratic flight make them very difficult to distinguish. These and other species not shown are listed at the end of this section.

Since most mammals come in shades of brown or grey, color is usually less important to identification than it is for, say, birds. Instead, such characteristics as overall size and shape; posture; shape and size of head, body and tail; and patterns of light and dark fur are more helpful. For this reason mammals are depicted in black and white line drawings. Pelage coloration is noted in the species descriptions.

The best times to see mammals are at dawn and dusk, when both nocturnal and diurnal types may be abroad. The worst time is midday, when even diurnal mammals may hole up. The most likely places to find mammals are near water sources or in areas where burrows, dens or nests are located. An observer who waits patiently and quietly in a concealed spot downwind from the observation area stands the best chance of success.

More often, however, one sees only signs of the beast: tracks, scat, nests and the like. Tracks are shown on Plates 58 and 59. Other distinctive signs are mentioned in the species descriptions, which also employ the following abbreviations and notations:

Lgth. = overall length from tip of nose to end of tail.
Tail = length of tail.
Abundance: Abun. = abundant, Com. = common, Uncom. = uncommon.
Geographic Distribution: S Rim = South Rim; N Rim = Kaibab, Kanab, Uinkaret or Shivwits plateaus; SN Rims = both rims; CAN = Inner Canyon.
Habitat: Aquat. = aquatic, marsh or open water; Ripar. = riparian (streamside vegetation); Grass. = grassland; Scrub = desert scrub; Wood. = pinyon–juniper or oak woodland; Forest = pine, fir or spruce forest.

The following mammals occur at the Grand Canyon, but are not shown in this guide:

Dwarf Shrew, *Sorex nanus*. Rare, N Rim, Grass. Similar to Merriam shrew (Plate 64).
Desert Shrew, *Notiosorex crawfordi*. Rare, S Rim and CAN, Wood. and Scrub. Similar to Merriam shrew (Plate 64).

Yuma Myotis (bat), *Myotis yumanensis*. Com., CAN.

Arizona Myotis (bat), *Myotis occultus*. Rare, SN Rims.

Long-eared Myotis (bat), *Myotis evotis*. Com. N Rim, Forest.

Fringed Myotis (bat), *Myotis thysanodes*. Com., S Rim; Rare, N Rim, Wood. and Forest.

Long-legged Myotis (bat), *Myotis volans*. Com., S Rim; Uncom., N Rim, Wood. and Forest.

California Myotis (bat), *Myotis californicus*. Abun., CAN; Com., SN Rims.

Small-footed Myotis (bat), *Myotis leibii*. Uncom., SN Rims.

Silver-haired Bat, *Lasionycteris noctivigans*. Rare, SN Rims.

Western Pipistrelle (bat), *Pipistrellus hesperus*. Abun., SN Rims and CAN.

Big Brown Bat, *Eptesicus fuscus*. Com., SN Rims and CAN.

Red Bat, *Lasiurus borealis*. Rare, CAN.

Hoary Bat, *Lasiurus cinereus*. Rare, CAN; possibly Com., S Rim.

Mexican Big-eared Bat, *Plecotus phyllotis*. Rare, SN Rims.

Townsend's Big-eared Bat, *Plecotus townsendii*. Rare to Uncom., SN Rims and CAN.

Pallid Bat, *Antrozous pallidus*. Com., CAN; Uncom., SN Rims.

Free-tailed Bat, *Tadarida brasiliensis*. Uncom. to Com., CAN; Uncom., SN Rims.

Big Free-tailed Bat, *Tadarida macrotis*. N Rim, Wood. and Forest. Abundance uncertain.

Nuttall Cottontail, *Sylvilagus nuttallii*. Com., SN Rims. Very similar to Desert Cottontail (Plate 62).

Northern Pocket Gopher, *Thomomys talpoides*. Com., N Rim, Grass. Similar to Common Pocket Gopher (Plate 62).

Pocket Mice, genus *Perognathus*. The following species are all very difficult to distinguish from one another. All resemble the Rock Pocket Mouse (Plate 64).

> Silky Pocket Mouse, *Perognathus flavus*. Rare, S Rim and CAN, Scrub.
>
> Long-tailed Pocket Mouse, *Perognathus formosus*. Com., rocky places, N Rim, and CAN Scrub north of river.
>
> Little Pocket Mouse, *Perognathus longimembris*. N Rim, sandy or gravelly places, Scrub and Wood.
>
> Great Basin Pocket Mouse, *Perognathus parvus*. N Rim, Wood.
>
> Merriam's Kangaroo Rat, *Dipodomys merriami*. CAN, creosote bush scrub. Similar to Ord's Kangaroo Rat (Plate 64).

White-footed Mice, genus *Peromyscus*. The following species are all very difficult to distinguish from the Deer Mouse (Plate 64).

Brush Mouse, *Peromyscus boylii*. Com., Grass., Scrub and Wood.

Pinyon Mouse, *Peromyscus truei*. Com., Wood.

Canyon Mouse, *Peromyscus crinitus*. Com., most places.

Cactus Mouse, *Peromyscus eremicus*. Com., CAN south of river; locally Com., S Rim and CAN north of river.

Long-tailed Grasshopper Mouse, *Onychomys torridus*. Near Vulcan's Throne. Similar to Short-tailed Grasshopper Mouse (Plate 64).

Wood Rats, genus *Neotoma*. The following species are all very difficult to distinguish from one another. All resemble the Bushy-tailed Wood Rat (Plate 64) except that their tails are not bushy. Stephen's Wood Rat has a densely hairy, but not bushy tail.

Desert Wood Rat, *Neotoma lepida*. Com., N Rim and CAN, Scrub and Wood.

Stephen's Wood Rat, *Neotoma stephensi*. Com., S Rim, Wood.

White-throated Wood Rat, *Neotoma albigula*. Com., S Rim and CAN, Scrub and Wood.

Mexican Wood Rat, *Neotoma mexicana*. Com., S Rim, Forest.

Mexican Vole, *Microtus mexicanus*. Com., S Rim, Grass. Similar to Long-tailed Vole (Plate 64).

House Mouse, *Mus musculus*. Human dwellings on S Rim, Exotic.

SELECTED REFERENCES

Bailey, Vernon. *Mammals of the Grand Canyon Region*. Natural History Bulletin no. 1. Grand Canyon, AZ: Grand Canyon Natural History Association, 1935.

Burt, William H., and Richard P. Grossenheider. A *Field Guide to the Mammals*. 2nd ed. Boston: Houghton Mifflin, 1964.

Hoffmeister, Donald F. *Mammals of the Grand Canyon*. Urbana: University of Illinois Press, 1971.

Hoffmeister, Donald F., and Floyd E. Durham. *Mammals of the Arizona Strip Including Grand Canyon National Monument*. Technical Series no. 11. Flagstaff, AZ: Museum of Northern Arizona, 1971.

Interpretive Staff, Grand Canyon National Park, *Grand Canyon Mammals Field Check List*. Grand Canyon, AZ: Grand Canyon Natural History Association, 1968.

Murie, Olaus J. A *Field Guide to Animal Tracks*. Boston: Houghton Mifflin, 1954.

19. BIRDS

Birdlife at the Grand Canyon is extremely diverse. Altogether, more than 280 species have been observed in the park. Of these, more than 200 are either nesting species or annual visitors. Some 40 species live in the area year-round. This large, varied avian population reflects the diversity of habitats found in the park, a diversity produced mainly by extreme changes in elevation over relatively short distances. In addition, the Colorado River attracts a large number of species that otherwise would be scarce or absent in the area.

For obvious reasons, the immense gulf of the Grand Canyon poses no barrier to birds, which occur on either side of the river wherever suitable habitat exists. The rims, however, are migratory barriers to some lowland species, largely because their preferred or essential habitats are not present at higher elevations.

The birds found within the Grand Canyon are mostly desert species that are widely distributed throughout the arid regions of the West. As a group, however, birds are preadapted, as it were, to survival in desert conditions. Though active during the day, the ability to fly allows birds to escape the heat. They can journey to watering places for a drink and a bath, migrate upslope during hot weather, ride thermals to altitudes where the air is cooler, or retreat to cool, shady roosts located well above the ground where temperatures are highest. In addition, birds have higher body temperatures than mammals: 104–108°F for most species. As a result, they can tolerate higher air temperatures. Since birds can fly to water, the overall aridity of the Inner Canyon seldom poses a problem. Though some species rely on open water for moisture, many others obtain sufficient amounts from the consumption of insects and other animal prey. Moreover, birds secrete relatively dry uric acid crystals rather than true urine, thereby conserving moisture.

At the other extreme, birds are also well adapted to the cold, snowy conditions found on the Kaibab Plateau during the winter. Feathers provide good insulation against cold and may be fluffed up to create additional loft. In effect, birds have their own built-in down parkas. Cold poses a problem largely to the extent that it limits food supplies. The same is true of snow.

Most species nesting on the Kaibab Plateau leave the area at or before the onset of winter. Many are summer residents that migrate out of the region to winter quarters where food is readily available. Other species remain in the park but winter in the Inner Canyon or on the generally warmer, less snowy South Rim. A surprisingly large number of species remain on the Kaibab Plateau throughout the winter, surviving on various types of food—conifer seeds and dormant insects, to cite but two examples—that remain available throughout the season. And since most of the summer residents have left the plateau, competition for these foods is greatly reduced.

In this century human activities at the Grand Canyon have created new habitats that have attracted birds that were formerly uncommon or absent in the area. The most dramatic alteration has occurred along the Colorado River. Before the completion of Glen Canyon Dam in 1963, seasonal flooding prevented the establishment of riparian vegetation. Since then, regulation of the river's flow has permitted a distinctive woodland community to develop quickly along its banks. This new riparian woodland provides nesting opportunities for such species as Lucy's warbler, Bell's vireo, willow flycatcher, hooded oriole, blue grosbeak and others, none of which were formerly common in the area. Of the 34 species added to the checklist of Grand Canyon birds since 1976, 11 were found along the river. In addition, the river and its perennial tributaries attract a surprising number of waterfowl and other aquatic or semiaquatic species. These include grebes, herons, egrets, coots, rails, gulls and shorebirds.

When the Park Service expanded the South Rim sewage lagoons in 1976, they became a popular resting place for migrants, including a number of species seldom found elsewhere in the area. These artificial ponds are among the best birding spots at the Grand Canyon.

IDENTIFYING BIRDS

More than 125 species of birds are depicted in this guide, including all nesting species and all fairly common to common visitors and migrants.

Omitted for reasons of space are uncommon or rare visitors and migrants, which are, however, listed at the conclusion of this introduction. The species shown here are those that an average park visitor is most likely to see. Serious birders, of course, with time enough to visit the area frequently, will probably see many other species as well, but they are likely to prefer for that purpose a field guide devoted specifically to birds. This guide is intended more for the casual observer less interested in the hobby of bird watching *per se* than in becoming familiar with various types likely to be encountered during a regrettably brief visit to the canyon.

Birds are grouped on the plates by family, though for various reasons the taxonomic order preferred by ornithologists is not consistently followed. Where males and females of a species have significantly different plumage, that of the female, which is usually much drabber than her mate, is either shown as well or briefly described in the text. Several species either come in more than one color phase or exhibit markedly different plumage during the nesting season than they do thereafter. Such species are usually shown only in the plumage they most commonly exhibit during their residence or sojourn at the Grand Canyon. In addition, birds of a single species often exhibit minor individual differences. Finally, colors and markings may appear different according to available light. The illustrations portray typical individuals seen at close range in direct, bright light.

In addition to plumage, features of importance to identification include general shape and posture; overall size; manner of flight; shape and color of bill, legs and feet; and habitat. Species descriptions indicate preferred habitats and point out those features by which one species can be readily told from similar types. Size is indicated directly on the plates (L = length).

Experienced birders also rely on behavior and song, as well as physical characteristics. For the inexperienced it is usually a handful simply to sort out field marks, so information on behavior and song is in most cases omitted here. In any event, attempts to render bird songs phonetically are rarely successful and are of limited use to most observers.

For successful birding, a pair of good, preferably lightweight binoculars is essential. A notebook for jotting down field marks or behavior for later reference is often useful, as for example when a bird flies away before one has located it in the guide.

Species descriptions employ the following abbreviations:

Cf. = Refer to
Abundance: Com. = common, Uncom. = uncommon, Irreg. =

irregular in occurrence, that is, present some years or seasons but not others. *Rare* is not abbreviated.

Seasons: Sum. = summer, Win. = winter, Spr. = spring. *Fall* is not abbreviated.

Status: Res. = resident, a year-round resident in the area; Sum. Res. = a species that nests in the area during the summer, but winters elsewhere; Vis. = visitor, one that resides in the area for a time, but does not nest there; Migr. = migrant or transient, a species that merely passes through the area.

Life Zone Distribution: L Son. = Lower Sonoran, U Son. = Upper Sonoran, Tran. = Transition, Bor. = Boreal (Canadian and Hudsonian zones).

Habitat: Aquat. = aquatic (on the water); Ripar. = riparian (streamside vegetation); Grass. = grassland; Scrub = desert scrub; Wood = pinyon-juniper or oak woodland; Forest = pine, fir or spruce forest, including aspen groves.

Species descriptions indicate only the preferred habitats of each species for the season indicated. Since birds are the most mobile of creatures, they wander widely and may often be found outside their normal haunts. This is particularly true after the nesting season. In addition, the seasonal status given for each species refers only to those times when the species is *fairly common* to *common* in the Grand Canyon region. Many species also occur in other habitats and seasons in lesser numbers, and one should therefore not be surprised to encounter a particular species at a time or place not indicated in the descriptions.

The following species occur at the Grand Canyon, but are not illustrated in this guide:

Uncommon to Rare Migrants and Visitors

Eared Grebe, *Podiceps nigricollis*

Western Grebe, *Aechmophorus occidentalis*

Pied-billed Grebe, *Podilymbus podiceps*

Double-crested Cormorant, *Phalacocorax auritus*

Green Heron, *Butorides striatus*

Great Egret, *Casmerodius albus*

Snowy Egret, *Egreta thula*

White-faced Ibis, *Plegadis chihi*

Canada Goose, *Branta canadensis*

Gadwall, *Anas strepera*

Pintail, *Anas acuta*

Green-winged Teal, *Anas crecca*

Blue-winged Teal, *Anas discors*

Cinnamon Teal, *Anas cyanoptera*

American Widgeon, *Anas americana*

Shoveler, *Anas clypeata*

Redhead, *Aythya americana*

Ring-necked Duck, *Aythya collaris*

Canvasback, *Aythya valisineria*

Lesser Scaup, *Aythya affinis*

Bufflehead, *Bucephala albeola*

Ruddy Duck, *Oxyura jamaicensis*
Swainson's Hawk, *Buteo swainsoni*
Rough-legged Hawk, *Buteo lagopus*
Ferruginous Hawk, *Buteo regalis*
Bald Eagle, *Aquila chrysaetos*
Marsh Hawk, *Circus cyaneus*
Osprey, *Pandion haliaetus*
Merlin, *Falco columbarius*
Virginia Rail, *Rallus limicola*
American Coot, *Fulica americana*
Killdeer, *Charadrius vociferus*
Common Snipe, *Capella gallinago*
Long-billed Curlew, *Numenius americanus*
Solitary Sandpiper, *Tringa solitaria*
Willet, *Catoptrophorus semipalmatus*
Greater Yellowlegs, *Tringa melanoleucus*
Least Sandpiper, *Calidris minutilla*
American Avocet, *Recurvirostra americana*
Black-necked Stilt, *Himantopus mexicanus*
Wilson's Phalarope, *Steganopus tricolor*
Northern Phalarope, *Lobipes lobatus*
Ring-billed Gull, *Larus delawarensis*
Yellow-billed Cuckoo, *Coccyzus americanus*
Lesser Nighthawk, *Chordeiles acutipennis*
Vaux's Swift, *Chaetura vauxi*
Calliope Hummingbird, *Stellula calliope*

Belted Kingfisher, *Megaceryle alcyon*
Western Flycatcher, *Empidonax difficilis*
Vermillion Flycatcher, *Pyrocephalus rubinus*
Tree Swallow, *Iridoprocne bicolor*
Bank Swallow, *Riparia riparia*
Rough-winged Swallow, *Stelgidopteryx ruficollis*
Barn Swallow, *Hirundo rustica*
Common Crow, *Corvus brachyrhynchos*
Winter Wren, *Troglodytes troglodytes*
Cactus Wren, *Campylorhynchus brunneicapillus*
Long-billed Marsh Wren, *Cistothorus palustris*
Sage Thrasher, *Oreoscoptes montanus*
Water Pipit, *Anthus spinoletta*
Bohemian Waxwing, *Bombycilla garrulus*
Cedar Waxwing, *Bombycilla cedrorum*
Orange-crowned Warbler, *Vermivora celata*
Nashville Warbler, *Vermivora ruficapilla*
Townsend's Warbler, *Dendroica townsendi*
Hermit Warbler, *Dendroica occidentalis*
Northern Waterthrush, *Seiurus noveboracensis*
MacGillivray's Warbler, *Oporornis tolmiei*
Yellow-headed Blackbird, *Xanthocephalus xanthocephalus*
Rose-breasted Grosbeak, *Pheucticus ludovicianus*

Evening Grosbeak, *Hesperiphona vespertina*

Purple Finch, *Carpodacus purpureus*

Pine Grosbeak, *Pinicola enucleator*

Black Rosy Finch, *Leucosticte atrata*

American Goldfinch, *Carduelis tristis*

Red Crossbill, *Loxia curvirostra*

Lark Bunting, *Calamospiza melanocorys*

Savannah Sparrow, *Passerculus sandwichensis*

Sage Sparrow, *Amphispiza belli*

Brewer's Sparrow, *Spizella breweri*

Harris' Sparrow, *Zonotrichia querula*

Fox Sparrow, *Passerella iliaca*

Song Sparrow, *Melospiza melodia*

SELECTED REFERENCES

Brown, Bryan T., et al. *Birds of the Grand Canyon Region: An Annotated Checklist*. Grand Canyon, AZ: Grand Canyon Natural History Association, 1978.

Grater, Russel K. *Checklist of Birds of Grand Canyon National Park*. Natural History Bulletin no. 8. Grand Canyon, AZ: Grand Canyon Natural History Association, 1937.

Johnson, R. R., et al. *Grand Canyon Birds Field Check List*. Grand Canyon, AZ: Grand Canyon Natural History Association, 1976.

Monson, G., and A. R. Phillips. *A Checklist of the Birds of Arizona*. Tucson: University of Arizona Press, 1964.

Peterson, Roger Tory. *A Field Guide to Western Birds*. 2nd ed. Boston: Houghton Mifflin, 1961.

Phillips, A. R., et al. *The Birds of Arizona*. Tucson: University of Arizona Press, 1964.

Robbins, Chandler S., et al. *Birds of North America*. New York: Golden Press, 1966.

Udvardy, Miklos D. F. *The Audubon Society Field Guide to North American Birds. Western Region*. New York: Knopf, 1977.

20. AMPHIBIANS AND REPTILES

Amphibians and reptiles constitute two distinct classes of vertebrate animals. Except that both are cold-blooded, with body temperatures that vary with their surroundings, they have little in common. They are lumped together here because there are too few species of amphibians at the Grand Canyon—only seven in all—to warrant a separate chapter.

AMPHIBIANS

Amphibians are partly aquatic, partly terrestrial. As a rule they spawn in water, which is scarce at the Grand Canyon. Eggs are deposited in jellylike masses or strings. Fertilization is external. They begin life as larvae (tadpoles) equipped with gills and tail. The larvae transform into adults, a process called metamorphosis, developing limbs and, in most cases, lungs. Metamorphosis usually takes place in a single season.

Frogs rarely venture from water even as adults and may be seen abroad during the day. Toads and salamanders are more terrestrial, returning to water largely to spawn. They spend much of the day holed up in burrows and other damp retreats, seldom appearing except on warm nights during or following rains. At the Grand Canyon, suitable conditions for activity and spawning occur from spring through fall. The rest of the year is largely spent in hibernation.

Most amphibians have moist skin produced by a thin coating of mucus secreted from numerous glands. Some also secrete a toxic substance distasteful to predators and irritating to the eyes and mucous membranes of humans. The mucous coating makes amphibians slippery prey, retards loss of body moisture and aids in respiration—for though all Grand Canyon species possess lungs, most also breathe to some extent through the skin.

Salamanders superficially resemble lizards but are readily distinguished by their smooth, moist skin and clawless toes. Toads and frogs are usually tailless, have moist skin—warty in toads, smooth in frogs—enlarged hind legs, webbed feet and clawless toes.

REPTILES

Reptiles of the Grand Canyon are terrestrial and distributed through all life zones. Thus far, 19 lizard species, 17 snake species and the desert tortoise have been observed in the area.

Reptiles are well suited to desert environments. Their tough skin retards moisture loss, while replacement water is obtained through their food. Though fairly tolerant of hot weather, they too have their limits. Most snakes will die if exposed for prolonged periods to temperatures much over 100° F. Lizards tend to have higher limits—often much higher—but in the Inner Canyon furnace even these limits are often exceeded. In hot weather most reptiles are active only in the morning and early evening and seek shelter during the hottest part of the day. Several species at the Grand Canyon are wholly or partly nocturnal.

Reptiles tend to be intolerant of cold weather. Most Grand Canyon species hibernate during the winter, which may bring freezing temperatures even to the Inner Gorge. Where winters are long and cold, as on the Kaibab Plateau, reptiles are uncommon or absent. At the Grand Canyon they are most abundant in the Sonoran zones.

Reptiles maintain remarkably constant body temperatures by moving back and forth between sunny and shady locations. During early morning, many snakes and lizards warm up by basking on rocks or open ground exposed to the sun. At dusk they commonly seek out rocks or pavement, which retain the day's heat long after sundown.

Most reptiles hatch from hard- or leathery-shelled eggs buried in warm, sandy ground. Some are born live: horned lizards, garter snakes and rattlesnakes, for example. In either case fertilization occurs through copulation. The young are born fully active and alert.

IDENTIFYING AMPHIBIANS AND REPTILES

Of the 44 species of amphibians and reptiles found at the Grand Canyon, 25 are shown in this guide. The remainder are listed at the end of this section.

Amphibians are seldom seen because they are scarce as a group, largely nocturnal and of local occurrence. The best way to see them is to explore along streams and ponds on warm summer nights after a rain. With the single exception of the tiger salamander, which is distinctive, identification may be difficult in the dark. A flashlight, of course, is essential.

Except in winter, there is virtually no chance of failing to see several species of lizards and, though less likely, perhaps even a snake or two. Rattlesnakes, however, are uncommon in the area and are of a retiring disposition. As a result, visitors more often worry about them than encounter them. Most reptiles in the Grand Canyon are fairly easy to identify. Some groups, however, consist of several quite similar species, and some species vary widely in coloration, with the result that it may not always be possible, without actually holding the animal, to make a positive identification. Do not, however, disturb or handle any reptile within the park. To do so is not only illegal, but may result in a painful bite or possible harm to the animal.

Abundance, life zone distribution and habitat preference are indicated in the species descriptions by the following abbreviations:

Abundance: Abun. = abundant, Com. = common, Uncom. = uncommon. *Rare* is not abbreviated.

Life Zone Distribution: L Son. = Lower Sonoran, U Son. = Upper Sonoran, Tran. = Transition, Bor. = Boreal (Canadian and Hudsonian zones of the North Rim).

Habitat Preference: Aquat. = aquatic (marsh or open water); Ripar. = riparian (streamside vegetation); Grass. = grassland; Scrub = desert scrub; Wood. = pinyon–juniper or oak woodland; Forest = pine, fir or spruce forest.

The following species of amphibians and reptiles occur at the Grand Canyon, but are not illustrated or discussed in the plates:

Amphibians: Frogs and Toads

Western Spadefoot Toad, *Scaphiopus hammondi*. Rare, U Son., Ripar., Grass. and Scrub.

Northern Leopard Frog, *Rana pipiens*. Rare, U Son. and Tran., Aquat. and Ripar.

Reptiles: Turtles

Desert Tortoise, *Gopherus agassizi*. Rare, L and U Son., Aquat., Ripar., Grass. and Scrub.

Reptiles: Lizards

Banded Gecko, *Coleonyx variegatus*. Uncom., L and U Son., Ripar., Grass. and Scrub.

Night Lizard, *Xantusia vigilis*. Rare, U Son., Wood.

Desert Collared Lizard, *Crotaphytus insularis*. Com., L and U Son., Scrub.

Leopard Lizard, *Gambelia wislizenii*. Rare, U Son., Wood.

Desert Horned Lizard, *Phrynosoma platyrhinos*. Rare, L and U Son., Grass. and Scrub.

Zebra-tailed Lizard, *Callisaurus draconoides*. Rare, L and U Son., Aquat., Ripar., Grass. and Scrub.

Plateau Whiptail, *Cnemidophorus velox*. Uncom., U Son., Ripar.

Western Skink, *Eumeces skiltonianus*. Uncom., Tran. and Bor., Grass.

Gila Monster, *Heloderma suspectum*. Rare, Ripar., western Grand Canyon.

Reptiles: Snakes

Western Blind Snake, *Leptotyphlops humilis*. Rare, L and U Son., Wood.

Coachwhip (Red Racer), *Masticophis flagellum*. Uncom., L and U Son., Ripar., Grass. and Scrub.

Western Patch-nosed Snake, *Salvadora hexalepis*. Uncom., U Son., Scrub and Wood.

Sonora Mountain Kingsnake, *Lampropeltis pyromelana*. Uncom., U Son. and Tran., Wood. and Forest.

Western Ground Snake, *Sonora semiannulata*. Uncom., L and U Son., Ripar., Grass. and Scrub.

Glossy Snake, *Arizona elegans*. Rare, L Son.

Sonora Lyre Snake, *Trimorphodon lambda*. Rare, L and U Son. zones.

Spotted Night Snake, *Hypsiglena torquata*. Uncom., Wood. and Forest.

Black-headed Snake, *Tantilla planiceps*. Rare, L and U Son. zones, Ripar. and Scrub.

SELECTED REFERENCES

Behler, John L., and F. Wayne King. *The Audubon Society Field Guide to North American Reptiles and Amphibians.* New York: Knopf, 1980.

Brown, Vinson. *Reptiles and Amphibians of the West.* Healdsburg, CA: Naturegraph, 1974.

Dodge, Natt N. *Amphibians and Reptiles of Grand Canyon National Park.* Natural History Bulletin no. 9. Grand Canyon, AZ: Grand Canyon Natural History Association, 1938.

Shaw, Charles E., and Sheldon Campbell. *Snakes of the American West.* New York: Knopf, 1974.

Stebbins, Robert C. *Amphibians and Reptiles of Western North America.* New York: McGraw-Hill, 1954.

———. *A Field Guide to Western Reptiles and Amphibians.* Boston: Houghton Mifflin, 1966.

Tomko, D. S. *Grand Canyon Amphibians and Reptiles Field Check List.* Grand Canyon, AZ: Grand Canyon Natural History Association, 1976.

21. FISH

Fish are cold-blooded aquatic vertebrates that lack legs but have conspicuous body and tail fins for swimming. Most are covered with scales and with a slimy coating of mucus to reduce water resistance. Fish breathe by taking water in through the mouth and passing it out through the gills. As water passes over the thin gill plates, dissolved oxygen is absorbed by capillaries and carbon dioxide is released. Young fish are either born live or hatched from eggs, depending on the species. There are more than 700 species of freshwater fish native to North America. Of these, only 11 are native to the Colorado River system, and only 7 are found in Grand Canyon National Park. Most of these species are found nowhere else in the world, having evolved under the rather unusual set of conditions offered by the pristine Colorado River.

Prior to this century the Colorado River was characterized by extreme muddiness and drastic seasonal fluctuations in chemistry, temperature, level, turbulence and rate of discharge. Each year the river carried more than 100,000 acre-feet of silt to its delta, at the head of the Gulf of California. On the average, discharge varied from a midsummer low of about 3000 cubic feet per second to a spring-flood high of 380,000 cubic feet per second. Most freshwater fish are unable to endure such wildly fluctuating conditions, which no doubt accounts at least in part for the small number of species native to the Colorado River system.

During this century, however, 20 dams have been built along the river, including Glen Canyon Dam just upstream from the Grand

Canyon. These dams have drastically altered the river environment above and below them. The principal changes in the Grand Canyon section of the river are briefly described in Chapter 3. They include: (1) elimination of seasonal fluctuations, since the flow of the river is now regulated upstream at Glen Canyon Dam; (2) reduction in turbidity because sediments are now trapped behind the dam, in Lake Powell; (3) reduction of summer water temperature because water released from the dam is drawn from the bottom of the lake; and (4) destruction of quiet backwaters that once formed during periods of low water.

In thus destroying the habitat of the native fishes, Glen Canyon Dam, as well as all others along the river, have brought these species to the brink of extinction. Native fish populations have been greatly reduced along the entire river system and in large reaches have been eliminated entirely. In the Grand Canyon, native species are largely confined to the mouths of permanent tributaries such as the Little Colorado River and Bright Angel Creek. Three native species—the Colorado squawfish, humpback chub and bonytail chub—are considered to be endangered species and are now protected by state or federal laws.

In altering the river environment, the dams also permitted the successful introduction of more than a dozen exotic species that formerly could not have survived in the river. These include trout, catfish, carp and several types of minnow, all of which may compete with and in some cases prey upon the native fish. Along with the new arrivals came a host of parasites formerly absent from the river and to which the native fish therefore have little resistance.

Today, rainbow trout now thrive in the Grand Canyon section of the Colorado, including its permanent tributaries. Bright Angel Creek offers especially fine angling. Brook trout are present in smaller numbers. Other game fish include sunfish, salmon and largemouth bass. Although the National Park Service stopped direct stocking of game fish within the park in 1967, exotics continue to be planted downstream at Lake Mead. Naturally, many of these fish migrate into the Grand Canyon.

The Park Service has implemented a management plan for the Grand Canyon fishery in cooperation with the Arizona Game and Fish Department and the U.S. Fish and Wildlife Service. One of the goals of this plain is to sustain and, if possible, increase native fish populations within the canyon. At present, for example, all fishing is forbidden at the confluence of the Colorado and Little Colorado rivers in order to protect the native humpback chub known to exist in these waters. Anglers must possess a valid Arizona fishing license to fish in the park. For information on where to obtain a license and on regulations governing angling in the canyon, inquire at park information centers.

The plates in this guide illustrate six native and six introduced fish species. Anglers are forbidden to keep native species, which should be carefully released back into the river. Anyone hooking a native fish should report the location of the catch to the Park Service. Such records may prove invaluable to future management of these rare species.

SELECTED REFERENCE

Minckley, W. L. *Fishes of Arizona*. Phoenix: Arizona Fish and Game, 1973.

22. BUTTERFLIES

The insect order Lepidoptera includes moths, butterflies and related types. In North America there are about 9000 species of moths and 800 species of butterflies. There is no single feature that separates all moths and butterflies, but moths tend to have stouter, hairier bodies and feathery rather than club-shape antennae. In addition the fore and hind wings of most moths are held together in flight by a small, curved spine or set of bristles called a frenulum. Butterflies lack this device. Most moths are nocturnal, while butterflies are more often abroad during the day. Moths therefore attract less notice and for this reason are not included in this guide.

LIFE CYCLE

Ninety percent of all insects, including butterflies, moths, beetles, flies, bees and other orders amounting to 90 percent of all insects, undergo radical transformations as they develop into adults. This process is called complete metamorphosis to distinguish it from the less dramatic anatomical changes (simple metamorphosis) experienced in the course of development by grasshoppers, true bugs and certain other insects. Complete metamorphosis includes four separate stages: egg, larva, pupa and adult.

All insects hatch from eggs. Those of butterflies vary greatly in size and shape and are usually ornamented with grooves, pits, ribs, knobs or other sculpturing. Each female butterfly deposits her eggs in a manner and pattern characteristic of her species. In most cases the eggs are placed on the particular type of plant or plants preferred or required by the larvae of each species. Within a few days the larvae—caterpillars— emerge from the eggs to begin feeding on the host plant.

Caterpillars are primarily eating machines. When not resting, they are ravenously consuming leaves or other parts of their host plants. Many caterpillars are serious agricultural pests, but the larvae of butterflies more often feed on deciduous trees or wild herbaceous plants. Like bees, however, adult butterflies and moths play an important, sometimes essential role in pollinating various plants and in this way more than make up for the damage wrought by their hungry offspring. This tidy balance does not apply to agricultural damage. Research shows, however, that disastrous crop losses from moths and other pests are often due, at least in part, to agricultural practices based on economic rather than ecological considerations.

In the wild, caterpillar populations are usually kept in balance by a large number of predators, including spiders and their kin, other insects, amphibians, reptiles, birds and even mammals, including humans on occasion. In response, caterpillars have evolved a variety of defenses. Some caterpillars make themselves inconspicuous by mimicking the leaves, twigs and other parts of the plants on which they feed. Others have developed a variety of feeding and resting habits designed to evade predators. For example, it's not uncommon for caterpillars to consume each leaf completely before going on to another. In this way they do not betray their presence through partly chewed foliage. Others are not so tidy, but are careful not to rest on the same shoots where they have been feeding. Other defenses evolved by various species include acrid or toxic body fluids, poisons stored in their shell-like body walls, and stinging or poisonous hairs or spines. Caterpillars so equipped often display gaudy colors to advertise their undesirable qualities, a strategy called aposematic coloration. At the same time, a number of perfectly tasty species hide the fact by mimicking the acrid or poisonous types. This type of mimicry also exists among adult butterflies.

Butterfly larvae come in a great variety of sizes and shapes, but most are smooth-skinned. The caterpillar of each species may be more distinctly marked than the adult, but since caterpillars are usually shy and inconspicuous, they are not depicted in this guide.

As a caterpillar grows it molts several times. That is, it sloughs off its old skin in favor of a new, more commodious suit. When the larva reaches full size, it typically attaches itself to a firm support, such as the stem of its host plant, by means of silky thread generated by its spinarets.

Then, during a final molt, it transforms into a pupa by developing a hard, mummylike case called a chrysalis. Moth pupae are in addition usually encased in a densely woven shroud of silken strands called a cocoon. During the pupal stage, the insect is inactive while it undergoes the radical transformation into an adult. This transformation is timed and directed by hormones, but external factors such as air temperature, length of day or humidity may trigger the process. Depending on the species, the change from pupa to adult may take from a few days to several months. Many species pupate in the fall, spend the winter in this fashion, and emerge as adults in the spring. Butterfly pupae, like the larvae, can be distinctive, but are not depicted in this guide.

Butterflies and all other insects have bodies composed of three segmented sections: head, thorax and abdomen. In butterflies the head includes the following parts: (1) two segmented antennae, which are typically slender and terminate in an enlarged "club"; (2) two compound, hemispherical eyes, each consisting of thousands of hexagonal simple eyes; (3) two jointed sensory organs called palpi located one on each side of the mouth; and (4) a coiled tubular proboscis which, when extended, may be longer than the body.

The thorax is the stout, middle section of the body. It consists of three segments, each bearing a pair of five-jointed legs. In addition, the middle and rear segments each bear a pair of wings. The abdomen is the slender, rear portion of the body extending backward from the legs. It consists of 11 segments, not all of which may be visible to the naked eye. Butterflies breathe through spiracles, a series of tiny openings located along the body. Oxygen passes into the blood and circulates through veins to all parts of the body, including the wings. Attached to the end of the abdomen are the genitalia: the ovipositor of the female and the claspers of the male.

Butterfly wings are membranous and densely coated with overlapping scales, which come off as "dust" when the insect is carelessly handled. The scales determine the color of the wings. Some scales may contain pigments, while others create the impression of color through the refraction of light. Other scales are modified into hairs. In male butterflies some of the scales also produce scents that probably play important roles in recognition and courtship.

Adult butterflies feed largely on flower nectar, which is obtained by uncoiling the proboscis and inserting it into the throat of a flower. Some butterfly species are quite selective, visiting only certain types of plants, often not the same type on which their larvae are found. Other species have rather catholic tastes. Adult butterflies drink nectar to sustain themselves, but they are usually short-lived compared to their larvae, and do not grow in size. Their function is not to eat but to reproduce. Normally there are one or two broods a year, and sometimes a brood may contain insects of only one sex. The flight season given for various species refers to the period after the adults emerge from their pupae.

BUTTERFLY ECOLOGY

The Grand Canyon influences butterfly populations ecologically in several ways. It can act as a barrier that prevents movement between the rims; it can act as a channel between the Great Basin Desert of Utah and Nevada, and the Sonoran and Mojave deserts of Arizona and California; and it can act as a refugium (an area to which a species is restricted) for native species or subspecies.

The Grand Canyon is not as effective a barrier to flying or drifting organisms as it is to strictly terrestrial species. Butterflies are not particularly strong fliers and are more subject to wind dispersion than are many other insects. Blown off course, butterflies may end up at the bottom of the canyon or on the opposite rim. Thus, it is rare for a species to be restricted to one side of the canyon; yet this is the case for the Grand Canyon ringlet (*Coenonympha ochracea furcae*) which inhabits only the south side of the park. Many butterflies have distinct habitat and food preferences, and these are indicated in the notes for Plates 86 and 87. Because of great differences in daily temperatures between the rims and the canyon floor some butterflies may be active along the Colorado River during the early spring and late fall, at times which are far from optimal for them at higher elevations.

The most noted North American migrant butterfly is the monarch (*Danaus plexippus*). From late summer through autumn it can be seen floating through the gorge along the river. It uses the Inner Gorge as a channel for its seasonal movements. Other species, searching for food plants which grow along the river, also use the canyon as a channel.

Several subspecies of butterflies are endemic to the Grand Canyon. These include the pegala satyr (*Cercyonis pegala damei*), the Grand Canyon ringlet, and the Grand Canyon swallowtail (*Papilio indra kaibabensis*). Another subspecies, Shellbach's fritillary (*Speyeria electa shellbachi*) is only rarely found outside the park. These butterflies show that the Grand Canyon can serve not only as a barrier and a channel, but also as an ecological sanctuary for its inhabitants.

IDENTIFYING BUTTERFLIES

Although a fair number of Grand Canyon butterflies can be easily identified "on the wing," as it were, the majority are readily distinguished only through the careful examination of hand-held specimens. Such features as genitalia, the vein pattern of wings or the presence or absence of hairs in one place or another may be essential to positive identification. Close examination, however, is not possible in Grand Canyon National Park, because collecting specimens is forbidden except by special permit. Therefore, the casual observer must be content to identify only the large, distinctively marked types that fly slowly, alight often and frequent habitats accessible to people. Smaller, drabber, more elusive species can usually be assigned to a particular family or occasionally a single genus, but rarely distinguished beyond that.

The plates in this guide emphasize the large, distinctive species types, though at least one representative of each family present at the Grand Canyon is included. Altogether, 18 species are shown. Species descriptions include—where possible—range, habitat, flight season, larval food plants and sundry features of interest. Much of this information and nomenclature is derived from John S. Garth's *Butterflies of Grand Canyon National Park*, the most recent work on butterflies of the park. Unfortunately, this publication is no longer in print. Other useful texts are mentioned below.

Species descriptions employ the following abbreviations:

Abundance: Abun. = abundant, Com. = common, Uncom. = uncommon.

Geographic Range: S Rim = South Rim, N Rim = North Rim, SN Rims = both rims, CAN = canyon, Gorge = Inner Gorge.

SELECTED REFERENCES

Garth, John S. *Butterflies of Grand Canyon National Park.* Natural History Bulletin no. 11. Grand Canyon, AZ: Grand Canyon Natural History Association, 1950.

Howe, W. H. *The Butterflies of North America.* Garden City, NY: Doubleday, 1975.

Mitchell, Robert T., and Herbert S. Zim. *Butterflies and Moths.* New York: Golden Press, 1964.

Milne, Lorus and Margery. *The Audubon Society Field Guide to North American Insects and Spiders.* New York: Knopf, 1980.

Tyler, H. A. *The Swallowtail Butterflies of North America.* Healdsburg, CA: Naturegraph, 1975.

PLATE INDEX

The numbers in bold-face type refer to the plates. When available, common names are used for the species listed. Less common species may be mentioned in the text, although they are not pictured.

GENERAL INDEX

INDEX